RICK HORTON

Laurence
Olivier

ON
ACTING

SIMON AND SCHUSTER · NEW YORK

Published by Simon and Schuster
A Division of Simon & Schuster, Inc.
Simon & Schuster Building
Rockefeller Center
1230 Avenue of the Americas
New York, New York 10020
Originally published in Great Britain
by George Weidenfeld & Nicolson Limited
SIMON AND SCHUSTER and colophon
are registered trademarks of Simon & Schuster, Inc.
Designed by Edith Fowler
Photo editor: Vincent Virga
Manufactured in the United States of America

10 9 8 7 6 5 4 3 2 1

Library of Congress Cataloging in Publication Data

Olivier, Laurence, 1907-
  On acting.
  Includes index.
   1. Olivier, Laurence, 1907- . 2. Acting.
3. Shakespeare, William, 1564-1616—Stage history.
4. Actors—Great Britain—Biography. I. Title.
PN2598.O55A36 1986
792'.028'0924 [B] 86-10037
ISBN 0-671-55869-2

To my children,
the next generation of actors

I would like to thank Gawn Grainger for editing the text of this book.

L.O.

CONTENTS

PART THREE
CONTEMPORARY INFLUENCES

PART FOUR
THE SILVER SCREEN

PART FIVE
REFLECTIONS

PROLOGUE

I N my autobiography, *Confessions of an Actor*, I thought I'd said everything about myself that needed to be said. I wanted to write my own book, as there seemed to be so many about me by other people on the market that I felt it was about time I put the real facts of my life down on paper as truthfully as I could express them, without the added trimmings of the sensational. Once it was finished, I felt that I'd got rid of a huge chore; the weight that had been sitting on me for two years was

suddenly lifted and I was free once again. I was no longer
chained to that monster machine which sat in the study
and waited every morning for my fingers and my brain.

Writing is not a glamorous occupation, as anyone who
has attempted it will know; it requires hard work and
self-discipline. It is lonely; it can be depressing; it creates
an unwelcome feeling of vulnerability. I have heard
writers complain of this before, but it always sounded
somewhat exaggerated: "Poor me, surrounded by my
solitude." Well, now I can tell you there is not a jot of
exaggeration in it; it is the stark truth. Writing *is* a lonely
profession; it is not romantic; it is a hard grind, a daily
grind, and anyone who succeeds in filling up a page is a
hero. It's rather like the man who kept banging his head
against the wall and when asked why he did so, replied,
"It's so lovely when I stop." That's how I felt when I
finished *Confessions*.

So why, four years afterwards, instead of looking at the
beautiful Sussex countryside and listening to the mid-
afternoon lark in between smiles and dozes, did I think
of burying my nose in blank pages again?

It was those Sunday evenings which did it. Sitting by
the fire, chatting late into the night. The how, why,
when chats—you know the ones I mean:

"What was it like when . . . ?"

"How did you find that character?"

"Why did you play it that way?"

Not the usual boring theatrical gossip—he's-sleeping-
with-her, she's-sleeping-with-him stuff—but discussing this
wonderful business of ours in detail from the proper

angle. Searching for origins, discussing beliefs, trying to explain what it was like for me to be up there inside the Shakespearean greats.

The more I talked, the more fascinated I grew with the way it had all come about. Of course it's always fun to talk about yourself. I don't think anyone can deny that. I realized that although enough had been written about me and my life, very little had been said on how it had happened, on what had been going on inside me when I tackled some of the great roles. Slowly I put pen to paper.

Any writer will tell you that the most depressing thing in the world to experience is that early-morning trudge to the dreaded typewriter, sitting down and then staring at the blank page. There it is, this whiter-than-white sheet of paper glaring back at you from the roller or desk, daring you to disfigure it with filthy black type or only just legible handwriting. The brightness of the white begins to affect your eyes. You sit down, you stand up, you look the other way, hoping that when you turn again some miracle will have been performed and the page will be full. You walk, you talk to yourself, you ask how you ever got yourself into this position in the first place. I'm an actor; why have I undertaken this?

The obstacles the writer sets in his way before he finally gets to the study are more than there are in the Grand National. There are papers to be read, letters to be relished, bills to be paid, checks to be signed. There are people to say hello to, instructions to be given; the day must be set in order. There are agents to be phoned, gardens to be seen, decisions about what you would like for lunch. Where are my glasses? where are my pens and pencils? I need my diary; I made some notes last night.

How the hell did Shakespeare do it? Do you think he went through the same beastly process, or did it just happen for him? Did he have a direct line to the muse? I would answer without hesitation, yes. No matter what, I don't think he would have been wrestling over a blank page for too long; otherwise half of the plays would never have appeared. He must have been writing at a great pace—almost nonstop, it would seem. Words flowed from him. Tradition has it that he wrote continuously: poem, act, great scene. To the rest of us mortals that does not seem fair . . . but then, no apportionment of genius seems that.

Perhaps Edgar Wallace had the easiest method of working. He would write a book in a day without putting pen to paper. He merely dictated everything into a machine, then off to the races. No fool, Wallace. He would be placing his bets while the rest of us would be only into the second paragraph.

Thinking of Edgar Wallace gave me an idea. Why shouldn't I use a tape recorder? Direct speech would give my words much greater impact. They would be fresh and clear, spontaneous and immediate in a way I could never hope to achieve on the page.

At first talking to a tape recorder seemed easy. Soon it became a bore and even lonelier than writing. I sat there reminiscing into a lifeless machine day after day. What I needed, I soon realized, was an audience. Someone to react to my memories, stimulating me to conjure up the past. I found the perfect foil in Gawn Grainger, who very kindly spent a great deal of time listening to me and who was the editor of this book, for all of which I am most grateful.

This is not a book for the gossips; it is purely and simply about acting and about how I feel it has come about for me. Luck and more luck. The right decisions; even more fortunately, the right opportunities for changes of style, and at the right times. It is hard for me to know to which I owe more: the apparent gifts, or the timing of my chances to exploit them. No matter what else I may or may not be, I am assuredly the luckiest man I know.

Part One

BEFORE
THE CURTAIN

CHAPTER ONE

Beginnings

WHERE do we start when we talk about the history of acting? Surely we have always acted; it is an instinct inherent in all of us. Some of us are better at it than others, but we all do it. The child plays games. The child cries when tears are the order of the day, endears himself to avoid criticism, smiles when necessary; he predicts what reactions we require. Look behind those eyes which are giving the beholder the laughter he expects, and you will see the veil of the actor. We have all, at one time or another, been performers, and many of us still are—politicians, playboys, cardinals and kings. We wear the robes that we have designed for ourselves, and then act out other people's fantasies. This is singular; this is the monologue; this is the one-man show.

Group acting, I think, was bound up in the beginning with religion. That was the original theater: dances to the gods for rain, for fertility; prayers and chanting, performing. In parts of the world, you can still see it now as it was. And in other parts of the world it is still done, but cloaked in subtlety.

Religious ritual was dominated by men. Women were left very much in the background. In fact, as we know, until comparatively recently women were not allowed to appear on our stages. If we go back to the Greeks, women were not even allowed into the Olympic theater; their presence was strictly taboo. There is a sweet story that I have heard somewhere. Apparently one reason for not allowing women in was that the men had to be naked in order to be free. The story goes that there was a newly married young woman who was madly in love with her husband. In order to be near him, she dressed as a young man to be admitted into the stadium. When her husband appeared and was successful in his performance, she rushed up to him and embraced him. Everything, naturally, came to a standstill. He said to her, "You fool, they will kill you for this." But so touched were the authorities that they did not put her to death, which was the usual punishment. I am sure she lived to a ripe old age and told tales of her feat to her great-grandchildren.

One thing about the Greeks that intrigues me is why they were naked. They were naked for running. Were they naked as actors to create an illusion of fitness, of speed, to streamline themselves rather like an Olympic swimmer of today—the smooth head parting the water? They shaved the hair on their bodies because it was considered unattractive. I have always done this myself if the part called for a show of legs. Maybe the nakedness was not for athleticism, but purely for absolute freedom. I wonder, what would it be like to perform completely naked? That really would be the test, wouldn't it? Nothing to cover you but your imagination. If it worked, I wonder what the audience would really see. The Greeks must have gone beyond that—beyond the naked man; way beyond. I have done it in front of a mirror—I suppose we all have at some time—and I have seen what I wanted to see beyond the nakedness, the emperor's clothes in reality. Imagination working atop imagination, audience and actor in one. Fascinating. But this again is singular: the mirror and the man.

I thought that acting must have begun as a colloquy between two people—first of all, just two—which was later followed by single acts, by recitations, bards and all that. Someone thought up the idea, and for years I believed it was the actors. I used to say, "Don't tell me actors didn't come before writers." Then I discovered, to my horror, that Thespis wasn't an actor, he was a producer. It was he who had the idea of two actors' having a colloquy. It was *his* idea. I still can't believe it, but it's true. He was a producer, not an actor. He simply said,

"Let's have a conversation; you say this and you say that. . . ." Maddening, infuriating. "Thespian" doesn't mean that to me.

On the other hand, I think he merely recalled his childhood. And if he did that, then I think we can safely say that the actor came first. Let's play mothers and fathers, doctors and nurses, cowboys and Indians. "You say this and I'll say that." Yes, I think it started long before Thespis. All Thespis did was point a finger at conversation and remind us of things that had gone before. He took the improvisation and turned it into a play. He gave the players parts.

If we go back to man's very beginnings, we will find that the actor comes first. The games people play are developed and molded until they eventually become the mirror in which society can look at itself. We ape, we mimic, we mock. We act. Most people put acting behind them when they reach puberty, and very often long before. But some of us leap the barrier of self-consciousness and spend the rest of our lives acting out the dreams of others. Nothing comes easily, and I don't think it should. The child finds it easy—but then, a child has a supple body and an open mind: fearless until taught fear; eyes wide, innocent and aware. That is a quality we should never lose, but sadly, we do. The child becomes daunted by the shadows of the future; then the child becomes the adult; then the adult becomes aware of his mortality. Shakespeare knew this, and so should the actor. The actor should be able to create the universe in the palm of his hand. I often think that could we creep behind the

actor's eyes, we would find an attic of forgotten toys and
a copy of the Domesday Book.

The complete actor, if there is such a being, would
have all this plus a row of telephone operators seated behind his forehead, waiting to plug into the next selection.
A good actor is working on at least three levels at all
times: lines, thought and awareness of the audience. A
great actor has this and more. He is able to plug in any
one of his operators at the flick of an eyelid. He is always
waiting to pounce at the slightest opportunity, wanting
to get at the audience's jugular. A lion, a tiger, a leopard—
there is something feline about him. But then, perhaps
he is more subtle than that, more capable of disguise—a
serpent. That's it: a serpent.

Kenneth Tynan once said of me that I use my talent
and neglect my genius. Well, I don't think there is any
room for genius in the theater. Genius, I think, is too
unreal. You can apply the word to other forms of art,
but theater deals primarily in practicability; there is no
room for genius. If you as a performer have a sudden
flash of genius, when do you express it? Do you keep the
members of the audience waiting patiently till Act IV,
Scene V of *King Lear* and then hit them with one flash
of genius and say, "That's all I can do today"? I don't
think so. I don't think they get their money's worth like
that. Apart from anything else, I think they'd be deeply
asleep by then, or boosting the bar profits. On the other
hand, if you're practiced, rehearsed and thoroughly
versed, you have something to offer. You know what the
lines are about, but you haven't waited for the final, ulti-

mate way of saying them or handling a single moment. Those things are still in the process of being tried out, and with any luck, one or two will happen. But you don't go on stage with intent to be a genius or saying, "I'm not going to be a genius tonight." You must produce something; that's the job. You must present a mirror or an echo; otherwise the audience will run screaming for their money back or shower the stage with tomatoes. You take care of the play and let the genius take care of itself.

To me acting is a technical problem. It's also an emotional problem. You've got to feel, which is a great test for the imagination. If you're an artist, you've got to prove it, and I regret that there have been times when I haven't managed to hide the technique. It should appear effortless. If you buy a diamond ring or any other wonderful bit of jewelry, you don't ask, "What was your technique in creating this?" If you did, the jeweler might say, "Why don't you mind your own business? You're not a jeweler."

Any actor will tell you that he would have great difficulty in describing his own technique. If I'm directing someone and I see he is in difficulties, I can suggest a technique that will help him. Sometimes it's almost ludicrously simple. You see an actor painfully searching for the reality of a character at a moment in the play, and yet it continues to elude him. So often you can get the most fantastic results by saying, "Darling, try twice the pace," and reality falls upon the actor like a cloak. Well, that's the trick that you learn with experience.

Ask a singer about his technique and he'll say, "Of course I'm perfectly in tune. I do happen to be gifted with the most glorious voice, and I've learned through years and years and years of solid practice and work how to place it."

Members of the audience must be respected; they must never be underestimated. It's very easy to sneer behind your handkerchief and wink at your fellows in the wings, but among that sea of faces beyond the footlights some will know. It is the same wherever you go, in all forms of entertainment: you respect them, they may respect you. They can be manipulated, of course, but that's something else. This they enjoy, this is why they are here; but they must not be handled clumsily or obviously.

I learned about audiences at a very early age. You had to if you wanted to keep the grown-ups awake on sleepy afternoons.

My sister shelters with cherishing love a large wooden packing case that was my first stage when I was about six. She still keeps it in the trunk room. It is about the size of the inside of a car, and I used to draw curtains in front of it. My father always bought Gold Flake cigarettes in fifties, in little circular tins, and I would cut them down and put a candle in each so that I'd have little footlights. And there, in my theater, I'd perform my own plays, entirely my own "works."

"Let's pretend," as I have already said, is the original impulse of acting. I didn't know about Thespis, and I'm certain nobody told me. But there it was, in a wooden box, lit by candles in cigarette tins: the first Olivier

Theatre. Of course, it becomes more difficult as the years move on. Acting really is a young enthusiasm, a childish excitement, a glamour that soon disappears. It is then that the hard work begins. The effort to improve yourself, to carve yourself into different shapes, to be successful, to be famous. What's the alternative? An office building and a bowler hat. In my case it might have been the Church. Mind you, that's not a bad auditorium.

The actor creates his own universe, then peoples it—a giant puppet master. The trick is to make the audience feel that they are observing reality, and this isn't easy, because to convey the word that has been placed in your mouth to a great number of people you have to exaggerate subtly, ever so slightly highlight. Lead the audience by the nose to the thought.

I hear remarks in the street or in a shop and I retain them. You must constantly observe: a walk, a limp, a run; how a head inclines to one side when listening; the twitch of an eyebrow; the hand that picks the nose when it thinks no one is looking; the mustache puller; the eyes that never look at you; the nose that sniffs long after the cold has gone.

Rhythms. Observe the speech patterns; keep them in your head, in your magic box. Store them until you need them, then use them. The way people walk down a bus or a subway train, one arm bent behind or both hands brought forward, elbows in as if in fear of accidental indecent contact. Then, in speech, the curious differences in lingual and dental contact. A weak R, the lisp that is just detectable. The plum that has somehow got itself lodged behind the epiglottis. The tongue that is too large for the mouth. The loose tooth, the false tooth. The adenoids that should have been removed in early years. The tight underpants that might raise vocal delivery somewhere towards the roof. The humble, the ingratiating, the toad. The jester, the minister, the king.

Try traveling on the London Circle Line underground. I worked on it as a gateman during the General Strike of 1926. It is exactly what the name says: a continuous circle round London, starting at A and returning to A. It's a favorite haunt for tramps in the winter, warm and snug, moving yet always returning to base. Get on, let's say, at King's Cross, and spend an hour returning to King's Cross, and observe. You will see more characters than you've ever dreamed of. It's quite astonishing. Go once in the early-morning rush hour and then again in the leisurely afternoon. Everything you need will be there.

I sometimes look at faces and attempt to place them in another period. Some lend themselves splendidly to this, and others not a jot. The modern man, he's impossible. You can't dislodge him at all. He is never older than the second that just passed. But period man, he's much more fun. You can recostume him in your imagination and place him wherever you will.

I like to think my face has always been like a blank canvas, ready to be shaped as I wished. It has always been my great joy to surprise an audience. Catch them on the hop. "My God, is *that him?*" I always had that

Jeremiah Lamenting the Destruction of Jerusalem, by Rembrandt

childish idea that they wouldn't recognize me one week from the previous week.

Galleries are another place where lessons can be learned. The National Portrait Gallery is a favorite place of mine. Here you can almost grow into the paintings. You can see how to shape a makeup by reading the highlights of the artist. In the Tate Gallery much can be learned from Gauguin, Van Gogh, Turner. If you're in Amsterdam, look at Rembrandt's *Jeremiah Lamenting*

the Destruction of Jerusalem: there is Shakespeare's Lear.
Well, a part of him.

The zoo: some actors swear by it, and spend hours
watching the animals. I agree this can help too, as witness my Othello, but to me the bars get in the way.
What we are looking at, observing, is captivity: the lion
or the tiger padding backwards and forwards, and dreaming of its native land. Captivity breeds its own particular
movement, and I think the only way to learn from animals would be to watch them in their natural environ-
ment. Observation in the zoo would work well, of course,
if you were playing a prisoner, but there aren't too many
of such parts around.

I once heard a story of a young actor who went to
London Zoo when he was about to play the part of the
Fool in *Lear.* He was standing in front of the baboons
when he became aware of someone behind him. He
turned and recognized an older actor. The older actor
looked at him for a moment and then pointed at the
enclosure. "When I played it," he said, "I was the one
up in the corner with the red bottom."

But when we talk of using animals as models, we are
going back to the dawn of drama, to dance and to rituals.
To the time when we performed as animals and donned
animal skins. They were very much part of our makeup
(not the Leichner kind): the bear, the lion, the tiger,
the elephant, the ape. We mimicked them leaping about
under the moon or the sun. We sacrificed them, we
hunted them, and always we lived beside them. They
might turn on us, we might turn on them—whichever

became hungry first. We were always an inch away from death.

So we had our drama, and played our games, and performed before the king. We bent over backwards to entertain the elders. We tumbled before the tribe and told tales, stood on our heads and juggled with beads. We beat drums and blew notes through horns; we swung on ropes and walked through fires. And above all, we danced; we beat out a rhythm with our bare feet on the warm earth. We worshiped the sun and the moon, and we performed rituals to make the corn grow and the rain fall. The actor was the center of the village's attention. Even then he wore the two masks, the mouth rising in smile or drooping in sorrow. He could make you laugh or cry, sometimes both at the same time. He was the mirror of his time, the newspaper, the radio. If you stood in front of him, he could show you yourself. If he performed well, he was applauded and showered with garlands and trinkets; if he performed badly, he was jeered and cast out—no different from today.

Well, there we were, drumming up our one-man shows, when along came Thespis. "Thespian" is too broad and flattering a term with which to describe our craft's practitioners. "Interpreter" is all stern judgment allows us; "artist" must be a rarely justified boast.

The actor has always been among us from dawn of man, and he always will be. And so it has gone through the generations—the actor's inherent instinct to survive. We still feel that at any moment the laughter will stop and the rain of tomatoes will begin. I don't think there has ever been any true actor who has not felt this. To this day I still feel it and know I will go on feeling it until I have given my final performance.

We actors stand by our present performance, not by our past. We are as immediate as the moment. We give you our feelings and hope you will return yours. We ask for acceptance; we are your servants.

Scratch an actor and underneath you'll find another actor.

CHAPTER TWO

Lessons
from the Past

BURBAGE, Garrick, Kean, Irving: four names that handed on the Shakespearean mantle to our generation. That's why today, performing Shakespeare, we can feel close to him; that his ink is still wet on the paper. Burbage did not know Garrick, Garrick did not know Kean and Kean did not know Irving, but it is the little cogs in between that make it all work, make it fascinating. Burbage created Hamlet and then, some time after, rehearsed a young actor, Joseph Taylor, in the part. Taylor played for the King's Company at the Globe and Blackfriars theaters. Being the second Hamlet and taught by the first, he must have automatically retained some of Burbage's original performance. Thomas Betterton played Hamlet and had studied with Sir William D'Avenant, who had seen Taylor. Garrick studied and learned from some of the older members of Betterton's company, and Kean from the survivors of Garrick's company, and then on to Irving. It all sounds very romantic, but looked at in this way it doesn't make William seem so very far away. . . .

Clearly Richard Burbage, the first Shakespearean actor, must have been good, for he was Shakespeare's favorite. No matter how well liked you are by an author, if he does not think you are doing justice to his script, he won't use you.

What was he like, this man Burbage? What was he really like? Was he good, or did he just happen to be around at the right time and in the right place? No, he must have been all right. William wouldn't have settled for rubbish. How extraordinary it must have been creating those parts for the first time. Hamlet, Lear, Othello. Did he know that four hundred years later actors would still be grappling with them? Were the two of them aware of the legacy they were handing on, or were they modern men concerned only with their time?

Of course, one thing to remember is that Shakespeare didn't know how marvelous he was. I wonder, did Burbage? Shakespeare had left Stratford and come to London. He got a job as a minor actor at the Globe play-

house, south of the Thames. The company soon found
him invaluable. He'd say, "Look, I've had an idea.
. . . I've got an idea about that scene." Then he'd give
them three or four sheets of paper which would turn out
to be magical stuff. After a while they would say to him,
"Look, Will, we need—oh, a good ten lines here. See if
you can make the situation—you know what the situation is—just—can you sort of put a cap on it with that?"
And Shakespeare would have this fantastic gift of doing
so.

When I say he didn't know how talented he was, I
think that would apply only to the early days. By the
time he was into his own stuff, I think he must have
been very much aware. He was inspired in the realms of
philosophy and philology; in almost everything he was
fantastically marvelous. I think it was an Elizabethan—I
was going to say fashion, but it was an Elizabethan gift,
the use of language. If there hadn't been a Shakespeare
or a Bacon, God knows what the English language would
have been like, or would be like now.

So Burbage was the interpreter and must have been
aware of what he was about. It is obviously difficult to
visualize what Burbage was really like, but here is a description that I came upon by Richard Flecknoe, which
would seem to give Burbage a seat on the throne of
Thespis:

> Burbage was a delightful Proteus, so wholly trans-
> forming himself into his part, and putting off him-
> self with his clothes, as he never (not so much as in
> the Tyring-House) Assum'd himself again until the

RICHARD BURBADGE.

Richard Burbage Edmund Kean

David Garrick Henry Irving

THREE ILLUSTRATIONS: VICTORIA AND ALBERT MUSEUM

play was done; there being as much difference between him and one of our common actors as between a Ballad singer who only mouths it and an
excellent singer, who knows all his Graces, and can
artfully vary and modulate his Voice, even to know
how much breath he is to give every syllable. He
had all the parts of an excellent orator (animating
his words with speaking, and with Speech and Action) his Auditors being never more delighted than
when he spoke, nor more sorry than when he held
his peace; yet even then he was an excellent actor
still, never falling in his part, when he had done
speaking; but with his looks and gesture, maintain-
ing it still unto the height, he imaging age *quod
agis*, only spoke to him: so as those who called him
a player do him wrong, with only this difference
from other mens, that is what is but a play to them,
is his Business; so their business is but a play to him.

(A *Short Discourse on the English Stage*, 1665)

Burbage's epitaph reads:

Hee's gone and with him what a world are dead,
Which he reuiud, to be reuiued soe.
No more young Hamlet, ould Heironymoe.
King Leer, the greued Moore, and more beside,
That lived in him, have now forever dy'de.

Well, fortunately, they did not die; they were handed
on. As I've explained, Burbage had schooled Joseph Taylor, who had been observed and remembered by Sir
William D'Avenant, who in turn tutored Betterton,
whose company, more than a hundred years after the
death of the first Hamlet, passed it on to Garrick.

It would appear that when David Garrick burst upon the scene, the theater had been lulled to sleep by sweet tones: beautiful voices, lyricism; romantic, hollow, sweet cadences signifying little. Garrick arrived on the scene and things began to change. No longer the sameness of tone: now there were sudden starts and ominous pauses—dare we say a hint of reality? Here's an extract from Garrick's contemporary biographer Thomas Davies, describing his debut in London:

> On the 19th of October, 1741, David Garrick acted *Richard III* for the first time, at the playhouse in Goodman's Fields. So many idle persons under the title of gentlemen acting for their diversion, had exposed their incapacity at the theatre, and had so often disappointed the audiences, that no very large company was brought together to see the new performer. However, several of his own acquaintances, many of them persons of good judgement, were assembled at the usual hour; though we may well believe, that the greater part of the audience were stimulated by curiosity to see the event, than invited by any hopes of rational entertainment.
>
> An actor, who, in the first display of his talents, undertakes a principal character, has generally, amongst other difficulties, the prejudices of the audience to struggle with, in favour of an established performer. Here indeed they were not insurmountable; Cibber, who had been much admired in *Richard*, had left the stage. Quin who was the popular player, but his manner of heaving up his words,

and his laboured action, prevented his being a favourite Richard.

Mr Garrick's easy and familiar, yet forcible style of speaking and acting, at first threw the critics into some hesitation concerning the novelty as well as the propriety of his manner. They had been long accustomed to an elevation of the voice, with a sudden mechanical depression of its tones, calculated to excite admiration, and to intrap applause. To the just modulation of the words, and concurring expression of the features from the genuine workings of nature, they had been strangers, at least for some time. But after he had gone through a variety of scenes, in which he gave evident proofs of consummate art, and perfect knowledge of character, their doubts were turned into surprise and astonishment, from which they relieved themselves in loud and reiterated applause. They were more especially charmed when the actor, after having thrown aside the hypocrite and politician, assumed the warrior and hero. When news was brought to Richard, that the Duke of Buckingham was taken, Garrick's look and action, when he pronounced the words, '—Off with his head! So much for Buckingham!' were so significant and important, from his visible enjoyment of the incident, that several loud shouts of approbation proclaimed the triumph of the actor and the satisfaction of the audience. The death of Richard was accompanied with the loudest congratulations of applause.

(*Memoirs of the Life of Garrick
with Anecdotes of Theatrical Contemporaries*, 1780)

The great theatrical volcano had erupted once again, and a giant was standing astride the London scene. Garrick was to rule until his death in 1779. He must have been very special indeed, towering above his contemporaries and blazing a theatrical path towards the next century.

> There is in Mr Garrick's whole figure, movements and propriety of demeanour something with which I have met with rarely in the few Frenchmen I have seen and never, except in this instance, among the large number of Englishmen with whom I am acquainted. I mean in this context Frenchmen who have at least reached middle age; and, naturally, those moving in good society. For example, when he turns to someone with a bow, it is not merely that the head, the shoulders, the feet and arms are engaged in this exercise, but that each member helps with great propriety to produce the demeanour most pleasing and appropriate to the occasion. When he steps on to the boards, even when not expressing fear, hope, suspicion, or any other passion, the eyes of all are immediately drawn to him alone, he moves to and fro among the other players like a man among marionettes. From this no one indeed, will recognise Mr Garrick's ease of manner, who has never remarked the demeanour of a well bred Frenchman, but this being the case, this hint would be the best description. . . .

This is an excerpt from a letter by Georg Christoph Lichtenberg. He goes on to say:

. . . He has complete command over the muscles of his body. I am convinced that his thick-set form does much towards producing this effect. His shapely legs become gradually thinner from the powerful thighs downwards, until they end in the neatest foot you can imagine; in the same way his large arms taper into a little hand. How imposing the effect of this must be you can well imagine. But this strength is not merely illusory. He is really strong and amazingly dexterous and nimble.

(*Lichtenberg's Visits to England*, Clarendon Press, 1938)

Garrick sounds the complete actor. He must have been astonishing to observe: ". . . The eyes of all are immediately drawn to him alone." Does this mean that the other members of the company were pretty dull? I don't think so. I imagine he was supported by good actors, but that *he* was up there with the gods.

Garrick took over the Theatre Royal, Drury Lane, in 1747, just six years after his London debut. He seems to have been a good manager and caring about the members of his company. He brought a discipline into the theater that hadn't been there before. Where things had grown shoddy and slapdash, he insisted on neatness and concentration. Actors had long been making up their own versions of the author's original—a sort of bastard version of improvisation. Garrick changed all this. He'd drop an actor, rather like a player on a football team, until he had learned to respect the audience and the author. What had happened was that actors had grown

lazy and probably in time had come to believe that their
versions of the text were the correct ones. We have all
done this at one time or another. What he eventually
achieved with his company was amazing ensemble playing. For confirmation of this, here's an extract from
Davies's memoirs of the time:

> . . . I need only mention one of the plays he re-
> vived; the *Every Man in His Humour*, of Ben
> Jonson, where all the personages were so exactly
> fitted to the look, voice, figure and talents of the
> actor that no play which comprehends so many dis-
> tinct peculiarities of humour was ever perhaps so
> completely acted; and to this care of the manager
> restoring this obsolete play to the stage may very
> justly be attributed its great success.

It sounds as though Garrick achieved the ensemble
playing that has since been emulated by such companies
as the Berliner Ensemble, the Moscow Art Theater, the
Abbey Theater of Dublin, the Royal Shakespeare Company and, I like to think, my own National Theatre
Company.

To achieve true theater, you can't have one man up
front and the acolytes with their backs to the audience
simply feeding the great star with lines. What you must
have is every character believing in himself and, therefore, contributing to the piece as a whole, placing and
pushing the play in the right direction. The third spear
carrier on the left should believe that the play is all about
the third spear carrier on the left. I've always believed
that. If the character is nameless, the actor should give

himself a name. He should give himself a family, a background, a past. Where was he born; what did he have for breakfast? Perhaps he had troubles at home, perhaps his wife has left him, perhaps his wife has just presented him with a new baby, perhaps he is saving for something—and so on. If the actor brings on with him a true belief in himself, we should be able to look at him at any moment during the action and see a complete three-dimensional figure and not a cardboard cutout. For an audience to be transported, they must see life and not paste.

The theater lost its ensemble playing after Garrick and didn't find it again until the great companies of Irving. In between came Edmund Kean, who was born in 1789 and was definitely a one-man band.

Kean's greatest asset was his dedication—something all actors must have. They cannot just turn on and turn off whenever they fancy. They must have dedication and determination, blinkered and concerned with nothing but the self that wants to get up there and act. They must be totally egocentric and prepared to climb, clamber, elbow, jostle and scythe their way through to the top. If, at the end, they still have friends, they are remarkable. Doesn't sound very attractive put like that, does it?

Edmund Kean had all of that and more, and he wore himself out by the time he was forty-four. What an extraordinary man he must have been—"the Sun's Bright Child." He walked from Birmingham to Bristol with his family in tow to gain employment; one of the children died on the road. He signed contracts, and unsigned contracts. He bulldozed his way through society—perhaps not a very likable man, except to the group of sycophants who drank with him in the Coalhole in the Strand. I imagine he must have been completely self-centered and, when not enjoying adulation, was out of his brains with alcohol. Yet in spite of this, the pleasure he gave has lived on through the years. Perhaps I'm a little hard on him; I mean, after all, I didn't know him. He really must have been very special indeed. What was it Coleridge said of him: "It's like reading Shakespeare by flashes of lightning"? He arrived on the scene and extinguished Kemble almost overnight. Hazlitt said of his Richard III:

> He gives animation, vigour and relief to the part, which we have never seen surpassed. In one who dares so much, there is little, indeed, to blame. The progress of wily adulation, of encroaching humility, was finely marked throughout by the action, voice and eye. He seemed like the first tempter, to approach his prey, certain of the event and as if success had smoothed the way before him. Richard should woo not as a lover, but as an actor, to show his mental superiority and power, to make the others the playthings of his will. Mr Kean's attitude in leaning against the side of the stage before he comes forward in a scene, was one of the most graceful and striking we remember to have seen.
>
> (A View of the English Stage, 1818–21)

Before the booze got to him he must have been quite startling: the little wild man, eyes blazing and brain full of poetry. He must have been very physical, athletic and strong. I think he was a tumbler when he was a boy.

The story goes that on his first night at Drury Lane,

an unknown playing Shylock, Kean was living on the south side of the River Thames and didn't have the money for the toll to cross the bridge. So he swam the Thames instead. I'm sure it's a huge exaggeration and probably didn't take place at all, but it's a lovely thought. He more than likely put the story about himself. There's nothing like a piece of romantic public relations. But even if he didn't do it, I'm sure that if it had been necessary, he would have done it. As, indeed, I would. Determination.

His first night at the Theatre Royal must have been quite extraordinary. He had not rehearsed with his fellow actors. That was according to the custom in those days; the moves were set and then the star would come in. No doubt he had a dress rehearsal, but even that is not established. If he had, he probably just walked the role, so nobody would have been aware of what was about to happen. He was entirely new to the London scene. Of course, the management would have seen him—probably in Dorchester, where he was very popular, and not just on the stage.

The Theatre Royal was looking for a new star. Everything was happening with the rivals at Covent Garden, but not at the Lane. It is said that on the first night the Theatre Royal was half full—probably half full with curiosity. News would have got about that an unknown was going to play Shylock. He must have been electric. In the interval, the thrilled audience from the Lane mingled with the audience from Covent Garden, and soon the word was about. By the end of the evening the Theatre

Royal was packed and cheering—and Edmund Kean was a star.

I like to think there is some truth in the story. I'm sure there is. So far as Drury Lane was concerned, Kean was a gamble—but what a gamble. He paid off in capacity box offices. He took the theater by the scruff of the neck and shook it back into life. He carried the Theatre Royal on his back and thrust it up into the big time again. He was a major star and a major classical actor.

Obviously we cannot believe everything that is written about him; no man is without bias, and none more so than critics. But somehow I feel there must be a lot of truth in what Coleridge and Hazlitt said. They were men who were respected in their time, and when you consider that Hazlitt went to see Kean play Richard no fewer than three times in 1814, twice in February and again in October, writing about it on each occasion, there must have been something worth watching. It is such a shame that the only records we have are on paper. There is a prompt copy of Kean's *Richard III* in the British Museum, in which the dear little assistant stage manager inserted the maestro's inflections. From this we can get a vague idea of how he performed rhythmically and where he paused, and what, perhaps, he may have sounded like. But the rest, like Kean himself, has gone in the flash of Coleridge's lightning.

So what did he pass on? I think his approach was probably the nearest we have to the modern theater of today. A reality. I think he burst through the romantic

form and presented a raw freshness that knocked the
audiences sideways, the audiences that had held up
Kemble as a god. I think he opened their eyes to the
truth and thrilled them out of the boxes.

Of course, in the early 1800s they were still happily
booing and hissing and throwing things—not always tomatoes. By the end of his life, Kean knew both sides of
his audience's face. Leigh Hunt said of him two years
before his death:

> Now, Kean we never see without being moved, and
> moved too, in fifty ways by his sarcasm, his sweet-
> ness, his pathos, his exceeding grace, his gallant
> levity, his measureless dignity; for his little person
> absolutely becomes tall and rises to the height of
> moral grandeur in such characters as that of
> Othello. We have seen him with three or four per-
> sons round him, all taller than he, but himself so
> graceful, so tranquil, so superior, so nobly self-
> possessed in the midst, that the mind of the specta-
> tor rose above them by this means, and so gave him
> a moral stature that confounded itself with the
> personal.   (*Tatler*, 1931)

In addition, there was about Kean a generosity. When
a friend asked Kean to help him out by appearing in his
benefit performance in Liverpool, Edmund agreed with
alacrity. He was to play Richard III to his friend's Duke
of Buckingham. They repaired, naturally, to the local
hostelry and talked about good times, bad times and old
times. By the time they got to the theater, they were
warm inside and in the head. After Edmund's first

speech the audience began to scream, "Mr. Kean, you're drunk!" After a long pause, he stared with those penetrating eyes at the hostile house and replied, "If you think I'm drunk, wait till you see Buckingham." This story has been told many times over the years and attached to other actors, but I believe it started in Liverpool about 1830.

I don't think Kean's mantle was picked up until Henry Irving came along; he was born five years after Kean died. Of course there were others in between. Irving didn't start acting at birth, or if he did, nothing is recorded. But I don't think they were in the same league. There was Charles, Kean's son, but he seemed to be suffering under his father's name, though he did make rather a good career for himself. Then, of course, there was Macready, but anyone who is remembered solely for his pause can't have been that hot. No, for me, the mantle came straight on to Irving.

Kean was Irving's idol, though, of course, he never saw him; but on the first night of *The Bells* he must have felt very close to him. Again, rather like Kean's Shylock, Irving's Mathias did not open to a full house. However, in no time at all it was the talk of the town ind Irving had the English theater in his hands. His determination must have been similar to his idol's. Once he was acclaimed, he became the master and champion of his profession.

Perhaps an example of Irving's determination and dedication is shown in the story of what happened on his

way home after his triumph at the Lyceum on that first
night, 15 November 1871. He turned to his wife, Florence,
and said, "Well, my dear, we too shall soon have our
own carriage and pair." After a pause, Florence apparently said something in the heat of the moment
which she may have regretted the rest of her life: she
said, "Are you going to go on making a fool of yourself
like this all of your life?" Irving told the driver of the
brougham in which they were traveling to stop. I believe
they were at Hyde Park Corner. Irving got out and raised
his hat, saying, "Good night, my dear. We shall never
meet again," and his wife completed the journey alone.
He never returned home, and he never spoke to Florence
again.

I think Irving and Kean must have approached roles
in a similar fashion, because both searched for the truth,
both had flashes of fire; but I imagine as human beings
they were very different. Although the Coalhole tavern
was closer to Irving's Lyceum than to Kean's Theatre
Royal—just a question of crossing the road—I don't
think the tavern's clientele would have seen much of the
great man. Irving became a leader of his profession in
every sense of the word, whereas Kean, when work was
done, only too quickly returned to a world of oblivion—
the Coalhole. Not that this affects either's contribution.
What was shown in both men's spotlit world was up-
lifting, exciting and unforgettable, and though they
never met, Kean's hand touched Irving's through the
voices of others. The five-year gap between a death and a

birth was bridged by Kean's contemporaries who had decided not to creep into their wooden overcoats with the assistance of John Barleycorn as Kean had.

The one thing the two great actors certainly had in common, apart from their talent, was that they both died penniless. But, as Irving said, he had "not been sent into this world to collect money."

My generation was brought up on the memory of Irving. To me he was a great idol, though I didn't see him, being born two years after his death. The hand-touching continues. Actors mimicked him and then passed their mimicry on to us. We were young men doing our own thing, but we all loved to sniff the past in our nostrils. When I was a young actor, Irving was clearly remembered. There was still a romance about his last night on a stage: how he had altered Becket's line "God's will be done" to "God is my judge"; and when he recited Becket's last line, "Into thy hands, O Lord, into thy hands," he had fallen to the floor, but upstage instead of downstage, his head towards the choir. Probably only half-truths, but nevertheless romantic enough to transport the listener to the wings of the Theatre Royal, Bradford.

In my company of 1963, I searched for actors who were as capable of playing Richard, Othello or Lear as I was. I was determined to surround myself with good actors and first-rate directors. I didn't want any wimps who would disappear into the shadows or, indeed, go the other way and shine out like a spotlit sore thumb. I didn't want someone who, as Beverly Baxter once said of

Kenneth Tynan when he was an actor, "waves at his friends in the audience and exits through the scenery." I wanted people who were prepared to outgun me; I wanted the new cream of the British theater, and I think I got it. Looking back at my company and seeing what has happened to them over the years, establishing themselves as leading actors in their own right, I think I succeeded. It has always been a thrill and a joy for me to see a new talent emerge, grasp the bit between its teeth and race down the course.

We should encourage and not stifle. I'm sure Garrick did this, and Davies's report confirms it. He surrounded himself with the best people of his day, and left the dross. Of course, there weren't as many actors around then as there are today, but because of that, I think there were probably more good ones than bad. I think the ones that were involved really wanted to do it. It wasn't a question of "Oh, well, if I fail my exams to become a doctor, I'll settle for acting." It was much more than that. Of course, a great many people were born into it—the family trade, as it were.

I heard a lady once say to her son, "But my dear, you surely don't mean you would become an *actor!*"—making it sound like Lady Bracknell's "A handbag!" Even in my youth the actor was still on the fringe of society. He was to be patronized rather than accepted; he was an amusement, a plaything still looked upon as a rogue and a vagabond. Romantic, but not socially enticing, all right for placing a discreet hand beneath the mistress's skirts, but not suitable for walking down the aisle and sharing a

golden band. Irving was the first individual actor to become socially acceptable, but even today there is an air
about the profession which says "wrong side of the
sheets." So in Garrick's day I believe you either were
born into it, or simply had to do it or die.

When Garrick took over Drury Lane, he was determined to make it the best playhouse in the land, and
not just a crown in which to set his own theatrical jewel.
He wanted the best and fought to get it. He was a great
one for rehearsing, which had really been unheard of before, a play being put on in five days at the most. Garrick
worked at each play for weeks, and would cut, rewrite
and add scenes if he felt it necessary. He would use the
ideas of his company as well as his own, which was the
start of true ensemble.

There is a story about the rehearsals of *Every Man in
His Humour*. An actor in the company called Woodward, considered one of the best comedians of his day,
appeared very attentive to Garrick's direction while rehearsing the part of Bobadil. However, during Garrick's
absence one morning, he decided to do it his way and
had the rest of the cast falling about and applauding his
antics. During this exhibition Garrick came in at the
back of the playhouse undetected and watched what was
going on. After a time he came forward and let his presence be known, much to the embarrassment of Woodward. There was a stunned silence. All looked to the
great man. He paused and stared back. The class had
been chalking on the blackboard while the teacher was
out of the room. He stepped up onto the stage and went

over to Woodward. Another pause; then, suddenly,
"Bravo Harry! Bravo! Upon my soul, bravo! Why, now,
this is, no, no, I can't say this is quite my idea of the
thing . . . yours is, after all . . . to be sure, rather . . .
ha!" Another pause. Woodward, embarrassed, replied,
"Sir, I will act the part, if you desire it, exactly according
to your notion of it." Another pause, and a smile from
Garrick: "No, no, by no means, Harry. Damn it, you
have actually clenched the matter. But why, my dear
Harry, would you not communicate before?"

If we are to believe it, and I do, we can hear the actors
still breathing in that company. The manager caught the
moment and used it. Instead of creating an embarrassing
scene or stealing away and pretending it had never happened, he took Woodward's idea and saw what he could
do with it. I'm sure, from that moment on, he had a
staunch ally in Harry Woodward.

The same has happened to me on more than one occasion. My actors at the National seemed to have an uncanny knack of doing devilish impersonations of me. I
believe there is still a tape around, though I have not
heard it, of an imaginary conversation on Waterloo
Bridge between myself, John Gielgud, Ralph Richardson
and Richard Burton, all done by one actor—who, need-
less to say, has gone on to become an international star
in his own right. I must do an impersonation of him one
day.

When his production of *Every Man in His Humour*
opened, Garrick was still only thirty-three, a young man
in his prime. It was said of Woodward's performance,

which had been encouraged by Garrick, that it was his masterpiece in low comedy.

Some thirteen years later, in 1763, Garrick, by this time well established as actor and manager, decided to make changes in the theater itself. He decided to be rid of stage spectators. Until then there had been two audiences, one in the auditorium and one on the stage. Often there were so many on the stage that the actors had little more than a pocket handkerchief to work on.

It was often the case that when an actor had a benefit, he would arrange for his friends to be in the stage boxes, making the occasion rather like a party. Consequently, there were some disastrous results. An actor called Holland was performing Hamlet for his own benefit and, on seeing the Ghost, reacted with such reality that his hat flew off. When Hamlet complained that the air "bites shrewdly" and was very cold, a female friend of Holland's who was a stage spectator calmly got up, crossed the stage, picked up the hat and replaced it on Holland's head. The house erupted in peals of laughter and the Ghost, without any more ceremony, left the stage, followed by a very embarrassed Mr. Holland.

Problems also arose over exits and entrances. If the stage spectators were present in force, it was often difficult to make one or the other. A certain actor playing Falstaff was apparently covered in so much padding that it took him a full five minutes to squeeze through. Sometimes the actor was greeted by his friends and held in conversation. So Garrick decided to remove the stage spectators, but came up against a lot of opposition, as it would mean a decrease in revenue and would certainly affect the pockets of the actors on their benefit nights. He and his partner, James Lacy, eventually got round this by deciding to enlarge the theater. If the space before the curtain contained as many people as had formerly filled the pit, boxes, galleries and stage, there could be no complaints. The enlargements were completed in 1762, and from that time onwards only the actors were allowed on the stage.

It then, of course, became the custom to entertain in the dressing rooms, and sometimes an interval could last as long as an hour and, if Royalty was backstage, even longer. But going to the theater then really was a night out, according to George Lichtenberg:

Hamlet has folded his arms under his cloak and pulled his hat down over his eyes; it is a cold night and just twelve o'clock; the theatre is darkened, and the whole audience of thousands are as quiet, and their faces as motionless, as though they were painted on the walls of the theatre; even from the farthest end of the playhouse one could hear a pin drop. Suddenly, Hamlet moves towards the back of the stage slightly to the left, and turns his back on the audience. Horatio starts, and saying, 'Look, my Lord, it comes,' points to the right where the Ghost has already appeared and stands motionless before anyone is aware of him. At these words Garrick turns sharply and, at the same moment, staggers back two or three paces with his knees giving way under him; his hat falls to the ground and both his arms, especially the left, are stretched out

nearly to their full length, with the hands as high
as his head, the right arm more bent, and the hands
lower and the fingers apart; his mouth is open; thus
he stands rooted to the spot, with legs apart, but no
loss of dignity, supported by his friends, who are
better acquainted with the apparition and fear lest
he should collapse. His whole demeanour is so ex-
pressive of terror that it made my flesh creep even
before he began to speak. The almost terror-struck
silence of the audience, which preceded this appearance and filled one with a sense of insecurity, probably did much to enhance this effect. At last he
speaks, not at the beginning, but at the end of a
breath, with a trembling voice: 'Angels and minis-
ters of grace defend us!'—words which supply anything this scene may lack and make it one of the
greatest and most terrible that will ever be played
on any stage. The Ghost beckons to him: I wish
you could see him, with eyes fixed on the Ghost,
though he is speaking to his companions, freeing
himself from their restraining hands, as they warn
him not to follow and hold him back. But at
length, when they have tried his patience too far,
he turns his face towards them, tears himself with
great violence from their grasp and draws his sword
on them with a swiftness that makes one shudder,
saying: 'By Heaven! I'll make a ghost of him that
lets me!' That is enough for them. Then he stands
with his sword held out so as to make him keep his
distance, and, at length when the spectator can no
longer see the Ghost, he begins slowly to follow
him, now standing still and then going on, with

sword still upon guard, eyes fixed on the Ghost, hair disordered, and out of breath, until he, too, is lost to sight. You can well imagine what loud applause accompanies this exit. It begins as soon as the Ghost goes off the stage and lasts until Hamlet disappears. . . .

I don't think I'd have approved of the applause at the end of the scene, but the rest sounds magnetic.

So there we have it. Burbage, Garrick, Kean and Irving. Great volcanoes, as far as I am concerned; heads high above the rest of the field. I believe that these four were the true innovators. They came along when the theater needed them and shook it into life again.

It would appear that I am dismissing the others in between, and I suppose I am, but that is not to say that they were not good. I'm sure some of them were very fine indeed—fellows like Betterton, Macklin, Quin, Phelps, Kemble and, of course, dear old "pause" Macready—but for me it was the four who built the signposts.

However, there was one man later whom I did see and who certainly had an influence upon me. It was 1924; I was seventeen, alive, active and full of tomorrow. I spent a lot of my time in those days sitting in the galleries of London theaters, looking down at the fashionable talent of the day, drinking in, remembering, learning. At this time a man came to London, a man who was very special, very immediate and very different. He was from another planet as far as my young eyes were concerned. I decided that for this man the gallery must be put aside; I needed to be in there, floor level, where I could see the eyes. I

spent the extra and stood in the pit. Through the whole
house there was a feeling of expectation. Whenever I
walk into a theater I feel that I am at home, and that
night it was even more so. I was tingling, nerve ends excited, eyes open, waiting. The last bar bell sounded, the
last empty seats were occupied, the front-of-house lights
dimmed, the chattering stopped and there was an ex-
pectant silence. A pause, a beat; then the curtain went up:

> Who's there?
> Nay, answer me. Stand and unfold yourself.
> Long live the King! . . .

Everyone waiting for Scene II.

> Let's do't, I pray; and I this morning know
> Where we shall find him most conveniently.
>
> Exeunt.

SCENE II

> Though yet of Hamlet . . .

On, on . . .

> A little more than kin, and less than kind!

There he was, the amazing Jack Barrymore, on stage
at the Haymarket. Everything about him was exciting.
He was athletic, he had charisma and, to my young
mind, he played the part to perfection. Although he was
American, his English speech was perfect. He was as-
tounding. He had everything going for him, including
startling good looks.

My Hamlets in later years owed a great deal to Jack
Barrymore. It seemed to me that he breathed life into

1924, Barrymore as Hamlet   SACHA/BBC HULTON

the character, which, since Irving, had descended into
arias and false inflections—all very beautiful and poetic,
but castrated. Barrymore put back the balls. I'm not saying he was next in line after Irving—I don't think he was,
or perhaps I did not see enough of him—but I think the
"old boys" would have approved of his approach. When
he was on stage, the sun came out. Some critics knocked

him for his way of speaking verse, as, indeed, was to happen to me in later years. They were wrong; I know they were wrong. He had a way of choosing a word and then exploding it in a moment of passion. Perhaps you did not always agree with the choice, but it was constantly riveting. He would vary his pace, but never gabble, was always understandable. There would be a sudden burst and then again a lull, rather like the wind freshening up before a squall. For my money he really seemed to understand Hamlet.

Barrymore was the top man in the American theater, a colossal talent: perhaps a little too leeched on by Hollywood, but then, that was a temptation that affected all our generation for a time. I'm sure that if Beverly Hills had been around for Burbage, Garrick, Kean and Irving, they would have boarded a fast ship to the New World before breakfast.

It would seem to me that Barrymore was the direct link with Edwin Booth, "the Prince of Players," probably the first of the great American actors. Booth's father, Junius Brutus Booth, was a contemporary of Kean's, so it's easy to see how things slowly match up, as in a detective story. The hand stretching down from Burbage finally crossed the Atlantic.

Not only were Kean and Junius Brutus Booth contemporaries, they also performed together, alternating the roles of Iago and Othello, both in Britain and in America. It is said that Kean used to upstage Booth by eating grapes during Booth's big speeches and digging the pips from between his teeth with his dagger.

Possibly true, but I'm sure Mr. Booth must have added a few touches of his own.

Perhaps I have quoted too much in this chapter, but I wanted you to be able to see through the eyes that were there. The past is one thing, but it is in the present that we live, and it is in the present that we perform.

We can learn from the past, and of course, so we should. We must retain and reject; but we must not forget the present.

Do we grow wiser as we get older, or have we just, like an old dog, learned a few extra tricks? I am seventeen going on eighty. I have learned, I have discovered, I have dismissed. I have led; I have been led, nose-ringed, by the past. In the end we must decide for ourselves; but it is making the right decisions that counts, deciding and holding on to your own beliefs, for it is you, and only you, at the end of the day, who can look after yourself. No one else really cares; you don't need glasses to see that self-preservation is on the menu. You must have the strength, the will and the determination of an ox, and you must believe in your own beliefs. Can a man preach from a Sunday pulpit and not believe? I think not, for if he does we will surely see the dust on his dog collar. We must, in the end, look to ourselves. We can take counsel, we can take advice, but in the end *we* must decide; it must be *our* decision. This is not to say we mustn't learn—we must. We must pick the brains of those who went before us; watch, learn and listen, research and discover; but above all, the final decision must be our own.

Moments will remain in our memory, things that we
have thought valuable, stored away somewhere in those
decaying memory cells. Of course, there will always be
a flavor of the past, for the past is a fact; but it is the
future we should be looking towards, because it is the
future that will be looking back at us. It is the future
that will be looking at yesterday, which is our present,
and in its turn will decide whether to retain or reject.
This does not mean that we should perform with one
eye on posterity; it does mean that we must perform
with integrity. Youth will always impersonate until it
has found its confidence and its own roots.

I am seventeen going on eighty. I will continue to
learn until all ceases to function. I know that the earth
turns and that the sun sets and the sun rises, but I must
always remember that somewhere in the shadows there
are new things to be seen.

Blazing away out there are the spirits of Burbage,
Garrick, Kean and Irving, lighting the theatrical sky
forever. Smiling, grinning, laughing and saying, "Follow
that!" I think that's how it will always be: "Who's on
next?" It's the music hall with the act numbers lighting
up at the side. It's not important to be top of the bill;
it's important to be the best.

Not everyone can join those giants who straddle the
theatrical world, grinning down at the Lilliputians, but
we can try. We must try. Above all we must be good.
That is all we can be, good. It is for other people to daub
the statue with what they will: genius, greatness or

whatever. But for this brief moment we are here, tread-
ing the mill that has been trod before, getting our ankles
wet and hoping that the horn will not be too green for
too long. Lead me by the nose, Richard, David, Edmund, Henry; lead me by the nose and then release me.
Let me make the judges think that I am the best bull
in the ring.

New actors, new waves, new ideas—it's all been done
before. What we forget is that every new generation is
the modern man. We are only watching things repeated
with different costumes, new settings, original surrounds.
However we look at it, it is still the same jewel, shining
from the crown, that was mined between 1564 and 1616.

> Good friend, for Jesus' sake forbear
> To dig the dust inclosed here.
> Blest be the man that spares these stones,
> And curst be he that moves my bones.

I like to think that some of our writers of today will
live, and somewhere in the next century they will be
mounting new productions in the orbital stations in the
sky. I am convinced that those great spinning metropo-
lises of the future will have a theater tucked somewhere
into their bosoms. In the next century, instead of going on tour to Manchester, Nottingham, Birmingham,
change trains at Crewe, it will be Orbital Station Two,
followed by Orbital Station Three. I can see the shuttle
from Heathrow now, blasting off the launching pad,
arrowing into space with a troupe of National Theatre
Players on board. Somewhere between here and Mars

an essayist or, perhaps, a computer will be discovering an actor for the first time: "Last night on Station Three we saw the most exciting Richard III since . . ."

Part Two

THE GREAT SHAKESPEAREAN ROLES

I HAVE lived with Shakespeare all my thinking life—the greatest dramatist of all time; to some the greatest poet, philosopher, man. With a flick of his pen, he can twist an audience from laughter to tears. His genius is unparalleled. He writes roles that any actor worth his salt would find the means to play by hook or by crook. He is matchless in wit, power, imagination, fire, philosophy . . . I could go on forever. But what he has above all is a magical sense of theater. His stories, though many of them are stolen and have been told before, are molded and fashioned in such a way that they shine as though they had been newly minted this morning. Whenever an actor comes to him, he should come with hunger and excitement. To make his language work from your brain to your fingertips is to fulfill your profession. You can come back to him time and time again, attacking the same role, and there will always be something new to discover. They say that even a bad actor playing Hamlet will get something right.

It has always been my intention to make Shakespeare as modern as possible. I don't mean in production: I mean to the ear. In my early days I was attacked for this—"Can't speak the verse"—but I was arrogant and confident enough to ride out this criticism, and I think I have been proved right. When *Henry V* happened, the audience knew what I was talking about. They weren't listening to someone singing an aria; they were hearing me set a man's thoughts before them as clearly as I could. On the first night of *Hamlet* at the Old Vic, Tyrone Guthrie, my director, came to the dressing room and said about my makeup, "Every inch a Hamlet. Think they'll probably fault you for the verse speaking, and to a certain extent they may be right, but I expect you will come to your own decisions about that in your own good time." I had to decide whether to rethink and obey the critics, or battle on and hope the critics might come to me.

An example is a production John Gielgud and I did of *Romeo and Juliet*. It's very easy, looking back, to criticize, but in those days there was a way of doing things. That was how they were *done*, and that was what the public came to see. They wanted their verse spoken beautifully, and if that was not how you delivered it, you were considered an upstart, an outsider. So I was the outsider and John was the jewel, and a shining one, too—deservedly so. John still has the most beautiful voice, but I felt in those days he allowed it to dominate his performances, and if he was lost for but a moment, he would dive straight back into its honey.

I thought his first Hamlet was wonderful, because he didn't allow himself to do that—he didn't sing. But as time went by I believe he sang it more and more. His fifth or sixth performance of Hamlet, as far as I was concerned, was a complete aria. For me this was a great disappointment. I said to myself, "That's wonderful in its way, but has he not gone backwards?"

His voice, of course, was musical enough to sell his performance to the people on the old grounds. He was giving the familiar tradition fresh life, whereas I was completely disregarding the old in favor of something new. Somehow I feel that he was a little led by the nose by his audience and by his acolytes. He was greatly admired, in fact adored, and like all of us at some time in our careers he believed his publicity. So by the time we did *Romeo*, I was considered by the Establishment to be his opponent. Everybody was in his favor, while I might have been from another planet. I can still remember some of the awful headlines. You always do, don't you? The good ones dance through your head and

1935, *Romeo and Juliet*. With Edith Evans as the Nurse, and John Gielgud as Mercutio; and with Peggy Ashcroft as Juliet

1940, *Romeo and Juliet*, with Vivien Leigh as Juliet

are forgotten in a day; the bad ones become indelibly stamped forever. Here's one from the *Evening News*: "A beautiful Juliet but . . ." Another said, "Mr. Olivier can play many parts; Romeo is not one of them. His blank verse is the blankest I've ever heard."

I made a terrible flop as Romeo because they said I couldn't speak verse. It was laughable from my point of view. I couldn't speak? I was brought up speaking; I'd been speaking verse since I was eight years old. But I didn't sing it, you see, and the fashion was perhaps to sing it.

What the hell! I think I was right, and I know that John will go on thinking that he was. Whatever the results, whichever side people come down on, we must have been fascinating to watch.

I wonder if he'd agree with me now—my outsider's approach that was so against the tradition of the time! The Establishment in those days must have thought me pretty mad; but on the other hand, they can't have thought me all that bad, for they went on employing me and the public continued to watch.

When I did my Hamlet I wanted to project this man's thoughts to people who had never had the opportunity to hear them before. Of course Shakespeare can be read, and indeed is—witness our school days. Reading him is better than nothing; but for my money, his plays must be seen. Presented by an actor, interpreted and projected from the other side of the curtain, that is where my job lies; that is the nature of my particular beast. You may not agree with my interpretation, but it is up to me to sell it to you as best I can.

Theater is more than a collection of effects, exits and entrances. The actor must take the audience on a journey. With tragedy, because the journey is predictable, the end must be cathartic. When you know what is going to happen, the point is twice as strong. It is a double realization. (This is also true of comedy. The second time you do the same gag, it brings the house down.) Rhythm and timing are needed to create effects which must also appear to be spontaneous: it is the seeming absolute spontaneity of reaction which makes the audience feel a moment of recognition, of new understanding. Reading may be better than nothing, but it is not the same as feeling and understanding Shakespeare's great lines through the interpretation of an actor.

Shakespeare was originally a popular playwright, a people's playwright; but as time and language changed so did our theatrical intelligence. We stopped listening. Perhaps the actor stopped making us listen. We have only to go back to Kean to find the theater full from pit to gallery with a cross section of society. They ate oranges in the stalls, and nobody had heard of matinee teas. Socialites may have waved from box to box, but not when Mr. Kean was on stage.

Somewhere in the wasteland of my early days Shakespeare had got lost or had been vocally abused out of all recognition. I hope that he is now back on the topmost pedestal where he truly belongs. He has been mutilated, mugged and masticated. He has been taken to the heights by some of our greatest actors, and to the depths by others. He has been translated, truncated, debased and musicalized. He has been quoted, quartered and pulverized; butchered, bullied and bashed beyond all recognition; misquoted and mismanaged; played by men, women and children whenever the fancy took them. He has challenged us all and won hands down. He has made fools of most of us at one time or another. There he stands, finger on cheek, quizzical, slightly bewildered, but passing the baton through century after century.

My God, I wish I'd met him, talked to him—but above all, heard and listened.

CHAPTER THREE

Hamlet

HAMLET is pound for pound, in my opinion, the greatest play ever written. It towers above everything else in dramatic literature. It gives us great climaxes, shadows and shades, yet contains occasional moments of high comedy. Every time you read a line it can be a new discovery. You can play it and play it as many times as the opportunity occurs and still not get to the bottom of its box of wonders. It can trick you round false corners and into culs-de-sac, or take you by the seat of your pants and hurl you across the stars. It can give you moments of unknown joy, or cast you into the depths of despair. Once you have played it, it will devour you and obsess you for the rest of your life. It has me. I think each day about it. I'll never play him again, of course, but by God, I wish I could.

The first time I was going to play the part, at the Old Vic, I felt that it was crucial to establish that Hamlet was bone-real from the very first word. I was determined to take the audience with me, to make them believe that this man lived. I knew that earlier players of this part had thought that Hamlet should begin on a strange note, but I decided it would be kindest to my audience to keep it simple, not to frighten them to death with the high theatricality of my opening.

Whenever an actor first attempts Hamlet, he should be aware that it's a sporadic collection of self-dramatizations in which he tries always to play the hero and, in truth, feels ill cast in the part. His imagination is working as though he were a hero, but his soul is working in the brave light of the author, who decided to write a play with a hero who wasn't a hero. Witness the soliloquy "How all occasions . . ." following hard upon his staring enviously at Fortinbras, the ideal man of the times.

Many years ago, when I was first to play Hamlet at the Old Vic, I went with Tyrone Guthrie, who was going to direct it, and Peggy Ashcroft, who was going to play Ophelia (but for some regrettable reason wasn't able to), to see Professor Ernest Jones, the great psychiatrist, who had made an exhaustive study of Hamlet from his own professional point of view and was wonderfully enlightening. His book on the subject was called *What Happens in Hamlet.*

We talked and talked. He believed that Hamlet was a prime sufferer from the Oedipus complex. There are many signals along the line to show his inner involvement with his mother. One of them is his excessive devotion to his father. Nobody's that fond of his father unless he feels guilty about his mother, however subconscious that guilt may be. Hamlet's worship of his father is manufactured, assumed; he needs it to cover up his subconscious guilt. The Oedipus complex may, indeed, be responsible for a formidable share of all that is wrong with Hamlet. I myself am only too happy to allow to be added to Shakespeare's other acknowledged gifts an intuitive understanding of psychology. Why not? He was the world's greatest man.

At one moment Professor Jones spoke, on the subject of myth and primitive painters' ideas of various occurrences, of a painting of particular psychopathic interest. It was *The Annunciation to the Blessed Virgin Mary,* which shows an angel blowing the pollen from a lily into her ear. He said, "Of course, the earhole is also the sign of vicious tendencies, possibly of a homosexual nature, you know."

In amazement I asked, "The *ear*hole?"

"Yes," he said, waited a minute, and then—very quietly (not for Peggy's ears)—"any orifice but the right one." I thought this very funny and could never get it out of my mind when I was playing Hamlet: the pollen going into the ear, blown by an angel from a lily.

I can't remember if Jones came to see the production; I don't think he did. But I warned him that he would not find the Oedipal theory overt, though, of course, it would be there. He said, "I wouldn't suggest you should make it overt, as long as you know about it. That's the important point. You're not supposed to tell the audience with every wink and nod that one of the reasons for your present predicament is that you wish you were still hanging on your mother's tits." A very entertaining man.

Speaking of finding new meanings in the text, its forever being fresh, I thought of one the other day. In the grave scene when Laertes is mourning Ophelia and the unknown figure announces, "This is I, Hamlet the Dane," I believe he is saying, "I am King"—echoes of his father, whom he must have heard at some time saying this in anger, maybe on a number of occasions. When I was playing it, I just thought the outburst was merely another show of temperament, another side of his self-expression. But no, he had to find other people to be all the time, and it didn't occur to me that at this moment it was his father. The audience wouldn't have known for a second what I was at, but it would have helped me greatly. There can be found a slight hint of it, but a sweetly tender one, during the duel with Laertes, when his mother drinks the poison obviously intended for Hamlet.

Hamlet's continual complaining throughout the play

is expressed directly to the audience, and he says almost in as many words no less than twice, "It's no good; I can't do it, can I? I wish I knew why. Am I a coward? Who dares pluck my beard? Am I this? Am I that? It's no good; I can't." Many people read into that the first pacifist; indeed, some remark that he's the first hero any author dared create from a hero who was no hero at all. But there are others, and I think this makes a marvelously firm argument for his Oedipus complex, who say he can kill his uncle/father when he is behind the arras, because he can say to himself he didn't know it was he . . . alas, poor Polonius. It is *after it is done* that he shouts victoriously to his mother, "Is it the King?" in the desperate hope he has done it without knowing it. He would rather act a part than do it: rather stab through a curtain than stab the King.

When Laertes has knifed him and death is a few breaths away, he is suddenly free to wreak vengeance because he has the innocent, pure reason of vengeance for himself, not for his guilt over his mother. Once he realizes he is about to touch hands with death, he is free, his guilt is expunged by his own murder, and he is able to feel, "You murder me and I'll murder you." For me that makes a final keystone in the arch of the argument for the Oedipus complex.

Though I believe this theory, I do not believe it to the extent of letting the play be just about that. The play is about a character who has that particular eccentricity, that particular thing *in* his character. When one thinks of audience after audience for nearly four hundred

1937, *Hamlet* at the Old Vic, with Francis Sullivan as Claudius

1937, *Hamlet* at Elsinore, with Vivien Leigh as Ophelia

years trying to work it out, it is fascinating. Shakespeare was simply pouring out all that was in his instinctive heart at the time; it is an extraordinary exploration into the human mind.

"The man in black" is always interesting; as an actor your job is to enable the audience to follow his journey from one characteristic to another, from mood to mood. The actor must be absolutely clear in his mind where he is going, whatever theories he has nursed (and over the years there have been many); in the end he must tell the story.

But the questions keep on coming up, and always will. Was Hamlet this? Was he that? Did he do this, did he do that? *Did he sleep with Ophelia?* In reply to this last, one old actor-manager, early in the century, said, "In *my* company, *always!*" As far as I'm concerned there was nothing platonic in the relationship: when it's played as brother and sister I have no time for it. Hamlet is not just imagining what is beneath Ophelia's skirts; he has found out for himself—"country matters"—for certain. "Get thee to a nunnery! Why wouldst thou be a breeder of sinners?" Ophelia's problem is that she truly believes that the four-poster will become permanent and legal, and that she will eventually wear the crown of Denmark. Hamlet's problem is that he wants to follow his mother to the bedchamber as well . . . and does? Most un-likely—but the Gertrude/Hamlet scene in the first pro-duction I did at the Old Vic went about as far in this direction as I dared suggest, or the Ghost's complaints would have been on a different score.

I had always decided that if I ever had the chance to lead a company I would start off with the big one, and in 1937 the chance came and I did. Of course, I was still not forgiven by a lot of the critics for my verse speaking, and there were still odious comparisons, as I suppose there always have to be. It may be that the young actor today has to suffer because my shadow has been left upon certain roles; not that I'm objecting, now, you understand. In those days Gielgud was the top dog when it came to verse speaking and his Hamlet was very popular, with me as with the majority of theatergoers.

I was determined to win through, and in the end, I think I did. But perhaps that's not for me to say. Truth . . . speak the truth, though the verse will not entirely take care of itself. Shakespeare knew what he was doing; he put the rhythms there and he didn't wish them to be ignored.

Looking back now, forty-eight years later, I find it difficult to see that performance with absolute clarity, though there is still a warmth that remains with me. People who have never experienced that walk between one wing and another will probably wonder what I mean by warmth. It gets into the nostrils and into the hair; it is a combination of electric light, glue, rancid paint and scent. It is like a favorite Teddy bear, or stepping from an airplane into the warm sun. Once experienced, it stays forever, calling the actor back again and again, like a siren's song.

Memory is one thing, but action is for the immediate

man. I still feel immediate. Every morning when I wake I think, To hell with the doctors, the temperature takers, the people who tamper with you like a prewar pressure cooker, telling you to sit in your wicker chair in high summer and muse. I should be out there where I belong, on the planks of wood that we call "the boards." I should be out there holding the old enemy at bay and trying to persuade them to believe it, to see it my way. I should be soaring away with my head tilted slightly towards the gods, feeding on the caviar of Shakespeare. Eyes telling all, and each member of the "congregation" thinking I am talking to him or her personally. I was made to perform, and it is not easy to be put out to grass, left to feed on memories and friendships. An actor must act.

Whatever people may have thought of my Hamlet, I think it was not bad. I know it was not perfection, but it *was* mine. I did it. It was *mine*.

My film interpretation of Hamlet was also all mine. I still think, after all these years, that the film stands up, much cut though it had to be, and I am still proud of it. A film can never show you what the actor was really like on the stage, but it can give you a very clear idea, and I have grown most wantonly partial to that medium. Its powers are apparently limitless.

Like any great play, *Hamlet* is totally adaptable. By this I mean it can be performed anywhere with anything. It can have a set, it can be played against drapes, it can be done before a brick wall. It lends itself to "the corner of the room." It was to this directive Sir Denys Lasdun was faithful in designing the theater generously named after me: "a large room with an audience embracing a corner of it."

I think one of the best performances I was involved in was probably at Elsinore in Denmark. Pouring, drenching rain meant that we could not open outside as we had intended to, and consequently, after a hurried discussion, it was decided that we would perform in the ballroom, which meant a rapid restaging. Tony (Tyrone) Guthrie, our director, was busy organizing things for the real opening, and something had to be arranged about seating for future performances, so he was heavily involved in administration. He left it to me to set it up and rehearse the new moves around the strange area that was now to accommodate us. As he went off, he said, "Fix it for me, Larry. Just place it all as you think best." So I did. All the movements had to be changed, so all the lovely invention was left to me. As you can imagine, I was thrilled to do it and, of course, enjoyed myself wildly.

There is nothing better than a group of actors being presented with a problem of this kind and having to improvise. When time is drifting away and the performance is getting closer, somehow the release of adrenaline creates an excitement that runs through everyone, from the leading actor/actress to the maker of the tea. The entire company pulls together with the one object in mind. It is at such times that you can ask for the impossible, and get it. "I'm afraid the only way you can play this scene is by hanging from the chandelier, dear boy." Without a moment's hesitation, the reply would come back, "Of course—no problem."

Great God! there is something amazing about them, the band of players. There is a comradeship that I have experienced only once elsewhere, but not so happily, in the Services.

Somehow every performance seems to be enhanced in times of unexpected difficulties; there is an edge, a fine edge that hoists the players, even the least inspired, onto another level. All the actors' motors have to be running, but in a low gear for greater acceleration. Nobody dares get a moment wrong. Whereas laziness, even boredom, may have crept in before—and this is very understandable when you think in terms of standing night after night on the end of a spear with somebody else delivering the dialogue that you feel you could do better—that boredom, for a moment, is forgotten and the contribution becomes genuine, energetic and electric. Everyone becomes a Thoroughbred, muscles alive and alert. The vibrations are high, and this will affect the audience as well. What they witness will be a night that they will always remember. "Were you there that night at Elsinore? I was." It is amazing how many people now think they were there. Rather like Harold Pinter's *The Birthday Party*, during its brief first run; if all the people who now claim they were there had in fact been there, it would have run for a year.

Whether or not what the audience sees is good we will never know, but the energy that is directed towards them will engulf them in its euphoric state. In Elsinore that night, the actors were heroes, every man Jack of them. I know—I was right in the middle of it. A dignity and excitement was achieved, an atmosphere in which no one falls on his arse unless it is intended. Everyone thrills with a sense of achievement and importance—and quite rightly. The "one for all" society syndrome. Above all, the performance was spontaneous.

I remember giving the stage at one moment to Torin Thatcher; he was playing the Ghost. We had erected a little stage for the play scenes and stuff, with some stairs that led up to it. I knelt by the stairs, facing away from the audience, and when, as the Ghost, he turned at the top, he found himself in this glorious solo upstage position. It was magnificent. I remember remarking to Tony Guthrie, "Wasn't it heavenly when Torin found himself so placed for his big scene with me?" and Tony replied, "Yes, it flowed through the ballroom like warm strawberry jam." I took that as a compliment.

It is a great night to remember, full of magic and memories. Some say it was the best thing they'd ever seen. Whether it was or not I'll never know, but it must have been something special. It rained, and because of this, the gods came over to our side. I think they always do, if handled with respect.

Enough has been said about Hamlet by others with better literary qualifications than mine; all I know is that he has a myriad of hidden problems you can never quite explain. He is utterly unlike Coriolanus, who is absolutely straightforward, with nothing of particular psychological interest. Coriolanus is himself; he knows it, his mother knows it. I can tell you how I crept inside him, inside Othello or Richard; but I cannot tell you how I crept inside Hamlet, the man. Hamlet just takes you by the hand and either treats you roughly or shows you the way to the stars. All I know is he captured me, and once he had, he never let me go.

Scholars have not stopped theorizing about *Hamlet* since the day that Burbage played its first performance. So what I feel about it, though important to me, is probably no more than a drop in the ocean so far as the academics are concerned, but it does have the special authority of the practitioner.

I suppose it must have been performed more times than any other play in the English language, with every performance at least slightly different, which is fascinating to think on. It is, without a doubt, the best play ever written, partly perhaps because it lends itself to so many changes and interpretations. The actor, however he plays it, well or badly, will get something right in his journey from the castle walls to his final silence.

I could see it and read it forever. Yes, the best play in the world.

CHAPTER FOUR

Henry V

I N my first season at the Old Vic in 1937 I wanted
to be completely different in every performance. This
is nothing new for an actor, of course—indeed, it is what
every actor should be about; but I was determined to
demonstrate as much versatility as possible. Something
that has always been part of my theatrical life: I like
to appear as a chameleon. Nothing has given me more
pleasure than knowing I have tricked my audience and
been on stage for more than five minutes without being

recognized. As I have always said, I am a character actor, not the leading man who seeks applause on his first entrance. I want the joy of dressing up, not applause for a handsome profile. So all my career I've attempted to disguise myself, probably to no better effect than I did in the double bill of *Oedipus* and Mr. Puff in Sheridan's *The Critic*. The joy of being an actor on that night was completely intoxicating. There are some occasions when you stand in the wings and cannot wait to get in front of the audience, and that was one of those moments. You can smell the excitement, feel the adrenaline coursing—like being drunk on spring water.

I have always looked for something new. That's what keeps the batteries recharged and the mind young; that's what keeps the cement from setting between the ears. I'm constantly looking, observing, storing the images away in my theatrical locker. A cough here, a blink there—all remembered, noted and put away in the mental drawer until needed, brought out, dusted and used. As Brecht said in one of his last poems, "You can make a fresh start with your final breath."

Thus it was that when I joined the Old Vic in 1937, I was looking for a way that I could show off my versatility. Why not jump in at the deep end? First Hamlet; then Sir Toby Belch, a complete contrast; and finally Henry V. Not bad for a first season, I thought.

All went well, apart from the odd critic's not approving my verse speaking, until it was time to get working on *Henry V*. Suddenly I panicked. I didn't think it was the play for me at that time. It seemed wrong; I was

1945, the double bill of *Oedipus* and *The Critic*. Left, making up for *Oedipus*, with Mr. Puff's wig on the dressing table.

frightened of the heroism. England had completely
changed in the 1930s: the whole atmosphere of the
country, which was frequently mirrored in the theater,
was opposed to heroics. Plays like *Journey's End*, which
had been so successful in the 1920s, would not have
survived for a week in the late 1930s. We had moved
away from all that, heads stuck firmly in the sand, rooting for pleasure—herds of people searching for truffles.
We were sophisticated and viewed the world from the
end of a cigarette holder. Little did we realize how soon
we would change. Shortly Germany would bare its teeth,
and our generation would become just as heroic as the
one that had gone to the trenches before.

It is strange looking back. It's rather like diving into
a pool, but in reverse, the body coming out of the water
feet first and returning to the high board, feet together,
arms stretched forward.

Having thought a great deal about *Henry V* and still
being very unsure, I spoke to my dear friend Ralph
Richardson, who as far as I was concerned was always
reliable with his advice. I trusted him, and I think he
trusted me.

"Henry the Fifth," he muttered, and thought for a
moment; then his eyes twinkled. "He's a scoutmaster."
He spoke in tones of disgust. He paused again, and
then in those unforgettable tones of his he said, "But
he raises scoutmastership to godlike proportions, which
Shakespeare always does." Another pause. "Of course
you must play him." So play him I did.

Rehearsals began, and still fearful, I started by com-

pletely undercutting Henry—something that I don't think
I can often be accused of doing during the course of my
career. I fought against the heroism by flattening and
getting underneath the lines; no banner waving for me.
"God for Harry! England and Saint George!" was not
going to ring out across the footlights as on a poor night
at a third-division *Gang Show*. I was being so natural
at one point that I think my fellow actors must have
had difficulty hearing me. The night scene really was
a night scene; my fellow actors were going to have no
difficulty sleeping—and if I had played it that way, the
audience, I'm sure, would have joined them.

One morning Tyrone Guthrie spoke. He had never
given me a great deal of direction; until then he had left
me alone, given me my head, and for this I was grateful. I remember with *Hamlet* he had let me go and
simply backed me up right through to the first night
and beyond. But, as I say, on this particular morning
at rehearsals he spoke.

He was a tall man and his looks were a combination
of Jonathan Miller and Charles de Gaulle—a very strik-
ing, dominating appearance. He had a habit of snapping
his fingers when he wanted attention. I think anyone
who ever worked with him will remember them as the
loudest finger snaps in Christendom. I swear that when
they snapped at the Old Vic, they could be heard outside the theater. *Snap*, they went, and the rehearsal came
to a halt.

"Larry . . . let's have it properly."

"Properly?"

"Properly."

"Tony, I am doing it properly."

"Like this . . . this is how I want it."

He went into "This day is call'd the Feast of Crispian. . . ." and as he built up towards the end, he vocally began to climb a ladder. Heroics, bloody heroics. I looked at him for a moment and saw that if he had been wearing the right hat, he could have done a good impersonation of Baden-Powell. He stopped and looked at me.

"That's the way to do it."

"Like that?"

"Like that."

"Tony . . . ?"

"If you don't do it like that and enjoy doing it like that, you just won't carry the audience with you."

He was right. I was fortunate to have him directing me and directing *for* me. I followed his eye. He knew.

So the Henry V which was to make me famous as an actor who could be heroic, and which I was later to film, began there at the precise moment when the fingers snapped and the "scoutmaster" recited the lines rather badly; he was no actor, but he pointed me in the direction I had fought against, and he was right.

I worked on the great arias, molded and fashioned them to me, and then from Guthrie's launch pad, took off. I was heroic—no one could have been more so—but I was truthful, I was not showing off; I played the man like a trumpet as clearly and truthfully as I knew how.

I'm not ashamed to say that I stole from people. I've

1937, *Henry* V at the Old Vic,
with
Jessica Tandy as Katherine

never been ashamed of that. If something is good then take it, borrow it, as you will. When young actors copy my characterizations, I am flattered, as I'm sure Irving would have been of the generation who impersonated him. It is not arrogance, it is understanding.

As I have said, I admired Barrymore and used much of his Hamlet in mine. In the case of Henry V I have to acknowledge some of Lewis Waller's performance. I was fascinated by his vocal acrobatics and I'm certain some of them lingered on within me—honed to my performance, of course, but still there.

> Once more unto the breach, dear friends, once
>   more;
> Or close the wall up with our English dead!
>
> (*Confident, encouraging, steady; lead them and prepare them.*)
>
> In peace there's nothing so becomes a man
> As modest stillness and humility;
>
> (*Hold them; let the words work.*)
>
> But when the blast of war blows in our ears,
> Then imitate the action of the tiger;
>
> (*Begin to feel that tingle in the base of the stomach; prepare, get ready for a change of gear.*)
>
> Stiffen the sinews, summon up the blood,
> Disguise fair nature with hard-favour'd rage;
>
> (*Stay in control but begin to feel the excitement. Then change the intonation.*)
>
> Then lend the eye a terrible aspect;

Let it pry through the portage of the head
Like the brass cannon; let the brow o'erwhelm it
As fearfully as doth a galled rock
O'erhang and jutty his confounded base,

(*Up a gear and beginning to move, the words
blazing in front of you.*)

Swill'd with the wild and wasteful ocean.

(*"Swill'd"*)

Now set the teeth and stretch the nostril wide,
Hold hard the breath and bend up every spirit
To his full height! . . .

(*Now we're really motoring, climbing vocally
but in complete control. The politician and the
hero.*)

                    . . . On, on, you noble English,

(*Patriotism*)

Whose blood is fet from fathers of war-proof!
Fathers that like so many Alexanders

(*Change the tune to as natural a one as is hu-
manly possible.*)
Have in these parts from morn till even fought,
And sheath'd their swords for lack of argument.
Dishonour not your mothers; now attest,
That those whom you call'd fathers did beget
        you!

(*Now take them with you; they want to come;
climb the ladder.*)

Be copy now to men of grosser blood
And teach them how to war! . . .

*(Now, like any good politician, speak to them
collectively in such a way that they think you
are speaking to them individually.)*
. . . And you, good yeomen,
Whose limbs were made in England, show us
    here
The mettle of your pasture. Let us swear
That you are worth your breeding; which I
    doubt not,
*(Got them . . . now hold them. Remember,
never give them everything.)*
For there is none of you so mean and base
That hath not noble lustre in your eyes.
I see you stand like greyhounds in the slips,
*(Moving up the ladder, pace, excitement, al-
most flying.)*
Straining upon the start. The game's afoot!
(NOW LET GO.)
Follow your spirit; and upon this charge
Cry . . .
(We're there.)
. . . "God for Harry! England and Saint
    George!"
(Take off.)

When it worked it was an amazing feeling—being in
complete control of body and mind, the whole machinery meshing perfectly. It was heroic, all right, but that
was what it needed; Tony Guthrie was right. Even the
critics were beginning to listen to me on a new wave-
length.

1945, *Henry* V on film, "Once more unto the breach . . ."

Within two years fighting began in earnest, and the antiheroic mood went out the window. When the war was under way I found myself on occasions going round military camps with a one-man turn that I had worked out. It was geared to whip up patriotism and was, I believe, very successful. It began with a poem on the death of General Havelock. Who the hell was he? I hear you say. Well, if you walk up Whitehall, turn and face Trafalgar Square, he's the one on the horse on the left-hand side. Sir Henry Havelock, a great hero in his time, having relieved the beleaguered British residency at Lucknow on 25 September 1857. He, along with Campbell and Outram, put down the Indian Mutiny. As Trevelyan says, he stamped out the flame in central India before it could spread. A year later the British Government had replaced the East India Company, and twenty years later Disraeli persuaded Queen Victoria to assume the title of Empress of India. For his deeds Havelock was cast in metal, placed upon a horse, and now resides in Trafalgar Square.

Anyway, I began with this poem, which was full of good old heroic stuff, and then went into

> This day is call'd the Feast of Crispian.
> He that outlives this day, and comes safe home,
> Will stand a-tiptoe when this day is nam'd
> And rouse him at the name of Crispian.

By now I knew how to pace it all perfectly and was able slowly to whip up my wartime audience of real soldiers, urging them forward with me:

> And hold their manhoods cheap whiles any
>   speaks
> That fought with us upon Saint Crispin's day.

During the applause I would hold my gesture and remain still. Then, when I felt the applause reach its peak and begin to wane, I would launch into "Once more unto the breach . . ." By the time I got to "God for Harry! . . ." I think they would have followed me anywhere. Looking back, I don't think we could have won

the war without "Once more unto the breach . . ."
somewhere in our soldiers' hearts.

When I made the film, I taught my horse to break
into a gallop at a certain moment in the speech, somewhere about "Be copy now to men of grosser blood / And
teach them how to war! . . ." The horse seemed to
know the lines as well as I did, and would prick up his
ears and go every time I got to "Saint George!" When
the film was complete, Arthur Rank, the producer, asked
what I'd like by way of a bonus, and much to his surprise,
I asked for my horse—which he happily gave me. I kept
him at Notley and rode him whenever I could. When
this was not possible, for exercise we used to hitch him
to the trap and take him to the station to meet guests,
petrol being rationed at the time. I remember on one
occasion going to meet Noël Coward, who was coming
for the weekend. I picked him up and there we were,
ambling slowly home through the perfect English countryside.

"Doesn't go very fast," clipped Noël.

"Want more speed, do you?" I asked.

"Yes," replied Noël.

"Hang on a minute," I said, and leaned over towards
the horse's ears.

"Once more unto the breach . . ." I started, and sure
enough, by the time I got to "Be copy now . . ." he
went into a gallop, and galloped all the way home.

So there you are: the part that I had fought against
fought for me. Henry took me by the hand and hurled
me into the theater history books.

My good fortune was with me again. Being at the Old
Vic at the right moment in time, and the good fortune
of having two friends like Ralph Richardson and Tony
Guthrie to advise me. What's wrong with scoutmasters?
Nothing. Especially when the scoutmaster is almost
omniscient.

Imagination. Prey on the audience's imagination. Play
with it like Plasticine. Mold it, break it, remold it. Fashion it, shape it, let it free. Take them away with you.
Weave tales and weave magic:

> Think, when we talk of horses, that you see them
> Printing their proud hoofs i' th' receiving earth.
> For 'tis your thoughts that now must deck our
>   kings,
> Carry them here and there, jumping o'er times,
> Turning th' accomplishment of many years
> Into an hour glass . . .

CHAPTER FIVE

Macbeth

W<small>E</small> have each our private idea of Macbeth, Hamlet, Othello, Lear; we have all of us read of, if we have not seen great performances of these parts; so that every actor who undertakes them has to pass through a triple ordeal, encountering, first, our imagination, kindled by Shakespeare; second our idealized memory of performances which used to please our, perhaps unripe, judgement; third, our conceptions of the great actors of the

past, gathered from the often extravagant panegy-
rics of contemporaries.

(William Archer, in *Brief Chronicles* by James Agate)

My initial view, as an actor, of *Macbeth* had been
formed by the first part I'd played in it, that of Lennox.
Later I was to see it through the eyes of Malcolm.

The first time I played the man himself was at the Old
Vic in the 1937–38 season. I was just thirty, very fit,
mentally very much in control and still bursting with
ambition. I was full of confidence. I had played Hamlet
at Elsinore and at the Old Vic, and I'd played Henry V
as though the part had been written for me.

I think *Macbeth* is one of Shakespeare's best plays,
and it is certainly one of my favorites. Shakespeare is always superb on the subject of death and on reactions to
horrifying or terrifying news. To my mind, "To-morrow
and to-morrow" is almost as great a speech as "To be or
not to be." *Macbeth* is compact, a perfectly rounded
piece. It tells a strong story at great speed and takes the
audience on a roller coaster of excitement. You can see
it a hundred times and it will still appear fresh. It is
visually superb, which made me wonder what Shakespeare would have given us had Hollywood existed in his
time.

The play is beautifully paced for the leading actor, as
witness the England scene, which gives him time to re-
lace his boots and take some deep breaths, preparing
himself for a thundering finale, which I gave it, and
which did not entirely meet with James Agate's approval:

Perhaps this is the place to say . . . and if it isn't
I shall say it . . . that I have been more 'got at'
over Mr Olivier's performance than by any other in
my recollection. Chelsea semaphored, 'Unable con-
ceive Macbeth as a gigolo.' Bloomsbury signalled,
'No use for Macbeth as a mountebank.' A young
gentleman in corduroy trousers and a velvet smok-
ing jacket opined to my face that Macbeth should
not be like a military colonel, retired. Reflecting
that what the young gentleman needed was an active drill-sergeant, I proceeded to turn a deaf, but
not altogether deaf, ear to another of the mincing
brigade, who suggested that the new Macbeth
shouted too loudly. I say not altogether deaf, because even the austerest critic is none the worse for
knowing what is being said by the mob . . .

It had been a deliberate decision of mine to join the
Old Vic company. I had approached them, and I knew
that as far as they were concerned I was quite a catch,
for I had a movie-star image that was capable of filling
a theater. I also felt, and still feel, that you are judged
entirely by your work in the classics. I wanted to be
taken seriously. I wanted to stand up and be counted. I
wanted to be conspicuous in the high court of the theater. To me, the Old Vic was the equivalent of the Old
Bailey. Here I would be judged for my classical work.
Here I would pitch my stand and stake my claim. Here I
could ease my way into the skin of the theatrical serpent,
the skin that had been worn by the masters from Burbage down to Irving and Barrymore. There it was,

pressed inside the leather binding with the name William Shakespeare written on the spine. There it lay, waiting to be molded, shaped, hurled into the air and caught again.

The director of my 1937 *Macbeth* was Michel St.-Denis, a star director full of wit and imagination, though on this particular production neither seemed to be on our side. When I told Ralph Richardson I was going down to the Vic, he asked, "What are you going to play?" and when I said, "Macbeth," he said, "You'll break your neck, my dear boy. You don't want to play Macbeth at your age; be very, very careful." It was what you might call a stylized production. Everything in godlike proportions. The makeups were masklike. I had a huge false face on, a nose that went down, a stuck-on chin and a putty forehead with vast eyebrows. The idea was to make something real through a highly poetic and unreal approach. I put myself entirely in St.-Denis' hands, but felt I was not good in such a theatrical production. I "made up" to play Macbeth, instead of letting Macbeth play through me. I had everything outwardly and not enough inwardly. I think, in that production, Macbeth was nearer my sleeve than my heart.

Though I have relied a great deal on makeup and appearances over the years, I still maintain that the real look should come from inside. Somebody was making me up once for *Khartoum* and he'd given me a false nose. Good, I said; fine. False cheekbones. Didn't know about that. False chin, false forehead. And I said, "You have to come back to the truth of this, and that is that it's

just me but twice the size; I don't see the object of it."
You cannot make up the lines by making up the face.
The look must come first from the head and from the
heart. What is added comes later. Remember the naked
Greeks.

Everything seemed to be against us. At the dress
rehearsal we reached cue three of the lighting plot at
three o'clock in the morning. There was no way we
were going to finish in time for the opening night. At
this speed we'd still have been rehearsing at Christmas.
They say there is a jinx on the play. I personally do not
believe it, but at three o'clock that morning I think I
might have been swayed. I remember Tony Guthrie
coming down the aisle during one of the waits. A certain amount of glee was showing in his walk. Perhaps
"glee" is too strong a word—more a feeling of "Told
you so." He spoke to St.-Denis, and as we all learned
afterwards, the first night, which was to have been the
next night, was cancelled.

No way, Guthrie said, could you keep the actors up
all night and through the next morning and expect them
to appear before row after row of vultures dressed as
penguins. So the first night did not happen.

Two nights later dear Lilian Baylis, founder of the
Old Vic, died. Some say, and I do not disagree, that her
death was brought on by the postponement of that first
night. To my knowledge it was the first time it had ever
happened at the Old Vic. Of course, for the supersti-
tious, it was the play—what else could it be? But as far
as I am concerned, it might just as well have been

Antony and Cleopatra. It wasn't the play that killed her, it was the footlights that overcame the might of that great lady. She towered above us all and departed quietly when her theater was silenced.

We did open eventually, and not to a great deal of critical success—yet the box office did the best business the Vic had ever done up until that moment. In the end James Agate was not too unkind:

> Since it would seem that, with the exception of Garrick, a great Macbeth has never been in the calendar, it is reasonable to expect that the new one should be lacking in perfect adequacy. It is a part demanding great natural and physical gifts, to which Mr Olivier at present can only oppose natural and physical shortcomings. He does not look like coping with Russian bears, Hyrcan tigers and rhinoceroses, whether armed or unarmed. His voice, which in the 'Tomorrow and tomorrow' and 'Sere and yellow leaf' speeches should vibrate like a cello, is of a pitch rather higher than the average. In other words, he is not a natural bass and has some difficulty getting down to baritone. All the same, he brings off some magnificent vocal effects, and his verse speaking has improved. Ideally, Macbeth might be likened to some oak, magnificent in outer shell but lacking in roots, and presently to be riven by the lightning of conscience. But nature has not so endowed Mr Olivier, who is forced to play the whole part nervously among the high tossed branches. . . .
>
> Mr Olivier will probably play this part twice as

well when he has twice his present years. Meanwhile he registers another step in a career of considerable achievement and increasing promise.

Of course, I was to play it again some years later, at Stratford in 1955, directed by Glen Byam Shaw, with a considerable degree of success. My voice was infinitely stronger and more powerful, and the extra chunk of life experience I had had since I'd first played the part really counted. The first time, I had played age through pure imagination; now I could bring knowledge to bear. I was also happy with the makeup and the costumes. I found that it was genuinely possible to make every second of Macbeth human despite all that murdering of children. By luck that second time I found a complete experience which belonged to the part and was able to get the right mixture of style and down-to-earth bone reality. I found the right cocktail, the right mixture, the right ingredients in the right proportion.

I remember once discussing the part with Anthony Quayle when we were both in *Titus Andronicus* behind the Iron Curtain. He'd asked me if I was finding Titus tough going. "It has," he said, "all the earmarks of a tough part." "Oh, God, yes," I replied. "But I suppose Macbeth is the worst, isn't it?" To which Quayle responded: "No. Macbeth is positive; he knows what he is doing and he does it. He is a much jollier part altogether for the actor. Everybody flogs you every time they look at you in *Titus*. You are bemoaning your fate throughout, and whatever happens to you is just another ghastly stroke of the knout, making you wail, 'Oh,

oh, oh, that this should happen to me!' Othello's another
part that's entirely composed of moaning, bellowing and
screaming against fate. Macbeth is much more fun." A
sentiment I would agree with.

I don't know why my second Macbeth came together then, but like everything in this extraordinary work
of theater, it did. It was my moment. This has happened
to me throughout my life. I have often been fortunate
to be in the right place at the right time. Blessed in that
way. A sense of timing was at work, almost an instinct.
But then, timing is made by the man, I think, and therefore man creates his own destiny. Take it or leave it,
my timing was right, and I accept that with gratitude,
whether it was man-made or God-made.

I was at my peak for the production at Stratford, and
at the right age; no masklike makeup was required. I
suppose it is an advantage in tackling all great roles if
the age is right. Of course, this doesn't seem to happen
with Romeo or with Lear. With Romeo you need the
understanding of an adult and with Lear the physique
of a younger man, though I did play Lear recently and
didn't seem to do too badly.

Being the right age at Stratford was an enormous ad-
vantage. I had the bellows and I understood the play.
Not that I had not understood it before, but somehow
I had grown into it.

1937, *Macbeth* at the Old Vic, with Judith Anderson
1955, at Stratford-on-Avon, with Vivien Leigh

CHAPTER SIX

Richard III

I THINK there is much that the public doesn't understand about acting. I think they understand baseball, cricket or football a great deal better. Let me try to explain. Naturally, if an actor is playing a baddie, no audience in the world likes him as much as they like the hero in the white hat, the man who makes them laugh or, best of all, the baddie who has them laughing with him. My ambition has been to lead the public away from the common trend of typecasting towards an appreciation of acting, so that they will come not only to see the play but also to watch acting for acting's sake.

Of the personae I've just mentioned—the baddie, the hero, the comic—Richard of Gloucester has them all, which is what makes him, as has always been true, such an attractive part to play. I mean, to be able to woo Lady Anne from hatred to acceptance in a five-minute scene is pure magic. There she is, on her way to bury her husband, whom Richard has killed, and he coolly steps in with, of all things, a proposal of marriage. The audacity is wonderful. To go from

> LADY ANNE. What black magician conjures up
> this fiend
> To stop devoted charitable deeds?

to

> . . . 'Tis more than you deserve;
> But since you teach me how to flatter you,
> Imagine I have said farewell already.

Incredible to give an actor such a scene to play. And then to round it off by giving Richard

> Was ever woman in this humour woo'd?
> Was ever woman in this humour won?
> I'll have her, but I will not keep her long.

You can't wait to get on the stage to play it.

Contrary to what I've just said, I didn't want to do the play when it was first suggested. I didn't know the play intimately; all I knew was that Donald Wolfit had just made a critical success of the part (a performance, incidentally, which I did not see until some time later and

then found disappointing). Whatever I did, I thought,
would result in my being the loser. *Peer Gynt* and *Arms
and the Man* were in the Old Vic repertoire at that time,
1944, and both were very successful—*Peer Gynt* sensa-
tionally so. Ralph Richardson knew what he was about.
I got the feeling that I was being asked to do Richard III
just to put me in my place. Looking back, I'm sure this
wasn't so, but like any other actor, I must be allowed
my paranoia. Anyway, John Burrell and Ralph, my codirectors at the Old Vic, insisted that Richard was the
ideal choice, and there was nothing I could do about it
except get on with it—so I did.

I began to study the piece and became more and more
aware of what a part it was. It began to grow inside me.
I had to find the character, and slowly he began to come
to me. I had a picture of him in my head, a painting, an
oil painting of what he ought to be like. I went around
for some time with this visual image of him. I never
believed that the real portraits of him were anything
like him; or if I did, I wasn't going to admit it. Nothing
was going to stop me from putting on that makeup.

My first makeup I don't think was very good. I had a
very long, sort of pointed nose, but somehow I had to
finish in there somewhere, so as to make a very unfor-
tunately unattractive small upper lip. I wanted to look
the most evil thing there was. But I also had to exercise
some other fluid that would win Lady Anne. I decided
to liberate in every pore of my skin the utmost libertin-
ism I could imagine. When I looked at her, she couldn't
look at me; she had to look away. And when she looked

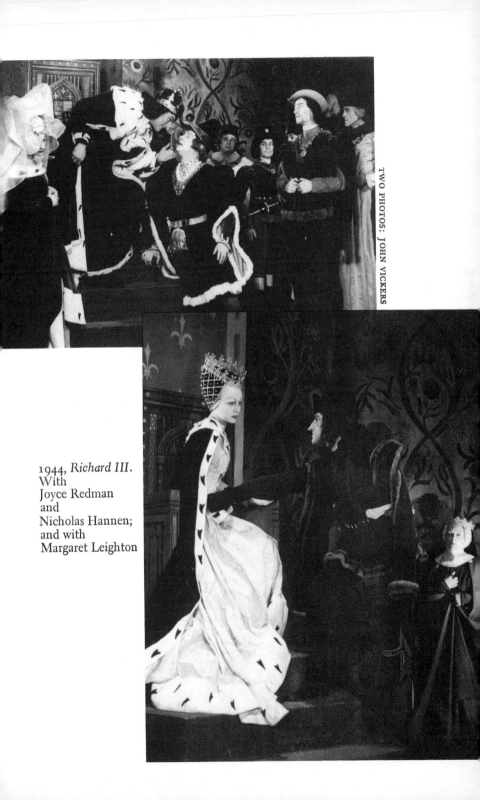

1944, *Richard III*.
With
Joyce Redman
and
Nicholas Hannen;
and with
Margaret Leighton

away, I would spend time devouring the region between her waist and upper thigh. Shocking maybe, but right, I felt. It was right for my Richard, and he was becoming my Richard by the minute.

Problems have always spurred me to find a solution; I welcome them. As Richard III I had to make the audience like me. They must be won over by his wit, his brilliantly wry sense of humor.

The excitement was beginning; the adrenaline. An actor, when he begins to sense that he is on to something, is a bit like a stoat coming out of its hole and smelling the morning air: the nose twitches and the body starts to tingle. The flash of lightning away in the distance, the thunder still muted, but coming, slowly coming. Everything begins to change: the taste buds improve, the sense of smell is more acute, the mind is constantly wrapping itself round the image which is to be created, then presented to an unsuspecting public.

I didn't read any of the books that were around defending Richard against the false rumor written by this tinkerer with melodrama named William Shakespeare, who got it from someone else, who got it from someone else, who got it from someone else. I just stayed with the man himself:

> Shine out, fair sun, till I have bought a glass,
> That I may see my shadow as I pass.

Usually in finding a character, I'm afraid I do it from the outside in. I know modern thinking decrees that you should do it from the very inside out, and that may be right, but it's not my way. I paint a portrait of the man in my mind's eye as if I were oil-painting it and say, "That's the man."

Then there was the voice. It came to me: the thin reed of a sanctimonious scholar. I started putting it on at once. It arrived and set the vision going: thin and rapierlike, but all-powerful. Somewhere between the bridge of the nose and the sinuses at first. It was easy to pitch, and it was perfect for the three sides I have mentioned: the hero, the villain and the ironic comedian. It was a sound that helped me formulate the character. I think I tried it at the first reading—yes, I did. But I had to exercise a lot before I started to know if I could take the big stuff on that voice without losing it. It was a bell ringing inside me: "Now is the winter . . ."—scholarly, yet deadly. The perfect hypocrite. From the first few words, you knew that this fellow was doubling up on himself. It had an edge that I had never used before, a mixture of honey and razor blades.

That sort of thin voice and that particularly pedantic way of speaking with that very thin voice, rather schoolmasterish, a little sanctimonious, was of course dead against the character, which made it a little more amusing, therefore more hypocritical, and somehow gave him, I felt, a strange authority. I'm sure that if a serpent could converse with us rather than hiss, we would recognize a certain similarity. It seems to me that even in a serpent's hiss there is a touch of a sexual smile. To my mind that is what Shakespeare's Richard had: venom coated with sugar. A veneer of smiling sophistication and wit, beneath which lay the barb to hook the fish.

1944, *Arms and the Man*, with Margaret Leighton

I suppose I must have heard the voice somewhere
before, maybe on a bus or a train, in a church or from
a politician's mouth—who knows? But there it is, and
has remained to haunt me ever since. It's amazing how
many people have copied it. I suppose I ought to be
flattered . . . I think I am. A lot of young actors, comedians, mimics—all, in my opinion, overshooting. If

I had used the voice that my impersonators attribute to
me, I don't think the audience would have taken me
very seriously.

Something significant happened to me a short time
before I played Richard. I was in Manchester playing
Sergius in *Arms and the Man*. One night, Tyrone Guthrie came to see it, and after the show he and I began
walking back to the hotel together. I remember the spot
vividly: we were under the canopy at the front of the
opera house. I still think of it whenever I'm in Manchester, walking to the studio from the Midland Hotel.
He stopped and said, "Liked you very much."

And I said, "Thank you. Thanks very much."

Hearing my tone, he asked, "What's the matter?
Don't you like the part?"

To which I replied, "Really, Tony, if you weren't so
tall I'd hit you."

He then asked me, "Don't you love Sergius?"

I replied, "Are you out of your mind? How can you
love a ridiculous fool of a man like that?"

At which he observed, "Well, of course, if you can't
love him, you'll never be any good as him, will you?"
Words of wisdom. I hadn't looked at it in that way
before. It taught me a great lesson. It kept echoing in
my head: ". . . if you can't love him, you'll never be
any good as him." Until then I'd never thought of
Guthrie in terms of teaching one how to act: I'd thought
of him only in terms of shoving people round you, or
shoving you. You know, placing people here or there,
making a lot of movement. He directed, it seemed to

me, purely by movement. His eye wasn't satisfied if something wasn't happening all the time, whereas I believe there are times when there should be complete stillness.

Guthrie didn't direct *Richard*, John Burrell did; but Guthrie's remark had inched its way under my skin. I will always be grateful. In Manchester for the rest of the run I began to love Sergius, and my whole performance seemed to get better and better. For the rest of my life, I would apply this. When I came to it, I loved Richard and he loved me, until we became one.

As we moved nearer the first night, 26 September, the voice and the character fused. Richard went with me everywhere. There he was, sitting on my shoulder— or I on his. The portrait, my personal portrait, clear as a full moon in my head. Actors (David Garrick) and playwrights (Colley Cibber) have tried to enhance the part over the years; Cibber's adaptation was the standard acting text for a century. "Off with his head! so much for Buckingham!" is not Shakespeare. And when Hastings is arrested by Catesby, Ratcliffe and Lovell and says, "The cat, the rat and Lovell our dog / Rule all England under the hog," that's not Shakespeare but a contemporary doggerel which adds to the play's image of Richard. A rare Shakespearean event, when the part's the thing and not the play.

As an actor approaches a first night the sense of excitement is extraordinary. As with a bullfighter, everything is geared towards the moment of truth with his audience. One second of mistiming and it's over. One

slip and they'll have you. Every waking minute the seconds are ticking away on your automatic time clock. You
have gone into the countdown. As the last week approaches, anything that gets in the way of your train
of thought is an irritation. An outside conversation (outside of the production, that is) is not welcome. Everything is homing in towards the raising of the curtain, and
if you've got it right—or think you've got it right—you
are not overconfident, but looking forward to the challenge. I could smell the play and couldn't wait to have
it wrapped round me like a cloak. Waking in the morning, showering, shaving, it was there: the twinge in the
gut, the knowledge that something was about to happen.
I had no way of knowing it would be a success—there
is no way of judging that—but I knew in my head that
I had almost completed the jigsaw.

They say we are mere shadows. I like to think of the
true actor as a skeleton. Bone, just bone, onto which
he places and molds the flesh, rather like a sculptor; but
he has an advantage over the sculptor because his crea-
tion is animated. He, the actor, can play the author's
tune. The image has been created, the vision has become
reality and words will flow.

My optimism was not shared by the rest of the company. Looking back, I can still feel their sense of despair.
The looks which said, "*Peer Gynt*, bless its darling heart,
is a sensational success . . . so is *Arms and the Man*,
but *Richard*—ah, well—two out of three is not bad." So
I just carried on, head down, planning, plotting Richard
himself. I think he might have been amused.

I had written Emlyn Williams and asked him if I
could borrow his beautiful gag which gained him a marvelous laugh: when Buckingham goes too far, Richard
suddenly turns over the pages of his Bible very, very
quickly. Emlyn wrote back, "Delighted that you think
it's worth copying." There's quite a bit of legitimate
borrowing in the theater.

I thought, too, about stagecraft, about placing, about
angles and lines. It was in this play that I used my back
to telling effect. I've always worked with my back. If you
have a scene with three people, place one and two just
beyond midway upstage, then the third below them
both, with his back to them; it's most effective—brings
reality to what would otherwise be a rather unreal group-
ing and creates the effect of conversation. Of course, you
can't hold it for very long; eventually you have to move
them around and change the pattern into some other
agreeable shape. But it is an excellent method of bringing reality to a scene of three people who might otherwise be strung out across the stage in an unnatural
straight line. Two can get down and the big shot stay
up, but I think it works best if two can be up and the
third stands below, with his back to them.

Suddenly we were there. A first night has its own evil
presence. It is curious the things that will annoy and
the things that don't. A professional is not annoyed by
stagehands being noisy; they cannot help this if there
have been many last-moment cuts and changes. Knowing the problems those boys are facing behind that backcloth or frontcloth, I just keep going straight on. Not

being confident that you are word-perfect is much more worrying.

Sometimes the audience gives such a feeling of friendly expectancy that they lift you to give a performance of tremendous verve: it's as if they were daring you not to fail, loving you to succeed. At others, they are leaden and seem to feel too much is being asked of their attentive powers. In a very large theater it can be almost impossible to exert a hypnotic influence: it is not possible to mesmerize more than a thousand people at a time. In February, you can face an absolute barrage of coughs as if the whole audience were a huge hospital for croup.

But this was the New Theatre, 26 September 1944. We were there and I was ready. Inside the dressing room I began to prepare. Over the loudspeaker I could hear the first trickle of the audience coming into the house. Nose on, wig on, makeup complete. There, staring back at me from the mirror, was my Richard, exactly as I wanted him. I'd based the makeup on the American theater director Jed Harris, the most loathsome man I'd ever met. My revenge on Jed Harris was complete. He was apparently equally loathed by the man who created the Big Bad Wolf for Walt Disney.

Makeup is a strange thing. I know that now it's not the fashion to wear it, but for me that's where a lot of the magic still lies. The smell of a stick of greasepaint— No. 5, No. 9, lake, 7½—still makes my scalp tingle.

I stood up and again looked in the mirror. The monster stared back at me and smiled.

By now the house was filling up, chattering and laugh-

Jed Harris

ing, getting ready to gorge itself and spit out the bones of any actor not coming up to its measure of the role. Me. . . . Richard smiled back at me again.

There was a spider somewhere inside my stomach, not a butterfly.

They say that an actor on a first night secretes enough adrenaline to kill an average person.

"Beginners, please." One last look and then away.

It is a strange feeling to stand in the wings awaiting that first moment of contact with the audience. Personally, I have never wanted to run away, but I understand people who have. There are some parts—few, but some—in which you can't wait to unleash yourself upon the audience, and this was one of them. I knew . . . and if they didn't agree with me, to hell with them.

I was in the slips and ready. The noise of the audience was still removed, but audible, which meant that the house lights were still up. I glanced round the stage. This was to be my world for the next three hours. Here I would plot, scheme, seduce and rise to the giddy heights of a crown. Here I would destroy Clarence, the Princes, Lady Anne, and cry for a horse in vain. I looked into the prompt corner and saw Diana Boddington, my stage manager, press the final bell for the bars. Far off I could hear it ringing.

Last questions: Was I prepared? Of course I was. The spider in the stomach again. God, I should have gone to the lavatory. Deep breath . . . perfect. Control . . . control . . . everything geared to a fine edge, sharp as

a razor . . . Come on, get that curtain up, I've been
here an hour.

I looked in the corner again. Diana pressed another
button and the chatter in the front of house slowly
ceased. The lights had dimmed and the warmers were
on the curtain. Yet another switch and a green light
winked. "Now," I thought. "Now." Up went the curtain
and there we were: the audience and Richard, face to
face for the first time.

The warmth from a full house is amazing. As the
curtain rises, it rushes across the footlights like a great
giant's breath. It fills your nostrils. Immediately you are
bathed in the heat of the lights, alone and vulnerable.

"Now is the winter . . ." I was inside the skull, looking out through Shakespeare's eyes.

I had married parts of the end of *Henry VI Part III*
with the opening soliloquy of Richard, and so, instead
of its lasting for a minute or thereabouts, it read for
fully six.

Halfway through, I knew. I knew that I was holding
the reins. When I said, "Can I do this and cannot get
the crown?" the audience made a sort of "hhhaaaa"
sound. I knew it had worked—whatever it was. They were
mine for another hour before I need start worrying.

I remember being in the wings at one moment and
saying to Beau (Nicholas) Hannen, "Smell it, Beau?"
A funny smell—like oysters. Success." I think he said,
"Yes." At another moment I passed Diana in the corner:
"Do you smell it?"

"Yes, I do," she replied. She knew these things instinctively. It was there, everywhere. The atmosphere was tingling. I had seduced Lady Anne and the audience as well.

It is on the second night that the reality of the first night is stamped indelibly on the brain. The people in the second-night audience have been told by the newspapers and by their friends that they are going to see something special, so they are excited but relaxed . . . and rather smug that they have got a ticket.

The repertoire had three successes, and I had my Richard.

CHAPTER SEVEN

King Lear

WHEN you've the strength for it, you're too young; when you've the age, you're too old. It's a bugger, isn't it? The Romeo syndrome in reverse. At least I had a crack at it at both ends of the scale. Pity I didn't play it at sixty as well. That would have been a great age, perhaps the perfect one.

I came to play Lear for the first time against my will. Ralph Richardson had an uncanny knack of claiming parts—he was a cunning old sod. What he'd do would be play the part on the radio first, which was very popular in those days, television still being an infant at the party, and in this way establish a right to do it. He did this with Cyrano de Bergerac, which I very much wanted to play. He had been an enormous success on the radio with it, and it therefore seemed only right that he should play it in the next season at the Old Vic.

I had to come up with a campaign plan, and as I was rooting around in the more dastardly areas of my memory, something came to me. Ralph had once said to me that although he felt he didn't really aspire to Shakespeare, there was one part he thought he could do and do well, and that was Lear.

I arranged to meet my codirectors at the Old Vic—John Burrell and Ralph—to decide what we were going to do in the next season. We sat down and began to plan out the repertoire.

"I would like to play Cyrano," said Ralph, knowing full well that I saw myself in the part.

"All right," said Burrell. "Excellent."

There was a pause and they looked at me. I waited for a moment and then, as though I'd had a sudden inspiration, I threw it in.

"Lear," I said. "I'd like to play Lear."

Ralph blanched. He knew I'd done it out of pure villainy.

"Absolutely," said Burrell. "I certainly can't see anything against that—can you, Ralph?"

Poor old Ralph had to reply, "No . . . no . . . no." I'd got him.

The next day we went to the pub for lunch as usual, the Salisbury in St. Martin's Lane. We sipped away for a bit and then, when I thought it the appropriate moment, I moved in.

"Good meeting yesterday, wasn't it?"

"Yes," said Ralph.

"Pleased?"

"Very," said Ralph.

"Think I'll make a good job of Lear?" I smiled at him. He didn't reply. He knew exactly what I was at. "Why don't we swap?"

"What's that?" he asked.

"I'll give you Lear if you give me Cyrano. Much better way round, don't you think?"

Those eyes searched into mine for a time, and then, very quietly, he said, "No!"

I'd never for a moment thought he wouldn't swap; I thought it was just a formality. I didn't want to play Lear—well, not yet, anyway—but there it was, signed, sealed and delivered. He would play Cyrano, and his Lear would be taken care of on another occasion. Alas, it never was.

There was no turning back. Not only did I play Lear for the Old Vic, I directed it as well. No half-measures for Olivier. If I was going to jump in, I might as well go the whole way. I was thirty-nine. We were still at the New Theatre in those days. When we announced the production, the advance booking was phenomenal, and several hundred playgoers failed to get tickets for the first night. Perhaps they all wanted to come and see me fall on my bottom. Well, I didn't. Naturally there were comparisons: Donald Wolfit had recently played it— but then, he never stopped playing it; and so had John Gielgud.

My production, when compared with Komisarjevsky's, did not come out favorably; but then, it's a hell of a play to direct and play the leading part in as well. Looking back, perhaps I should have left the directorial side to someone else, but I was flying high in those days.

I always start studying a part at once. First I exercise my vocal cords and my cord muscles by shouting full out in the open air, probably to an audience of cows. I try to extend my vocal range and make sure I can manage eight or more lines without pausing for breath. Then I practice the role in detail to myself. It is a great mistake to take up rehearsal time with technical matters. By the first rehearsal of *Lear* I knew exactly where to take a breath, how to light and shade my voice, and how to tonalize it at certain moments in order to get the utmost variety. The actor must keep an audience engaged by constant changes of inflection; he must keep them forward in their seats; he must have an acute sense of when he is boring them, when they are about to yawn or look at their watches, wondering when the interval is coming; he must know the instant he has lost their interest.

When I get to the actual rehearsal I like to work full out, to try my complete range, so that I can eventually produce my final performance by a process of selection.

In my production I made the court appear one that was well used to the sudden whims of Lear and his pas-

1946, *King Lear*, with Alec Guinness as the Fool

sion for authority. I made him finicky, almost childlike, and the court was prepared to humor him. I set this up before my first entrance, so when I made my appearance I was able to cast a critical and fussy eye over the dress and position of my guards. I think by doing this I gave the part more plausibility.

I suppose my performance may have leaned a little more towards Gielgud's than towards Wolfit's. Wolfit stressed the senility of the character, whereas in mine the octogenarian's body still pulsed with life and passion. I was able to get tremendous power vocally, so in the storm scene the thunder and lightning were in the King himself as well as in the elements. I felt that one of the greatest moments in my performance was my distraction before the storm: "A tremendous tantrum of impotence," Ken Tynan called it, "full of crazed emphases and teasing fullness of tone."

> I will have such revenges on you both
> That all the world shall—I will do such things—
> What they are yet, I know not;—but they shall be
> The terrors of the earth! . . .

Audrey Williamson said:

> . . . the sheer torrential sound of it swept across the senses like Niagara, but in all this raving music one could still hear the tortured cry of a drowning man. The sudden drop of the voice at 'O Fool, I shall go mad,' clutching at the jester for support and wild, broken flight from the scene wrung the heart as no other Lear at this moment has succeeded in doing.   (*Old Vic Drama*, 1946–47)

Most kind of the critics. It's always heartwarming when someone else says it. It was actually an extremely successful production, and I came out of it with a great deal of credit, which I think surprised several people and was an added bonus to me since I hadn't wanted to do it in the first place.

Frankly, Lear is an easy part, one of the easiest parts in Shakespeare apart from Coriolanus. We can all play it. It is simply bang straightforward. Not like Romeo, for instance, with whom you spend the whole evening searching for sympathy. But then, anyone who lets an erection rule his life doesn't deserve much sympathy, does he?

No, Lear is easy. He's like all of us, really: he's just a stupid old fart. He's got this frightful temper. He's completely selfish and utterly inconsiderate. He does not for a moment think of the consequences of what he has said. He is simply bad-tempered arrogance with a crown perched on top. He obviously wasn't spanked by his mother often enough. It is crass stupidity that governs him. I mean, to turn away like that from his favorite daughter—what kind of idiot is he? Mind you, I suppose Shakespeare knew what he was about; by getting Cordelia off the stage he was able to save the management money. In his day the boy actor who played Cordelia would double as the Fool. That makes rather interesting ripples through the piece, does it not?

That first production at the New Theatre I enjoyed enormously. It didn't tire me, although the pundits always say it's the most exhausting role in Shakespeare. Nonsense; I disagree. Of course, I had youth and vigor on my side, but not for a moment did I find it tiring. I enjoyed every performance thoroughly. Of course, I had to wear the age on my sleeve, and looking now at some of the photographs in close-up, I suppose I did look a little like Clapham Junction, but I'm certain the

overall appearance and interpretation were well worth
a ticket.

Naturally, with energy on my side I was able to give
"Blow, winds, and crack your cheeks!" everything that
my bellows allowed. I was determined to be heard in
Trafalgar Square, and I'm sure the effect was electric,
for I stood in jet blackness shot through with lightning.
It was only later, when I came to play the part again,
that I realized such excess wasn't necessary. Age teaches
you that. Age gives you the authority anyway. Something
well worth remembering when tackling the part: you
do not quake and quaver and nod like a toy dog in the
back of a car with age. Age is something else. Age has
a dignity, almost a serenity, and when anger comes from
age it does not have to be shouted. It explodes with
authority. A look, a smile can be just as chilling. Of
course Lear has to rage, I'm not denying that, but it's
well worth looking at how much vocal anger is necessary.
The austere command of years can be conveyed just as
powerfully, perhaps even more so, if played with steely
calm.

I suppose one of the reasons people say it is an exhausting role is that it is usually played by an elderly
actor. The audience spend most of the evening on the
edge of their seats fearing that the performer will have
a seizure at any moment. They are breathless with anticipation. Was that stumble part of the action or was it
real? When he put his hand to his heart, was it to feel
if it was still in motion? Was that a crack of the voice

or was it the beginnings of the death rattle? This is cruelty; the poor old man shouldn't be forced to do it. The management should be reported to the Royal Society for Prevention of Cruelty to Aged Actors.

At the end of the evening, when the ancient star inches his way down to the center of the stage and nods his tired head towards his exhausted public, he does not realize that the appreciation, the tumultuous applause, the accolades that are hurled towards his deaf ears are not for his rendering of the Bard's great lines, but come out of relief that he is still standing and has not left for the Great Greenroom in the Sky.

Of course he is shattered, and of course it is the most exhausting part in Shakespeare. The poor old bugger nearly dies every night, but he loves it. Try and stop him from doing it, just try.

There is nothing more tempting than to hang on to the curtain at the end of a long evening and let the audience know that you have given your all for them, just for them. This was the night and the only night when you sweated blood to give them the definitive performance. Tonight you and they shared something special. This performance was for their grandchildren. You know the bow—we've all done it. It goes something like this:

Eyes take in the gallery, hold for a moment.

Eyes take in the upper circle, hold for another moment.

Eyes to the dress circle, longer hold; more money here.

Eyes to the stalls, even longer.

Then to the left and to the right, for the boxes. Treat the boxes as if there were Royalty seated in them.

Then slowly let the head come down completely, chin almost on chest. Play the modesty.

Then the questions.

Is this really for me? This applause that I hear, can it be for me?

I can't believe it. What have I done to deserve this? I am only a mere player, your humble servant.

Wait for a moment, then play the modesty again. Arms outstretched to the company on either side. Without them, dear audience, without my fellow players, I am nothing.

Wait for another beat and then move forward.

Hand on heart, then final bow.

I would stay with you longer my dear audience, but I am exhausted. I must leave you now.

By this time they should be on their feet. If not, you've got something wrong.

My God, those old actors knew how to do it!

One of the first productions of *Lear* I saw was in Los Angeles, when I was living there before the war. It was given by an actor called Randle Ayrton, who was then a famous British star. He was with the Stratford-upon-Avon company, and they took this particular production of *Lear* out to the States. It was considered quite a good production. I went to see it with my mother-in-law, who knew him. I was still married to Jill Esmond at the time. We went backstage afterwards to bandy the compliments and exchange the usual pleasantries. My mother-in-law gushed all over him.

"You were just like the Old Man," she said. "Just like the Old Man."

(Irving even then, so long after his death, was still referred to as the Old Man.) Of course he was; he'd based it on him, hadn't he?

Listening to the compliments flying, I came to a decision. I vowed to eradicate all knowledge of the Old Man from the public's memory forever. I was determined to become the Old Man myself. Let them impersonate me fifty years after my death. My will was granite. I was determined to be the greatest actor of all time.

My last performance of Lear, on television in 1984, I must leave for you to judge. It was not geared for the theater, though of course its origins were there. Strangely enough, I still didn't find it exhausting.

I was thinking the other day of Shakespeare's own basic description of all his tragedies. Surprisingly enough, it is said by the one man who could not make up his mind, but who really knew how to say something. Such a brain.

> HAMLET. So oft it chances in particular men
>   That, for some vicious mole of nature
>   in them,
>   As, in their birth,—wherein they are not
>   guilty,
>   Since nature cannot choose his origin,—
>   By the o'ergrowth of some complexion,

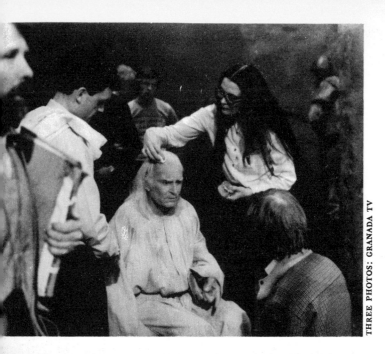

1984, making *King Lear* for television

ZOE DOMINIC/CAMERA PRESS

> Oft breaking down the pales and forts of
>   reason,
> Or by some habit that too much
>   o'erleavens
> The form of plausive manners, that
>   these men
> Carrying, I say, the stamp of one defect,
> Being nature's livery, or fortune's star,
> Their virtues else—be they as pure as grace,
> As infinite as man may undergo—
> Shall in the general censure take corruption
> From that particular fault. The dram of e'il
> Doth all the noble substance often doubt
> To his own scandal.

Well, there's your Richard, there's your Hamlet, there's
your Macbeth, there's your Othello . . . and your Lear.

Sometimes I wonder if I have not become a little like
Lear myself. Is it now possible that I have placed a part
of his clothing upon me? I wear an invisible theatrical
crown, which I like, am very attached to and will not
give up. Just as I was determined to eliminate Irving and
let the Old Man's spotlight rest on me, the Young Man,
now I have in turn become the Old Man and somebody
somewhere must be thinking the same thoughts that I
had in Hollywood all those years ago. Well, whoever you
are and wherever you are, if you want it, you'll have to
come and get it. But I warn you, it will take more than
physical strength and cunning to get it. First you have
to dust clean the blackboard of the chalk of memory.
But begin, whoever you are; do begin. You must, if you
believe, and you will not succeed if you do not believe.

But just remember, as you come tiptoeing along the passageway to the chamber of gold, that you will find an old man standing at the entrance, legs apart, back straight and erect, eyes piercing, barring the way.

ZOE DOMINIC/CAMERA PRESS

1984, with John Hurt as the Fool

CHAPTER EIGHT

Othello

WHEN it was announced that I was going to
run the National Theatre Company, a letter arrived on
my desk one morning from Kenneth Tynan, then drama
critic of the *Observer*. Tynan had not endeared himself
to me over the years, because he had constantly attacked
Vivien Leigh for her performances—to my mind, with
no justification. Vivien was a very fine actress, as can be
witnessed still in films like *Gone with the Wind* and

A Streetcar Named Desire. But it seems to me that the critics have never been able to accept beauty and talent. You can have one or the other, not both. She had both.

As far as Tynan was concerned, she could do no right, and this I found offensive. It is so easy to attack, much easier than to praise, and Tynan's pen was brilliant and often dipped in acid. As it happened, he was always generous towards me, which didn't help when Vivien and I were performing together. There is little joy in getting a good review when your other half is getting a bad one. But apart from his blindness towards Vivien, it has to be said that he was one of the finest dramatic critics of the twentieth century: I put him up there alongside Shaw. His premature death was a great loss to the arts in general, for whether criticizing or merely being involved, he was a major influence on what has now become our modern theater.

His letter that morning simply said that he was prepared to give up his Fleet Street world if I would take him into the National as literary adviser; he wanted to join the other side of the footlights. As you can imagine, I was very surprised. I arranged a lunch, and we talked. Ken became my dramaturge.

What has this got to do with Othello? One of the conditions that Ken gave me was insistence that within five years of his joining us, I would perform the role. It had never occurred to me. Iago was the big part, as far as I was concerned. I had already played Iago and really didn't fancy approaching the play from the other fel-

1962, with Kenneth Tynan

low's point of view. If I take on Othello, I told Ken, I don't want a witty Machiavellian Iago. I want an honest-to-God N.C.O.

I'd played Iago with Ralph Richardson the first time round. Poor Ralph, he was not born to play the Moor.

His Othello was as boring an Othello as has ever been, and I was in like a jackdaw, stealing the goodies. I played Iago entirely for laughs. No menace, no danger at all. I thought, rather than play him like a sixteenth-century villainous character, it would be more interesting and acceptable to play him terribly sweet and as charming as could be. I felt that he would seem more dangerous and plausible this way, and that everybody would believe him "honest Iago." And I played up to it. I believed that that was what people thought I was: honest. Then, when I got to the soliloquy, I'd have my syringe ready and let the audience have it straight up the arse.

It didn't work critically, but it did work for me. And of course, it didn't work for poor old Ralph.

1938, Iago

ANGUS MCBEAN/
MANDER AND MITCHENSON

So when it was suggested that I play the Moor, I naturally had reservations, knowing, as I did, the play from Iago's point of view. I felt that Othello was a loser from the word Go. I had this fantasy, and I like to think that it's probably very near the truth, that Shakespeare and Burbage went out on a binge one night, each trying to outdrink the other, the yards of ale slipping down their throats and thickening their tongues. Just before one or other slid under the alehouse table, Burbage looked at Shakespeare and said, "I can play anything you write—anything at all." And Shakespeare said, "Right. I'll fix you, boy" and wrote Othello for him. I'm sure something like that must have occurred.

It's a very badly designed role; for instance, there are too many climaxes, far too many. Working on the assumption that Othello's first reaction to Iago is "Come on, I know you're after Cassio's lieutenancy . . . I'll get the truth out of you—come on," this starts Othello on a higher step than Iago. But in getting the truth, Othello trips himself up, becomes jealous without being aware of how it began and goes completely over the edge. He rants; he roars like a cornered bull, the picks hanging from his neck, blood dripping, waiting for the *coup de grâce.*

In the middle act there are some very fine pieces: "Like to the Pontic sea," and the "Farewell the plumed troop" speech. But soon come the fits and the raging again, saying things like "I'll tear her all to pieces!" "I will chop her into messes!"—all demanding that you scream at your utmost.

It is very easy to show off and bellow away like a dying moose. "Look at me, audience, I can bellow more mightily than anyone has bellowed before." How often, as a beginner, one has done it: bludgeoning an audience into defeat, bursting eardrums with the throttle full out; big is beautiful. In the last scene you kill Desdemona—a huge top—and follow with two or three tremendous outbursts in a very short space of time. At your death, the quiet sigh of the audience, "Thank God . . . thank God . . ." and they leave, scratched behind the ears.

No, I thought, this is one hell of a difficult part. It's Iago's piece. There he is, the bugger, sitting on your shoulder and quietly winking at the audience. But all this said, the challenge was out. Tynan had insisted, and let's face it, there's nothing more flattering for an actor, no matter how much he has achieved.

One of the innermost, and at the same time overtly conscious, determinations of my life has always been to make the modern generation understand what I am doing. I knew I could not play Othello in any detached way; I would have to put every single throb of my tiniest vein right into it. I knew I would not be able to fulfill myself in the part, or the part in myself, unless I did so. It was not a role of which I would be able to rid myself when I took off the makeup.

If you're wise, you always take off the part with your makeup; you forget about it. People who can't do that suffer very much, and I don't think it's good for them. I don't think it's even good for the work to go on thinking about it afterwards. But rehearsing is a different problem; I'm not talking about periods of rehearsal. Of course you think about nothing else, day and night, in those circumstances. But in playing a part, if you've given it everything you've got, you ought to sit down and have a nice drink; that's what I say.

As Othello, I would have to start quietly, to come onto the stage first as the most real person the audience had ever seen; then, bit by bit, when I'd won their confidence, I would be able to start riding them. Only then would they accept my roaring. Through careful timing and delicate use of rhythm I would give the audience seconds, moments, tiny instances of recognition of the absolute truth of the situation. By spontaneous reaction I would make the audience feel illuminated, not by a *new* sensation but by a half-suspected sensation of truth that they had only subconsciously been aware of before. When that happened it would be like a flashing mirror for them. But I would have to work hard to achieve such an effect.

I would not care if people tittered when I rolled around on the floor in what critics would be bound to call the wrong place, because I would know that the audiences were building up to a much larger dose of catharsis later on. If I roared and screamed and behaved grotesquely and the audience laughed, I would know I'd relieved their tension. They'd come back better for the end, more tragically receptive.

I began to think about the play again, and look at it from Othello's point of view. I began to sniff around the man, like an old dog inspecting yesterday's bone.

I began to read the play and reread it, worming my way into the text. Scratching at the veneer I had left on it from my previous experience of Iago's point of view, chipping away and getting back to the bare, fresh page. Throwing off the harness of a previous production.

To create a character, I first visualize a painting; the manner, movement, gestures, walk all follow. It began to come. Pictures and sounds began to form in my mind, subconsciously at first, but slowly working their way to the surface. You keep the image in the heart and then project it onto the oil painting. I say "oil" rather than "watercolor" because for me, acting will always be in oils.

I was beginning to know how I should look: very strong. He should stand as a strong man stands, with a sort of ease, straight-backed, straight-necked, relaxed as a lion. I was certain that he had to be very graceful. I was sure that when he killed in battle, he did it with absolute beauty.

Black . . . I had to *be* black. I had to feel black down to my soul. I had to look out from a black man's world. Not one of repression, for Othello would have felt superior to the white man. If I peeled my skin, underneath would be another layer of black skin. I was to be beautiful. Quite beautiful.

Throwing away the white man was difficult, but fascinating. Of course, you can never truly do this, but there were times when I convinced myself that I had. The oil painting.

A walk . . . I needed a walk. I must relax my feet.

1965,
Othello on film,
with Maggie Smith
as Desdemona

Get the right balance, not too taut, not too loose. Walk
with poise. It wasn't working. I couldn't make it work.
The movement, the rhythm that I needed wasn't there.
I watched, I studied—nothing. I should walk like a soft
black leopard. Sensuous. He should grow from the earth,
the rich brown earth, warmed by the sun. I took off my
shoes and then my socks. Barefoot, I felt the movement
come to me. Slowly it came: lithe, dignified and sensual.
Lilting, yet positive.

I felt that Othello spoke quite differently from any
other character in Shakespeare: he speaks like a foreigner
who's learned the language too carefully. His moral
attitude is also that of somebody who has studied to
impress. The Senate think he is clear, pure, full of cool
courage. He's concocted this perfect cocoon exterior:
he is the statue of a perfect man. But the statue is flawed:
Shakespeare gives him one fissure. The fissure cracks and
the statue breaks. He is too jealous: the fault is self-
deception. He's the greatest exponent of self-deception
there's ever been. Othello's self-conscious dramatization
of himself as the noble warrior leads him to ignore
reality.

The voice. I was sure he had a deeper voice than mine.
Bass, a bass part, a sound that should be dark violet—
velvet stuff. A careful way of speaking, a Moor who
didn't speak Venetian naturally. A bell . . . sometimes
your body can become a bell. A superbly shaped instrument for sounds to be echoed round, shaped, then sent
soaring away towards the attentive ear.

The voice was of great importance. I began to work

on it every day. I had to lower it, and slowly I surely did.
I was becoming the text. I was forgetting Iago, "honest Iago."

I gave a full-blooded, all-out rendering of the part at
the very first rehearsal, and from then on I tried things
out extravagantly, way over the top. Hands, eyes, body,
a kind of self-flagellation. I have done this most of my
acting life, grasping the nettle early on and making a
fool of myself.

The company realize right away how embarrassing it's
going to be and I save a hell of a lot of time. I am not
doing it for the company. If you are frightened of making a fool of yourself, if you start too subtly, too cozily,
giving just little glimpses of what the part might become,
you create huge barriers for yourself later on. You must
be open, naive, prepared to charge down every alley that
presents itself, until you lock into the ones that you and
your character need.

Often, by mistake, you'll stumble on something and
it will be exactly what you want, and you hold on to it,
keep it and cherish it. Often an accident happens and
there it is: the man, the man you want. That's him.

In the handkerchief scene, I intended angry insistence.
It developed into imploring anger. It was right.

Then the rose: I did not whip Iago's face with it, but
stroked him gently, as if to say, "Come on, you're pulling me leg. I'm not for that." Othello wasn't so simple
that he couldn't tell when Iago was being a bit of a
humbug. It was an absolutely realistic touch, which the
audience appreciated.

On the other hand, you mustn't let this self-indulgence carry you away. This is a pitfall, as I've said earlier, that can become a bear pit. Once in, never to be seen again. You must always be like a jockey on a racehorse, knowing that the slightest movement, change of balance, will disturb the machinery. On the other hand, you must let the horse know where he is going—where you want him to go, not where he wants to go. Bit between his teeth and he'll return to the stable, not the winning post. You hold on to the reins, guiding subtly, never letting the neck stretch out. Always keeping something back.

It doesn't matter how big the acting is, how loud you're roaring, it must never be absolutely at the top of your range. If you hit the ceiling then you let the audience see the measure of you, and you're done for. You look weak, instead of strong, and they think, "He's straining himself . . ." and you're finished. Always keep something in the reserve tank.

An audience will encourage you to show the extent of your powers, willing you and wooing you to do so, but an audience is like Iago himself: once having got you to open your heart, it will eat your entrails. You, the actor, must always be on top. Show a glimpse, flirt, live dangerously, but never take your trousers off. Let them think that you are always just about to. Let them beg. Let them come back for more. Always the encore.

So the ranting and roaring did take place, but only in the confines of the rehearsal room. Those four walls splattered with the blood and tears of actors past and present, fingering their way skyward like stripped trees on an autumn backcloth. I roared, I ranted, I embarrassed my fellow players. I honed and hewed, and fought with William Shakespeare. Round after round, some days losing bitterly, some days with a glimmer of what might be. Words coming, words going. Some days not a syllable could be remembered. Other days everything as clear as daylight.

Working on the voice, lowering it, lowering it.

Getting more used to the feel of the rehearsal-room floor through bare feet. Knowing what it was like to be at one with the bare boards, the earth beneath, the sky above. Slowly moving towards the opening. The play becoming less of a play at times and more of a reality. Moments when I think I am Othello, when I am convinced I am black.

Beware . . . I tell myself to beware. Come back to the text, do not drift. You are good only if you are in control. Every moment you must be in complete control.

Sometimes I begin to think that Shakespeare is playing Iago and I am playing Burbage.

On the first night, I was in the theater several hours before, creating the image which now looked back at me from the mirror. Black all over my body, Max Factor 2880, then a lighter brown, then Negro No. 2, a stronger brown. Brown on black to give a rich mahogany. Then the great trick: that glorious half-yard of chiffon with which I polished myself all over until I shone. Pancake makeup looks powdery, and when you sweat it is apt if you're not careful to break out in little rivulets, but if you use this wonderful bit of chiffon, it gleams a smooth ebony. The lips blueberry, the tight curled wig, the white of the eyes, whiter than ever, and the black, black sheen that covered my flesh and bones, glistening in the dressing-room lights.

> RODERIGO. . . . never tell me! I take it much
> unkindly
> That thou, Iago, who hast had my purse
> As if the strings were thine, shouldst know
> of this. . . .

Roderigo's first lines came echoing over the dressing room speakers. The curtain was up.

Deep breaths; stand the way a strong man stands, with a feline ease. Straight-backed, straight-necked, relaxed as a lion. Kill with beauty. . . .

I am . . . I am, I . . . I am Othello . . . but Olivier is in charge. The actor is in control. The actor breathes into the nostrils of the character and the character comes to life. For this moment in my time, Othello is my character—he's mine. He belongs to no one else; he belongs to me. When I sigh, he sighs. When I laugh, he laughs. When I cry, he cries.

Remember, do not show them the complete iceberg. Do not scratch behind their ears. Keep them there, riveted, until you decide to let them go. Hold them in the palm of your hand. Your pink palm. How pink it seems when framed with black. . . .

Black skin—white costume—red rose . . . the first line comes.

'Tis better as it is.

Dear Ken, your contract is fulfilled.

CHAPTER NINE

Antony
and Cleopatra

I N 1951 I had the St. James's Theatre and was talking
one day with Roger Furse about what we should do next.
Roger was a brilliant designer, and he and I had worked
together for years and indeed continued to do so until I
formed the National Theatre in 1963.

"I really can't imagine," he said, "why you and Vivien
don't do *Antony and Cleopatra* and *Caesar and Cleopatra* in repertoire."

It hadn't occurred to me before, but the more I

thought about it the better the idea seemed. I knew
Vivien would be wonderful in the Shaw, but I wasn't so
certain about the Shakespeare. As it turned out I needn't
have had any worries at all. She was brilliant, and in my
opinion the best Cleopatra ever. She was radiant and
beautiful and shone through the lines as if they had been
specially written with her in mind. My Antony was not
bad either, though some critics didn't seem to agree with
me. But at this period in my career it didn't matter;
Vivien and I were sailing, we were set in the galaxy, and
fortunately, everyone wanted to see us. There was a tremendous feeling of optimism in the air. The war had
been over for six years, we had grown used to peace,
there was a Festival of Britain on the South Bank; the
population seemed to be on an upward surge, and Vivien
and I were twinkling above it. Within a week of the an-
nouncement of the forthcoming productions at the St.
James's, we were sold out for the twenty-six-week run,
and we were thinking about going to America.

I'd never really thought a lot about Antony—as a person, that is. I mean, really, he's an absolute twerp, isn't
he? A stupid man. But thank God Shakespeare didn't try
to rectify that; if he had, there would have been no play.
Not a lot between the ears has Antony. Now, Cleopatra,
she's the one. She has wit, style and sophistication, and
if she's played well, no Antony, however brilliant, can
touch her. There she stands, the golden Queen of the
Nile, towering above the play and toying with her soldier
lover. She has the good sense not to tell him of his short-
comings; but then, why should she? It was a purely physi-

1951, *Antony and Cleopatra*

cal relationship. Two very attractive human beings determined to do wonderful things to each other. Result
. . . suicide. There is nothing cerebral about their love: it is pure passion, lust and enjoyment. And why not? How would you feel alone in a chamber with that lady? I don't think you'd want to discuss the *Times* crossword. You'd keep inclemency to the bedroom and not use it as an adjective to describe the clouds outside.

So there he is, little Antony, Julius's friend of twenty years earlier, grubbing around the Nile and making a cock-up of everything. The young man who had orated so brilliantly over Caesar's body now a middle-aged lapdog. I often wonder what the relationship was between Caesar and Antony. I think one of Antony's problems was that because he was a nobleman, he thought he would automatically have an honorable character, but he hadn't. The greatest and the noblest he wasn't. But what a fantastic final speech, wonderful last lines. Strangely enough, they make me weep to say them now:

> . . . the greatest prince o' th' world,
> The noblest; and do now not basely die,
> Not cowardly put off my helmet to
> My countryman—a Roman by a Roman
> Valiantly vanquish'd. Now my spirit is going.
> I can no more.

Haunting, quite haunting. As I say, they make me weep now; but I never wept on stage.

Though I call him a twerp, it's still a great part. You've got to see that it is and follow it through. The one thing you mustn't do is play it for sympathy, this you must beware of, and it's a very easy trap to fall into. Once you try to wheedle your way into the audience's pocket you've had it. You may as well pick up your toga and go home. The actor should remember to leave the heroics in the forum in the other play with Caesar's body. This Antony is very different.

I once had the chance to play the Antony in *Julius Caesar*, but only for a brief moment and not completely. It was many years ago, when I was with the Lena Ashwell players—the "Lavatory Players," as I christened them, because we played town halls and swimming pools where the only changing rooms seemed to be the lavatories. *Julius Caesar* was to be my last play with them. During the run of it I was asked to take my talents elsewhere, having been dismissed for disorderly conduct on stage, as I explain in *Confessions of an Actor*.

I was playing the part of Flavius, not exactly the most taxing role in the world, and Crowds. You've got to have Crowds in *Julius Caesar*, no matter how small. Somehow I don't think I was a very good Crowd, for I spent most of my time trying to make the other actors giggle, which of course eventually led to my downfall.

At that time I was fired from several jobs for giggling myself. I couldn't help it. Noël Coward broke me of it when we were doing *Private Lives* by deliberately saying, "Look, you're a giggler and I'm going to cure you. I'll tell you how I'm going to do it. I warn you. I'm going to make you giggle all I can, and between Gertie and me we can do it anytime we feel like it. We can kill you. And you know it. Now, I'm going to go on doing that, and at the end of each performance, every time you do it, I'm going to tick you off in front of the entire cast and staff, and you are going to learn not to." It took seven months.

Anyway, back to Lena Ashwell.

There we were, sitting in our cubicles, waiting to bring the Bard to whoever came to that particular swimming pool that night. Can you imagine arriving with your swim trunks, and towel tucked under your arm, only to discover that the pool has been boarded over for the evening and atop it are Lena Ashwell's bonny band of troupers? I think we'd have been better off performing an aqua show. The acoustics were wonderful if you didn't mind the echo, echo, echo. And the scenery, as you can imagine, was minimal. As I say, there we were sitting in our cubicles like seals in the slips waiting to give our all in front of a handful of deaf pensioners and exploding children who were only too well aware how their own little foghorns could echo back to them, when it was discovered that our leading man (Godfrey Kenton), who was playing Antony, hadn't turned up. All eyes to the understudy—me.

"Larry, Godfrey's not here."

"Not here?"

"Not here."

"Ah."

"Do you know it?"

"Backwards . . . and Brutus and Cassius. . . ."

"Well, you're playing Antony until he gets here . . . forwards."

"What about Flavius?" For whom I was already toga'd.

"Flavius too. Act One beginners, please."

I went out in front of the swimming-pool patrons and began:

> FLAVIUS. Hence! home, you idle creatures, get
> you home! . . .

You can imagine the sort of reaction that drew. I finished the scene—somewhat hurriedly, I imagine—then moments later reappeared as Antony. I had gone up in stature, stepped out of the crowd and into the breach.

Not a bad part, Antony, but he doesn't really come into his own until the forum scene. Until then the character is just warming up, getting ready for the big oratory. Caesar was duly killed and my big moment was almost upon me. I was really looking forward to it. Let me get at it; I'll stir those nodding zombies in the front row. They'll tell their grandchildren they heard Olivier's "Friends, Romans, countrymen . . ."

I was about to begin. What a speech! I was going to ring it out round the pool from the top diving board to the back of the empty balcony. I was going to play it so well that it would remain in the heads of those who witnessed it forever. Stories would be told years hence of this night when Antony had come alive in a swimming pool. People who had not been there would pretend that they had:

> I was there that night when young Olivier stepped
> in and gave us the definitive Antony. I knew then
> that a star was born. It must have been the same

feeling as witnessing the first performance of Irving
in *The Bells* or Kean as Shylock. I knew a major
actor had arrived. When he began his big speech,
the atmosphere was electric, the hairs stood up on
the back of my neck as I became aware that I was
seeing something very special. What a privilege to
have been there at that moment! I will never forget
it. . . .

Suddenly I looked into the wings and there was this
frantic ticktack man. It was Godfrey. He'd arrived and
was dressed and was wanting to come on. For a moment
I thought of refusing to leave. I mean, what could he
do—what could anybody do, for that matter? I was there,
I was in possession of the boards, I could squat and only
a hook would get me off. It seemed such a shame to
deny the audience the magic that I was prepared to give
them. More frantic arm moving from the wing. Should I
deny not only them but also their grandchildren who
would sit on their laps in fifty years' time and hear the
story? Surely my duty was to posterity.
    "Get off, it's my turn."
    Another beat . . . a pause . . . very tempting . . .
    "Get off . . ." The whisper was getting louder.
    What the hell . . . I'll play it another time . . .
I'll show them. But of course I never did. Slowly I made
my exit. A new shape and voice took over the role and I
went back into the Crowd, and I don't believe that any
of those nodding geriatric gnomes or nose-picking ado-
lescents noticed. They were dreaming of days gone by or

1951, *Caesar and Cleopatra*

days to come, and the mighty Caesar was forgotten forever.

So you see, I knew something of the early Antony when I came to play the later one.

I decided not to direct when we did *Antony and Cleopatra* at the St. James's. I felt that acting in both plays would be enough without the hassle of the production as well, so Michael Benthall undertook the direction, and did a fine job.

I gave Vivien one note or tip at the first rehearsal. "Darling, do me a favor," I said, "just try and lower your voice a whole octave." And she did. Something I did myself as Othello. She lowered her voice and it captured the performance. Something she was to do again later when she played in *Streetcar*.

After her success in the Shaw, the press were waiting. Her real tussle is to follow, they said, for Shaw makes the most brilliant comic role for Cleopatra in the first act, but after the middle of the play she doesn't get one laugh. He loses interest in Cleopatra and fastens his interest on Caesar; he just adores Caesar. Bad playwriting. But it happens occasionally to authors that they create a part, lose interest and unbalance the proportions of all the other aspects. But Vivien surmounted this problem and made it in the Shakespeare part too; she made it with top honors. They had underestimated the lady, she was brilliant. As I have said, it was as though the Bard had picked up his pen and for a moment looked down the centuries and seen her. The gods had given him a glimpse of four hundred years on; down at the end of the telescope he had seen Vivien dancing.

I think the vocal note was the only one I gave her. She knew how to play the part. She seized it, fashioned and formed it, then showed us the magic.

As I look back at this chapter, it must seem that I have brushed Antony aside by calling him a twerp. This does not mean that it is not still a great part. It is; it is a wonderful part, and one which I look back upon with relish. I really wouldn't have missed him for the world. There are glorious passages of writing and poetry. It's a hell of a part to play. His final two scenes, the one with Eros and then the one with Cleopatra—wonderful moments of poetic tragedy:

ANTONY.   Since Cleopatra died,
    I have liv'd in such dishonour, that the gods
    Detest my baseness. I, that with my sword
    Quarter'd the world, and o'er green Neptune's back
    With ships made cities, condemn myself to lack
    The courage of a woman . . .

Not bad, eh? His use of language is staggering. His descriptions are deadly accurate and set forth with such economy. A great, great gift.

It's a wonderful part. But just remember, all you future Antonys, one little word of advice: Cleopatra's got you firmly by the balls.

CHAPTER TEN

The Merchant
of Venice

My Shylock owed more to Benjamin Disraeli than to Fagin, physically and mentally. There was to be no stropping of knives on the soles of shoes, no fingering of the sharpness of the blade, no splitting of hairs with the curved edge, no spitting of oaths onto the courtroom floor, no rolling of eyes to the deaf gods.

I was determined to maintain dignity and not stoop physically and mentally to Victorian villainy. Not for me the long, matted hair, invariably red; the hooked nose; the bent back. I had got all that out of my system playing A. B. Rayam in Somerset Maugham's *Home and Beauty*. That image of Shylock I had always seen as a caricature and an easy way out, making mock not only of the Jewish people but also of Shakespeare himself. He is too good a writer to be dealt with in that way, though over the centuries it has been a popular way of performing the part: the red wig begging to be hissed from the gallery, the more boos the better; the audience backing Gratiano, that embryonic fascist.

I wanted to find something else—again the old search for reality. In this I was greatly helped by Jonathan Miller, my director at the National Theatre in 1970. First of all I wanted to find a setting for *The Merchant of Venice* which would give it a feeling of dignity and austerity. I hit upon 1880–85, that period when the Victorians had found their maturity. Tall hats and frock coats; a time of clean and polished fingernails. Fortunately, Jonathan and my other associates agreed with my vision.

In the early days of rehearsal I remember Jonathan being ruthless in his criticism of some of my line readings. It came as quite a shock to begin with, until I slowly began to realize what he was at.

"You're not going to say it like that, are you?" Echoes of Guthrie.

"Why not?"

"Can't you think of some other way of doing it?" Guthrie again.

"I don't really see why, Jonathan."

"Because people will say, your audiences will say,
'There you are—Olivier all over.' "

"Yes?"

"If you want to stamp yourself vocally all over the
role, just be Olivier being Olivier, then go ahead. You
don't need me for that."

Slowly he made me see myself as others saw me. He
wanted to help me out of it; I'd made a mountain out
of mannerisms and had ended up impersonating myself.
It's a habit that old actors fall into very easily. Miller
opened my eyes and made me look in the mirror again.

It was a good lesson to learn, and one so easy to miss.
As in every business, once you have become a success
people are more inclined to be sycophantic; everything
you do is perfect: it must be—you are the leader. If you
are wrong, a whole dynasty collapses; therefore you must
be right. Any criticism, any rumbling of dissent is made
some way off, out of hearing. This doesn't happen so
much in the theater as it does in other businesses; in the
theater there is much more equality; in a way, you are
only as good as your last job. Mind you, having said that,
perhaps I'm wrong: maybe it does happen as often in
the theater; perhaps it was happening to me and I just
went merrily along thinking I was right and must be
right because nobody told me I was wrong. I'm not saying that what I had done in my early days at the National had fallen into Olivier doing Olivier—far from it:
I'm saying that when I started the rehearsals for The
Merchant I had obviously slipped into this error; Jonathan spotted it and had the courage to point it out.

By the time I had reached the National I was not only the leading actor but manager of the whole setup as well. I had very fine associate directors, but when it came down to it, I was the boss. I was approaching sixty and had been at the top of my profession for some years, so it couldn't have been easy for people to summon up the courage to come and tell me I was wrong. They did, of course, in administration, but when it came to the acting I was the "guv'nor." Naturally there were arguments about the choice of plays, and indeed as I have said in my other book, the scales did not always come down in my favor. But when it came to acting, I knew best, and if I didn't, it was not for them to tell me. This sounds arrogant, and I suppose it is; what I'm really trying to say is that my ear was open, but no one chose to whisper into it until Jonathan Miller.

Inevitably old actors do repeat themselves. It's so easy. If it worked before, it will work again. I don't think I consciously thought in this way; in fact, I didn't. If I had, I'd have stopped it right away myself. No, it was definitely in the subconscious. I suppose, when a little tiredness creeps into the bones, some aid from the past doesn't go amiss. I had been well known for my inflections over the years, the changing of pace, the sudden surges of power, so why not pluck a few moments from the past?

As I say, when Jonathan pointed the finger, it came as a bit of a shock. For a moment I returned to school, my satchel full of embarrassment. Here was I, the one actor who had always prided himself on his originality, and here was a young director telling me I was as original as yesterday's newspaper. For a moment my mind flashed around some of my contemporaries. I paused. "He's right," I thought—a deep breath—"he's right." And I trust that from that moment I stopped living in my own image and began afresh.

I had seen George Arliss play Disraeli in a 1929 movie, and it suggested shades of the Shylock that I wanted to give. So again, without embarrassment, I must acknowledge another actor. You must remember that when I say I've used other performers to unlock the gates for me in certain roles, it is always my interpretation in the end. I am not a mimic, I am a purveyor of plays.

So the process began again, the process of molding and building and becoming a character. I studied and watched in trains, buses, streets, taxis. I observed the populace. Soon I became aware that the so-called Jewish nose was to be seen more frequently on Gentile faces than on Jewish ones. This pleased me because, as I have already said, that was not the way I wanted to play it. Then suddenly I saw what it was. The mouth: it was the mouth that was different. Larger, much more sensitive, much more mobile. A visit to the dentist was necessary.

I had teeth made that totally altered the shape of my face. They pulled my mouth out and pushed my upper lip forward. Suddenly there he was, my Shylock. Months of sitting and staring at noses that didn't exist, and there it was all the time. The mouth was the thing. The moment I saw it in the mirror, I knew I was right.

It was a lesson well learned. Don't look for the ob-

1970, Shylock

vious. If anything, that's usually the caricature; go the other way, be more subtle in your choice. Look for the mole, the tic, the wart, the walk, the handshake, the smile. Mouths are very interesting and can be altered so easily. By doing this you can completely reshape a face and create a character. Thin lips, fat lips, crooked lips, harelips and so on. Just look how much a face is changed by a mustache, change the mustache and again the character changes. What has happened to the actor's face between entering the dressing room and coming out again tells the story. Try whitening the face as an experiment. Reduce your face to nothing with a white Pancake, and then add one thing and see what you make of it. Dab on a spot and see what it does. Take it away again and add an eyebrow, take the eyebrow away and add a mustache, and so on. Very interesting what you may discover. For instance, have you ever thought of playing a character who has just shaved off his mustache? That feeling of nakedness on the upper lip: the fingers flick to it frequently to see if it really has gone. Nobody, of course, in the play will refer to it, but it will add something to your performance which might just give it an extra depth, a little more color, make it just a little different.

There are a million things you can add to the makeup of your mind. And these are the things which will eventually make your character exist. I'm not suggesting that an actor go over the top; that would only be deeply irritating to the audience and your fellow actors alike. But experiment and see what you find. The mouth and the eyes are all-important.

So I had my new teeth and I immediately felt right.
My only concern was that Jonathan Miller might take
one look and confiscate them. But I think he was so relieved that I hadn't put on a false nose, he willingly let
me keep them.

Part of my Shylock was based on an uncle of mine, the
first Lord Olivier—I am the second. Uncle Sydney was
part of the first Labour Government of 1924: he was
Secretary of State for India. He was a remarkable man.
He was twice Governor of Jamaica, which was quite a
feat—to have two innings at the one job, as it were. He
was obviously very popular and well liked.

I remember he came to stay once, and Father had spent
the few household pennies on vintage port and good
food. Uncle Sydney was to have the best. He had a beard
and looked quite Jewish, which in his early days created
a slight problem, for in spite of Disraeli's success, it still
made life difficult for politicians.

There was a dignity and bearing about Uncle Sydney
that was an enormous help in my search for Shylock. I
remembered it and used it.

My performance remained contained in uprightness
and civility until Jessica was stolen away, and then, with
justification, slowly went demented. To take the daughter was like carving the heart out of Shylock, and this I
tried to emphasize in the role. The departure of his
daughter turned his brain. Once this happened, he was
prepared to sue, to destroy. Once she had gone off with
a Gentile, as far as he was concerned she was dead. The
pound of flesh was nothing compared with the abduc-

1973, with Joan Plowright as Portia

tion. He had been raped by a pack of Christian dogs. From that moment onwards I let the fury and the rages come.

It was during the run of *The Merchant* that I suffered badly from the actor's nightmare: *stage fright*. I wonder if that had anything to do with my performance's becoming fresh, open and naked again. It's always possible.

Let me give you a brief insight into stage fright. It comes in all sorts of forms; I suppose it's always there, but most of the time it hovers unseen. It is an animal, a

monster which hides in its foul corner without revealing
itself, but you know that it is there and that it may come
forward at any moment. A shadow in a lightless room,
it's lurking there in the back of your brain cells, an insubstantial presence that refuses to go away. At any moment
it will push a finger forward and knock over the "opera-
tor" who is waiting at your "exchange" for the next message to be received, translated and sent to another part
of your body. The next message can't get through. Stage
fright is like the character in *The Turn of the Screw* who
never appears: he is always waiting outside the door, any
door, waiting to get you. You either battle or walk away.

For people who haven't had it it is very difficult to
understand. To the young actor who is full of optimism
and energy it is a joke. I'm certain I didn't believe in it
when I was young and hopeful. I don't suppose I even
gave it a thought. But suddenly there he is: the bogeyman comes along and tries to rob you of your living. He
can come at any time, in any form. The dark shadow of
fear.

Sometimes the process can begin in bed at night, the
night before a performance. Hot and cold sweats suddenly wake you; your brain leaps into top gear, thinking
of the performance to come. The logical fighting the
illogical.

"I don't know the lines. Dear God, I don't know the
lines."

"Of course you do. You know them backwards."

"That's not the point. I don't want to know them
backwards. I just want to know them."

"You know them. You know you know them."

"Let me just go through them again."

"What's the point? Sleep—you really must sleep."

"To hell with sleep. I'll go through the whole blasted script, that's what I'll do. I'll go through the whole thing."

"It's pointless."

"I'll write it all out in longhand. I'll go through it syllable by syllable."

How like a fawning publican he looks!
I hate him for he is a Christian. . . .

Next—what's next? For God's sake, what comes next?

"Relax."

"I'll get up . . . I'll get up and walk round the house. I'll recite the whole play out loud until it is so bored with me, it will reside in my memory box forever."

And up I'd get, the hot sweat having turned to cold.

"Panic . . . that's all it is. People get like this in the early hours of the morning . . . it's a well-known fact."

"Come on back to bed . . . you'll feel better in the morning."

"Maybe you're right . . . maybe. I'm really very tired. . . . I need to sleep."

Back to bed, feeling cold now, blankets pulled up round the ears. Sleeping in fits and starts. Sudden moments of wide-awakeness, and other moments of deep sleep. Nightmares . . . black holes . . . bright colors . . . Suddenly it's morning.

As I have said, it comes in many forms, creeps up and

swamps you like a shadow, and just when you think you've conquered it, there it is sitting at the end of the bed grinning at you.

There is the kind of stage fright that begins when you are waiting in the wings and you can hear your cue approaching. The heart starts to pound and you can feel it at the base of your spine. It is nothing like first-night nerves—it is way beyond that. The breathing becomes affected: the breath becomes shorter when you want to make it longer and deeper; and all the time this wretched cue is getting nearer. You try to calm down, but the sweat breaks out again. The voice in the head starts to ramble.

"I should have stayed in the dressing room . . . why do I subject myself to this? I've done it all . . . I've done everything . . . why don't I stop now, while I'm on top?"

The cue is getting nearer.

"I'm not going to be able to go on . . . I'm rooted to the spot. Somebody has nailed my shoes to the floor. My legs are made of lead. I'm alone—oh, God, how alone I am! Nobody understands this . . . nobody."

Cue nearly here.

"I'm going to walk out into that bright glare and be utterly exposed. Walk out? Nonsense. I can't leave here. I'll never move again. I'm going to be rooted to this spot forever."

PORTIA. . . . If he have the condition of a
saint and the complexion of a devil . . .

"If I don't go on now I'll never go on again."

PORTIA. . . . I had rather he should shrive me
than wive me . . .

"This is the theater where I have played Hamlet,
Richard, Henry. . . . This is my theater . . . my beloved theater. This can't happen here . . . I will not let
it happen here . . . I am in control . . . I have got to
be in control . . . I am . . . I am . . ."

PORTIA. . . . Come, Nerissa. Sirrah, go before.
Whiles we shut the gate upon one wooer,
another knocks at the door.

"Now . . . that's it . . . now. The next lines to be
spoken are mine. Move . . . move . . ."

The thumping at the base of the spine is now almost
painful. This is what it must be like to give birth.

I go forward. Slowly I go forward.

"Shylock . . . you're Shylock. Am I? Am I really? I'm
not . . . I'm just me . . . stage-frightened me."

Suddenly I'm there. The wing is left behind and I'm
on.

I have given instructions to the other actors not to
look me in the eyes. My company—what a thing to do to
them. But I had to. The one thing an actor must do is
look his fellow actor in the eyes, and I have asked my
fellow players not to.

SHYLOCK. Three thousand ducats—well.

"I've said it . . . the line's out. I've said the first line.
God, supposing I fall over? I've got the feeling I'm going
to fall over.

BASSANIO. Ay, sir, for three months.

"I mustn't fall over."

SHYLOCK. For three months—well.

"Second line out . . . I've said two lines. Why can't I get rid of this lack of balance? Lack of sense of balance."

BASSANIO. For the which, as I told you, Antonio shall be bound.

"Relax . . . that's all I've got to do . . . relax."

SHYLOCK. Antonio shall become bound—well.

"What happens if I fall over now? Balance . . . come on, balance."

BASSANIO. May you stead me? Will you pleasure me? Shall I know your answer?

"The lines are echoing. I'm in an echo chamber. . . . 'Shall I know your answer?' What is my answer? Calm—stay calm. My heart is racing. Speak . . . it's your turn. What is it? What do I say? I know it . . . I know the lines. . . . What is it . . . what is it? Come on . . . come on. . . . I've been here for an hour . . . I've paused for an hour. Why aren't they coughing? Anything . . . just say anything. . . ."

SHYLOCK. Three thousand ducats for three months, and Antonio bound.

"I've done it . . . that's the right line. I've done it."
Once you have experienced stage fright, you are always aware that it could be just around the corner waiting for you, just waiting for you to get cocky and overconfident. So you treat the body and the brain with much more re-

spect, and you remain conscious always of the shadow in the corner.

I find the play horrid and cruel, and none of the characters likable. Shylock is just better-quality stuff than any of the Christians in the play, who are heartless, money-grubbing monsters. But I have much to thank the play for. It finally put down my stage fright. Now I can say, "I have been there, I have looked over the edge, and I have returned."

People have asked me about the cry that I let out off-stage when Shylock exited after the court scene, mortified by the judgment. I wanted something to remain ringing in the ears long after I was in the dressing room. Something that would stay with the audience through the sweetness and light of the final romantic comic scene. I used to leave and deliberately lose my footing in the wings. I'd fall forwards and smash the palms of my hands on the concrete floor. Then the real pain would make me cry and sob like a child. A dramatic way of doing it maybe, but an effective one. There he was, his dignity gone, a case lost, because he was a Jew. The trip offstage drove him into infuriated grief. Many of the great actors of the past had finished the play on Shylock's final exit: Kean for one. I didn't, and wouldn't even if it had been suggested. Shakespeare wrote the play to finish in Belmont, and finish in Belmont it should, but Shylock should remain. Beneath the humor there should be a sad shadow of a destroyed man. For me the cry did it.

Part Three

CONTEMPORARY INFLUENCES

CHAPTER ELEVEN

Knights of the Theater

I'VE known Ralph Richardson and John Gielgud for many, many years and we've acted together on innumerable occasions, lately more often on the screen. Hollywood would send for us, the three knights, in the hope that our names would increase the mogul's box-office receipts. I don't know that it ever did, but I suppose it may have.

You can hear them now in their high-rise Californian offices, can't you? "What we need is a bit of class. . . .

1985, *Wagner* with Ralph Richardson and John Gielgud

Get me one of them Limey guys with a handle to his name. . . . Better still, get me three." And there we'd be, the threesome: Ralph, John and Larry. I'm not knocking it, believe me; there were times when it was very useful. Even now I can look at an acre of land with satisfaction and say to myself, "Ah, *Such-and-Such* bought that. . . ."

It's difficult to talk about contemporaries. I don't know why I am doing it, really. I should be talking about how it was done, not whom it was done with or what others were doing at the same time. Yet it is difficult to avoid it. We actors beg to be adored, appreciated, admired, so we must every now and then be allowed to be discovered with our trousers down. There are always going to be tales about actors that will amuse or shock their public—usually apocryphal, but fun. We all have skeletons in our wardrobes. The actor quite deliberately sets himself up for this kind of treatment; we are the Aunt Sallys of the world.

Looking back, I suppose we all took ourselves rather seriously; when we let the humor and the vulnerability creep in, we get much closer to the truth. This was especially true of John Gielgud in his early days. Now that he appears to regard himself with a sense of humor, he has become a much finer actor. Once he threw off the finery and took an honest look at himself in the glass, his acting became much richer and more truthful. His performances in *Home* and *No Man's Land*, for instance, showed him at his stunning best. He is a character actor, and it is good to see he's got holes in his socks. He has a delicious sense of humor, and at last he is letting it grin through. He no longer needs the No. 5 and No. 9 and the voice that wooed the world.

I remember when we worked together in that early production of *Romeo and Juliet*, how I was the whipping boy and John was the adored god. At that time John was king of the West End; he was already a huge star and quite rightly enjoyed it. I don't say that with any envy, for indeed I was a star as well, but I was still considered a movie actor. I was more of an upstart, I suppose—in

the eyes of the Establishment, that is, not in my own
eyes: certainly not in my own. I have always had that rod
of steel in my makeup; flexible, but there. I have always
very much believed in myself, as of course every actor
must.

John is a very sweet man who is forever saying terrible
things about me and wonderful things about Ralph. He
probably wouldn't agree with this, and I've more than
likely got it all wrong; I mean I'm sure he's fond of me
really, but somehow something still niggles in the back
of my mind. He harks back every now and again to how
terrible he thought I was as Romeo; but that was more
than forty-five years ago. Surely you don't have to harbor
unpleasant thoughts about people for forty-five years? I
know that my Romeo, to say the least, was controversial,
but it was also ultimately a success.

At the time, of course, opinion was very much out of
my favor. I was a slightly bigger success than John as
Mercutio, but he made a vastly bigger success than I did
as Romeo, and that hurt because Romeo was what I saw
myself as. The theatrical world had not yet reached the
"Wouldn't it be fun if it were a bit more real?" idea.
Never mind about "Wouldn't it be more fun . . . ?"
We should have been asking ourselves, "Wouldn't it be
right to find reality?" For it is not a game of charades,
this acting world of ours; it is an everlasting search for
the truth. We must never allow ourselves to be blinkered
by sights from the wings. We must guard our talents
from false adulation. We must insist on holding a piece
of rock in our palms and not bright-colored plastic.

We were, and indeed are, very different actors and people. I will always be an active actor, and John a passive one. I'm a peripheral player who goes out to the character, whereas he stays in the center, finds something in the part that will suit him, then pulls it in towards himself. I went for the physical—the heroics, if you like—whereas John was always the poet, the ephemerist, head upturned towards the stars. I always appeared to be firmly astride this earth, eyes level on the horizon. Two very different actors, both with one thing in mind: success. I don't think I'd have wanted to play Richard II, and I don't think John was molded to play Richard III. It might have been fascinating if we had; but only for us, a collector's item. Mind you, I'd have given him a merry ride as Bolingbroke.

John has a dignity, a majesty which suggests that he was born with a crown on his head; on the other hand, my persona is that of a man who has plucked the crown up and placed it on himself. I am Bosworth Field and Agincourt, and John is Pomfret Castle.

Today, for me, John has somehow completed the acting circle. He has found his center; he is a brilliant character actor. The pain behind the glasses in *No Man's Land* was electrifying . . . the bare soul covered with a thin veneer of sophistication. You could see the clouds passing across his face like a day in an English acre. The sun popping out on the odd moment giving a facade of warmth and happiness . . . not a summer sun, a winter sun. That performance created a reality I've always fought for.

1944, *Uncle Vanya*, as Astrov, with Margaret Leighton as Elena and Ralph Richardson as Vanya

Ralph was one of the finest actors of this century; pound for pound he could take on anyone in the theatrical ring. He was brilliant, and I think would have stood shoulder-high in any century. Come to that, I think, pound for pound, he could have taken on anyone in the boxing ring. He had amazing strength and poetic gentleness. He could play gods and common men with equal majesty. I loved him dearly and find it very difficult to believe that he has gone. Somehow I always expect to

find him in the next room or round the next corner, or to
hear him screaming up the back lane on his beloved
motorbike. He was larger than life, but at the same time,
was able to present life with complete clarity and truth.
He could take a line and twist it and make it remain in
your head forever. He had wonderful, generous features—
God! what an actor's face. Broad, bold and easy to read.

A fine, incredible man and a most dear friend. We
laughed together, dreamt together, drank together, worked
and played together. We were rivals in the best sense of
the word, and for a time we ran a theater together, which
during that period I think was the best around. Peer
Gynt, Richard III, Cyrano, Henry V, Falstaff—we were
pretty special. I learned a lot from him, our friendship
going back as far as Barry Jackson and Birmingham days.
I suppose, in a way, I was a bit like Hal to his Falstaff.
He was an established actor in the company when I
joined, so we all looked up to him with a great deal of
respect. He was the leading man.

Ralph was equally at home in comedy or tragedy: he
wore the mask of both. He could take you from a moment of high comedy into deep tragedy with a nod. The
audience loved him, and the camera treated him with
the adulation of a young lover. It adored him, and he
seemed to adore it. He molded it round his performances
like warm putty; it was as though it had been invented
just for him. I can see him now on the cliffs watching
the sea gulls in *Breaking the Sound Barrier*, or standing by
the fireplace in *The Heiress*, the camera seeming to fit
round him like an old and deeply loved armchair. He even

smoked a pipe as though he'd invented it. I only have to think of him for a moment and I can hear his voice. He was warm and what the public might call ordinary and, therefore, quite exceptional. That was his ability, that was his talent; he really was a man for all seasons.

When the theater set off on its new path, led by George Devine and the new young directors and actors, he took it all with ease in his great, giant steps, and after a time you began to feel that he had changed the course of the theater entirely on his own. His performance in Pinter's *No Man's Land* and Storey's *Home* were classics on their own. Finely tuned moments of theatrical magic. He could at times hold an audience in the palm of his hand and bend down and whisper an earful of delights. He could take you through *Peer Gynt* and make hours seem like seconds, with a wry brain and an eyeful of smiles. He was a conjurer, a magician. He was Everyman with a touch of—dare I say it?—genius. He spoke poetry with the air of someone who had just written it, and made you feel you were hearing it for the first time. Of course, he was always aware of the verse, but this was his cunning: he made you feel that it was taking care of itself. His voice had such clarity; he chose his words with great care and placed them where others would fear to tread. He had the ability to make it look easy—always the sign of a great artist. With Ralph it all looked so simple. I often got the impression that his audience wanted to be up there with him, the whole process looked so enjoyable. He could make believe better than most. I always used to think he was on another planet.

I remember his first entrance in R. C. Sherriff's *Home at Seven*, a play about a businessman who had disappeared for twenty-four hours, during which time a murder had been committed. He brought the complete character on stage with what appeared to be no effort at all. You sat there and thought, "This *is* the man." He didn't have to speak, he *was* David Preston, the perfect city businessman. You could see him on the morning commuter train with *The Times* rolled under his arm, the furled umbrella and the bowler hat. You knew what his desk at the office was like; you knew how he drank his tea.

Ralph was a great after-dinner speaker; he seemed to be a natural. Give him the opportunity and he'd stay there all night. He had enormous wit, and his timing was as accurate as Big Ben's. I think perhaps he would have made a great comic in the music halls. He throve on his audience. When Ralph was on the bill at a charity concert or a memorial, you always added ten minutes to your original timing; once his anecdotes started, he couldn't stop. Not that anybody wanted him to; his hearers were only too happy to sit at his feet and be mesmerized by his charm.

The most amazing and outrageous things would happen to Ralph. I'm sure he wouldn't mind my telling you the story of his two visits to two houses we once had. He's probably told the story himself countless times, and much better than I can place it on these pages, but I'll tell you all the same.

The first house was a darling place called Durham

Cottage, which Vivien and I were very proud of. He came down for dinner with his divine wife, Meriel Forbes, known to us all as Mu—a wonderful lady. The three of us, Vivien, Mu and I, were very much aware of dear Ralph's taste in wines—a pretty poor one at the best of times—and we had a priceless bottle of burgundy which we intended to consume without the assistance of the merry monarch. So what I did was place a bottle of champagne in front of him and say, "There you are, Ralph, that's yours. As soon as that's finished, there's loads more. You don't have to stop drinking because you've come to the end of the bottle. When you've finished that one, just get tucked into the next." His eyes twinkled and everything seemed settled. The three of us wine fanciers got stuck into our burgundy and purred a lot. All was right with our world.

The trouble was that Ralph took me seriously and didn't stop when he had consumed the first bottle; consequently he got gloriously pissed. Everything would have been fine, except for one thing. It was Vivien's birthday, 5 November—Guy Fawkes' Day—and as a treat, Ralph had brought some fireworks, which he always loved.

We had not been in the house very long, and everything was absolutely perfect as far as we were concerned: freshly painted and pristine, newly furnished and looking, we thought, impeccable. Even the outside was looking splendid. The garden had just been started; there was a little pond with a fountain and the right things planted round it. I've always been in love with gardens.

Suddenly, at the table, Ralph sat bolt upright and exclaimed: "Fireworks!"

I panicked.

There was a pause. He grinned at me and then stood. "Fireworks."

I attempted a smile, the burgundy turning to acid, and inquired, "Fireworks?"

He winked. "It's Vivien's birthday and Guy Fawkes' joy day; can't let that go without a bang or two, can we?"

I knew I was beaten.

"Ralph, how sweet you are," Vivien said. "What a lovely thought."

"Right," he said.

I jumped in: "Outside, Ralph, all right? They'll be fine outside. This is all so new, and we're proud of it. The ladies can watch from the window."

"Oh, my dear fellow," he said, and started to laugh. He gave my face a playful slap—he always slapped one's face much too hard. I thought, "Here we go, I've had it, there's nothing I can do." And so he started. He began by letting off squibs from the dining-room windowsill and, of course, scarred it with huge burns. He then nailed a Catherine wheel to a beautiful weeping cotoneaster and I could see the poor tree dying before my eyes. He stuck them on the mantelpiece, he stuck them on the walnut bureau, he stuck them everywhere.

After a time my anger began to come to the surface, and despite his absolutely bemused state, he began to sense my disapproval. He suddenly stopped and looked round at us all. He paused for a moment and then

grabbed Mu's hand and said, "Come on Mu, best leave
these people" and burst through the French windows,
shattering the lock and a couple of panes of glass. Once
in the garden, he really hit the heights. From the French
windows he found the pond; stepped into it, knocking
the statue over; then stepped out again, leaving a dead
goldfish or two in his wake. Then he proceeded to move
on down the garden. He passed through a hedge of lilac
that I had just planted, a bumbling, grumbling bear, and
then on to the front gate, which he pushed through and
slammed shut, and the handle fell off. He then disappeared into the night.

It really was very funny; there's no way it could have
been staged with such perfection. Every gag was used in
what might have been the original hasty exit. Dear
Ralph.

The next time he paid a visit we had moved from
Durham Cottage to an even more splendid place, Notley
Abbey. Notley was near Thame, halfway between Strat-
ford and London, and was very, very beautiful. Of all the
houses I've lived in over the years, Notley is my favorite.
It was absolutely enchanting, and enchanted me. At
Notley I had an affair with the past. For me it had mes-
meric power; I could easily drown in its atmosphere. I
could not let it alone; I was a child lost in its history.
Perhaps I loved it too much, if that is possible.

It had been built by Walter Giffard, Earl of Buckingham, during the reign of Henry II, "in order that the
souls of the King, his Queen Eleanor of Aquitaine, his
own soul and those of all his family, might be prayed for

in perpetuity." Whenever I returned to Notley after a
period away, I felt safe and secure. I had my castle.

When Ralph came down he was truly on his best behavior after Durham Cottage, and it seemed he was determined to be the most enthusiastic guest we'd ever had.
He insisted on seeing everything.

"My dear Laurence, you must show me everything.
You must take me from top to bottom and show me
every single detail. I insist."

"Right," I said. "Let's start with the frescoes and the
ceiling of the part of it that was the Great Hall." And
off we went.

The hall was filled with Latin quotations all going
round and round. A dado of Latin quotations. There
were very pretty colors, and some of the walls had tiny
violets stenciled on them. I knew this would be a favorite
haunt of mine, somewhere I'd always like to show people
if they were remotely interested in the period. It was
fascinating.

To get there I used to go up the tower and then across
one room which had been turned into a sort of boxroom,
and then along a bit where I'd floored just a sort of passageway and nothing else, so you can imagine it was a
trifle precarious.

Ralph would stop every few minutes to admire something deeply. "Oh, it's beautiful. Oh, Laurence, what a
marvelously fortunate fellow you are. Oh, isn't it beautiful," and so on. We stopped at one point on the passageway that I'd floored, and Ralph looked at something
in particular—can't think now what it was. He looked

for some time, scrutinizing every detail, playing the part of the Historian; at any moment, I thought, he's going to produce a magnifying glass. After a pause, he said, "Oh, my dear fellow, the wonder of it, oh, the beauty . . ." At this moment, bound in the cocoon of his absolute rapturous pleasure, he stepped off my carefully laid passageway and went straight through the ceiling into the spare bedroom below.

What a man! I adored him.

Over the years I often asked him for advice, and he was always very much to the point.

"Ralph . . ."

"Hullo, dear boy, how are you?"

"Ralph, shall I go to the Old Vic?"

"Think it's a very good idea."

"Thanks. Goodbye."

My *Richard III* had been an enormous success at the Old Vic with, as I have already mentioned, *Peer Gynt* and *Arms and the Man*. Naturally, after their successes, Europe and America beckoned. We were asked to perform all three in Paris and New York.

Ralph had played the first night and the last of the season at the Vic, with *Peer Gynt*, and I felt that it was now my turn to kick off on the tour, and so I put it to him that I should go first:

"Old cock, I'm sorry . . . but you played . . . you took the first night of all and the last night of the first season with your play. Now, in Europe, it's my turn. I'll be the first, if you don't mind."

Poor fellow had to agree. I knew full well that the first

1945, *Peer Gynt*, as the Button Molder

off in Paris, or wherever we played in Europe, would be the big one in the critics' estimation. They'd recognize that that was top. I knew what I was doing, all right. So when the season closed in London, we set off for Paris with the "sweet smell" still in our nostrils.

We opened, and *Richard III* was an outstanding success. After the cheers and the wining and dining, I returned to the hotel, treasuring my triumph and thinking

1944, *Arms and the Man*, with Ralph Richardson as Bluntschli

what a clever fellow I was to have gone first. I was sitting in my hotel room at a desk by the window, writing a letter to Vivien, full of my first-night glory, when a strange thing happened that I never really got to the bottom of. I hadn't seen much of Ralph after the show; he'd obviously headed off to do his thing, as I had mine.

I'd got to a part of the letter which read "I'm worried Ralph has . . ." when I suddenly heard this noise on the pipes outside. I went to the window and looked out. There, below me, I could see a figure attempting to climb

up the drainpipes in my direction. On closer inspection
I saw that it was a disheveled, inebriated Ralph.

"Ralph," I yelled, "do you want to kill yourself?"

At first he didn't seem to hear me, so determined
was he.

"Get down, Ralph, get down."

He suddenly looked up towards me, paused for a moment, hesitated, *grinned*, and returned to the earth. He
disappeared, and I went downstairs to let him in. Before
I could ask him where he'd been, what had happened,
what was the problem, he pushed me roughly aside and
walked up the stairs.

"Get out of my way," he mumbled. Perhaps he
thought I was in *his* room, I don't know.

We'd had sort of friendly quarrels before, but they
were always all right. Perhaps a little deadliness behind
them, no more. We'd always had a jealousy, a rivalry,
about what we could do and what we could not do. We
were forever trying to outgun each other, which was
healthy and good for business; but somehow this night
there seemed to be something more involved.

He stood still for a moment, then suddenly lunged towards me and picked me up in his arms like a baby.
Within strides, he had crossed the room and was onto
the balcony. I thought, "It'll stop now; the joke's over."
But it wasn't. He moved with me in his arms across the
balcony and held me over the edge. I couldn't believe it
was happening. Here I was, a fully grown man, not without strength of my own, being held like a child by my
best friend above a Parisian street.

When you know there is nothing between you and the hard cobbles sixty feet below except a pair of strong arms, time really does stand still. I knew that if I struggled, he would let me go, and so I remained as still and as calm as I possibly could, which isn't easy when your heart is running at a hundred miles a minute. Supposing he slipped? Supposing he got tired? Oh, hell! It is true, everything does rush before you. What a way to go, halfway through a letter to Vivien. . . .

Very quietly I spoke. "Ralph . . . I think we'll both look very silly in the morning."

Pause. Nothing.

"Why don't you pull me back?"

Still nothing. In the silence I could feel him breathing.

"Look . . . why don't you pull me back, like a good boy? I'm beginning to feel really nervous."

Another pause. Then slowly he brought me back in. He set me on my feet inside the balcony and we both stood there looking at each other. I saw in his eyes that if I'd done anything other than I had, he'd have let me go. For a brief moment he'd wanted to kill me.

We moved back into the warm room. I closed the balcony windows behind me. It was wonderful to smell the stuffy, centrally heated air instead of the cold Parisian night.

I said, as casually as I could, "That was a rather dangerous one, wasn't it, Ralph?" He admitted that it had been, then quietly left and went to his own room. I just sat there, not being able to believe what had happened.

The next morning we sat together at breakfast. Over coffee I repeated, "Ralph, that was rather a near one, wasn't it?"

He said, "Yeah." He bit a piece of toast and then continued, "Yes, we were both very foolish. It was a double fault."

I couldn't believe what I was hearing . . . a double fault! He held me over a balcony and threatened to drop me, threatened to spread my life all over the pavement, and it was my doing? There are some thrills you can do without.

What a man! Looking back, I laugh sometimes to think what the consequences might have been. If he'd dropped me, I'd have been acting with Henry Irving much sooner than I'd anticipated, and a short time afterwards Ralph would have joined me, having done a brief dance on the end of a rope. There would have been no more Old Vic as far as we were concerned. But then, maybe that wouldn't have displeased some people.

Whatever else, he was a great man. I treasured him dearly, and he will be with me forever. They were golden days, and we were the golden boys, blessed with God's sunshine.

Watching John and Ralph spark off each other over the past few years on stage and on screen has been a real joy: the contrasts rich in flavor, like eating a good meal, looking at a fine painting or listening to Mozart. They were so in tune, though able to descant to each other at will, like a brilliant double act. That wicked glimpse

1945, *Henry IV, Part II*, as Justice Shallow with Ralph Richardson as Falstaff

from Ralph at the audience saying, "This is my turn; look at me," and then John, with complete authority, gently steering the eyes back in his direction.

They were in such charge of their acting machinery, would that they could have gone on forever; but now, sadly, the elder of the party has gone and the two-man band has been reduced to a single turn again.

It was a dream to watch them, all guns blazing, and we must be grateful to the inspired managements who had the insight to put them together.

CHAPTER TWELVE

Breakthrough

I TALKED earlier of timing and I think it is important, not just in acting but also in life itself. I have somehow always had a nose for the way fashion might go; I have always attempted to be there at the precise time the old order changeth, whether it be for the better or not. That is why, I think, I have managed to remain an accounted success for most of my life. I have continually sniffed the theatrical air searching for the winds of change.

When I first saw *Look Back in Anger,* I didn't really take to it at all. "Angry Young Man." So what? A new term coined by journalists to sell newspapers. . . . And yet, at the same time I did sense something was happening. I felt that this might well be one of the theater's great turning points. It wasn't the play itself so much as its articulateness, the new sense of drama it projected. The theater seemed to have a new message, and if so, this message must be respected.

Sometimes you'll find yourself somewhere by chance or by mistake, and your awareness, for some reason unknown to you, becomes doubly acute. A badly lit alley, and halfway along instinct tells you this is dangerous. Do you go on and out into the blind side, or do you retreat and return to the place you know? You cannot flip a coin; you must make a firm decision: the middle is mugger's paradise, you must either skulk back or leap on. I know what I do. It's because of this that I've been able to enjoy my working life for so many years. It has been magical, and I wouldn't have had it any other way. Let's face it, it's much better than going to the office.

I think I am what I might term an immediate man, always ready for the next second of life. Someone once asked me, "What's it like to know that you will live long after you're dead?"

I replied, "Where's the glamour in that? Westminster abbey is just as cold as any village graveyard. Nobody wants to die."

Using that immediacy, I have always been prepared to

turn on a sixpence, like a boxer reading the eyes of the opposition. Guard always up and, if hit, never show it. Smile.

It was suggested that I should see *Look Back in Anger* again, which I did. It was on this second occasion that I became certain Mother Theatre had given birth to a monster which was spitting, clawing and elbowing its way through the tradition that the previous generation had built and settled for. The child was transforming everything, and almost overnight. It was out of nappies before most of my generation was aware it had been born. Not only was it out of nappies, it was here to stay and would have an effect on acting as well as on plays being written.

Of course, I do not perform as a new young actor does. If the new generation were required to do what I do now, they would have extreme difficulty, because it took a long time to arrive at where I am. But I feel that if they were to teach me their job, they would find that I could grasp it quite quickly, because I'm well versed in my work.

I went backstage afterwards and, having exchanged the usual formal compliments, I was introduced to the man himself. "Larry, this is John Osborne. . . ."

The writer is the recorder of our times, the actor the interpreter, and it is the producer's job to fuse them. In this case, George Devine.

I have never felt old-fashioned. Inside myself I am seventeen, with red cheeks. But I felt that to the youth at the Royal Court, as my wife Joan later corroborated, I

seemed Establishment, and probably set in my theatrical
ways. She said she would be both socially and politically
opposed to me at that time, to anybody who was fright-
fully well groomed or too glamorous for his own good.
They said I couldn't really act. You had to be in jeans
and sweaters to have talent. When I finally came in, of
course, and started acting, I was just an actor in shirt
sleeves and with sweat on my brow. But at the time, their
resentment was very understandable. I was aware that at
that time Vivien and I were known as the Royal Couple
of British Theatre. Not that we didn't enjoy it; but all
my life, as I have already said, I have been prepared for
change.

I was not the "king" about to bless the people from
my throne of talent, I was a worker like everybody else. A
man of other people's letters. So I didn't need much encouragement from George Devine. I knew where I was
going. I took the banner of my generation to them. I was
in there long before John Gielgud or Ralph Richardson
knew it existed. I said to John Osborne, "God, I wish
you'd write a play for me one day."

The first act of *The Entertainer* was sent to me in
New York. I read it straightaway and decided that the
part for me was that of Billy Rice, the old father. I found
him fascinating. You could feel the music hall in his old
bones, and I believed I could do something rather special
with him.

I called George in London and told him I was interested, and I imagine he conveyed my interest to John
Osborne. I heard John quoted later on as saying that he

never writes with any particular actor in mind. Maybe
this is so; I cannot argue with what he claims to be true.
All I can say is that when the rest of *The Entertainer* arrived in New York, nobody but me was going to play the
part of Archie.

Billy was a good part, a magnificent part, but when I
read the completed script, Archie leaped off the page at
me and he had to be mine. I called George immediately
and told him that *The Entertainer* would be my next
project.

It was a glorious part, such a change. I was getting so
stewed up with my image of doing a sort of classical role
in the theater, or if it wasn't classical, a costumy role,
that I had simply become completely bored with myself
as an actor, knowing that the public must know what to
expect and were getting just that every time they came
to see me. It was absolutely deplorably depressing, made
me awfully sulky about life and utterly discontented with
my work—a way I'd never expected to feel.

Almost at once I began to steep myself in the old
music-hall tradition. It wasn't too difficult because it was
there in John's play—that, and so many other things. The
play was enormous, a huge canvas. The winds of change
were there, all right. I was in step with the new wave, in
step and marching. The recorder, the interpreter and the
producer.

What an amazing man George Devine was. I felt he
was my closest friend. He had tremendous vision and insight. When you look back and see what happened at the
Royal Court in Sloane Square in the 1950s, you cannot

fail to be astonished at the achievements. What a sad and premature loss his death was.

So the "king" came to the Court, not the Court to the king.

The play had been written with superb technique . . . that wonderful scene about the cake, her sense of violation when she finds a piece of the cake has been cut. However, I had a problem with the telling of rotten jokes because it was very hard not to win the audience over too soon. To begin with they were charmed and amused by my sallies, captivated by my virtuosity; but gradually I had to build on the sense of sadness, tiredness and threadbareness until there wasn't a laugh anywhere in the house. Then I knew, Well, that's come off. However, it was no good struggling to put them against me from the beginning, no good at all. I had to be extremely slow to reveal what an unsympathetic character I really was.

I will always be grateful for those days and look back on them with affection. Archie Rice: there he stands in the bright spotlight, alone, laughless but smiling. A bowler hat, a cane, eyebrows, a gap in his teeth, and dead eyes. . . .

I suppose wherever I go there will always be a piece of Sloane Square in my heart.

I talk as though the Royal Court had been new to me. That is not exactly true; I had played there twenty-nine years before. But what it represented in 1957 was very new to me. I had appeared there in 1928 with the Birmingham Repertory Company, from January to May, playing Malcolm in a modern-dress *Macbeth*, the title role in *Harold* (Tennyson), the Lord in *The Taming of the Shrew* (offered me palpably to check if I'd got a swollen head) and the Young Man in *The Adding Machine* (Elmer Rice). Strange that I should have returned as *Archie* Rice.

Archie, the song-and-dance man reduced to appearing twice nightly in a nude revue, lecherous, corrupt and blue with a talent for destructive self-analysis. I always saw him as an intelligent man aware of his failure, pushing it under the carpet under a haze of gin. He knew where he was and what he'd become, and the only way to cope with it was to abdicate all responsibility. I thought John Osborne had put the whole of contemporary England on stage with one amazing sweep of his brush. It was an epic painting, and the strokes were brilliantly bold.

I have always found the music hall fascinating. Such courage, such bravura, the painted smile on the comic's face when the house is laughterless and all the mackintoshes want are the stationary nudes. There's theater for you. The broken heart that floats in a sea of gin. The staring eyes with nothing behind them. Clowns have always made me want to cry.

The music hall, variety, vaudeville—whatever you will —has always been close to my form of theater: the "legitimate" theater, as it is called. What a ridiculously stupid expression. "Legitimate," "straight"—does this mean that variety is "illegitimate" and "bent"? Why do we need to put everything into pigeonholes? Surely we are all one, we are all entertainers, from Henry Irving to George Robey.

Robey's diction was superb. Those music-hall boys had no mike and their consonants used to hit the back wall of the biggest theater in the world *smack*. You never heard anybody say, "I couldn't hear" in those days.

The difference between the stand-up comic and the actor is that the comic has his colloquy with the audience. It is still two-way traffic; it's still a dialogue, not a monologue. The comic without his reaction is dead, so the audience must become his feed. To watch a truly great comedian perform is just as exciting as to watch a fine Hamlet—if not more so. The comic lives dangerously; he is always on the razor's edge. One moment of mistiming and his audience will turn on him. They are sitting there, waiting. Laughing—and waiting.

The music hall was nearer in atmosphere to the theater of the last century than to that of today. Oranges were still consumed, peel everywhere, and the air sweet and sticky. Nuts were crunched underfoot, and the audience was constantly on the move from the bar to the lavatory and seat. Some people just came in to see a favorite act and then depart again. It was rather like a cinema, I suppose, or television, but here the moving pictures could talk back, and here you could throw things at the moving pictures without being arrested. It was all part and parcel of the entertainment.

It is sad to think that by the time Archie Rice came along the music halls were nearly gone. There were just a handful left in England. The Chelsea Palace had become a store, the Collins Music Hall in Islington had become a lumberyard, and the Met, Edgware Road, perhaps the most famous of them all, had disappeared into new architecture. Gone, all gone. Bingo halls and bowling alleys. The comedians had to find their way into the clubs or television. So there was not much left for me to observe. The music hall was crumbling, like the Empire —which, of course, was John's central point.

Getting inside Archie was not as easy as I had at first thought. There he was on paper saying, "Come on, come and get me, I'm easy," waving a hat and raising his eyebrows. And indeed, to play him from the surface would have been simple—but it would be a great disservice to John. I had to get under the bowler hat and behind the dead eyes.

Starting a part is always exciting, a journey into the unknown. There is always that slight tremor somewhere inside, not knowing what the end result is going to be. No matter how hard you work at preparing a part, nothing will really happen until you get into that empty rehearsal room and begin, nervously, to flex your muscles. This is where you start to blow into the character's mouth and see if the heart will begin to pump. No matter how experienced you are, the first get-together always makes the nerves jangle. There is always the inevitable chat beforehand, trying to postpone the moment when the scripts are opened and the author hears the lines for the first time other than in his head. Nobody knows if it is going to work, no matter how good you feel the piece is. The words have to stand up and be counted.

Everyone still putting off the moment. Banal banter, nobody really listening.

"Hullo, how lovely to see you."

"And you . . . and you. . . ."

"Have you seen Fred recently?"

"No; have you?"

"No. . . ."

Pause.

"Pity."

"Still drinking, I suppose."

"I suppose. . . ."

"Shame."

"Could have done so many things."

"She's left him."

"Has she?"

"Long time now . . . can't say I blame her."

What the hell are we talking about? W*ho* the hell are we talking about? The stage manager indicates the coffee. Coffee is taken. Black, white, sugared, whatever.

"Biscuit?"

"Thanks."

Crumbs in the mouth, coffee too hot. Perhaps it would be better if we didn't do a read-through. Nonsense. Why should I be nervous? I've done it all before a million times. I'm up there where a lot of people would like to be. I have no reason to be nervous; I'm a star. It's not working. I *am* nervous, I'm bloody nervous. Think of all the first nights, all the parts that I've played over the years. Think of . . . I mean I'm fifty, I've been at it for most of my life. I was born an actor. Look at it this way: *they* are nervous, *they* are the puppies, you're an old dog. Be quiet and drink the coffee.

"How's *The Sleeping Prince*—sorry, *Prince and the Showgirl*—going?"

"Fine."

"Finished?"

"Yes."

"What was she like?"

"Mmmm?"

"Marilyn Monroe?"

"Oh."

She must be nervous; otherwise she wouldn't be asking me these silly questions. Archie Rice—think about Archie Rice.

"I think she's very talented."

"Yes." Think whatever you like.

"Vulnerable?"

If only you knew. Is Archie Rice vulnerable? Has he got any talent? Did he have any talent? How aware is he of his position? Did he ever top the bill? Did he ever love Phoebe? Did he ever love himself? Suez . . . what did I think of Suez? Is that relevant? Everything is relevant.

"She's obviously much brighter than her publicity would have us believe."

I must get a book on music-hall songs. I must go and see some more acts, bad ones. The pier, perhaps. I could try the pier. I'd really like to know what it feels like to be up there alone. It's not the same in Shakespeare. In Shakespeare when the soliloquy comes you're cozy in the character. The comic's up there all alone with his trousers down and wrapped up in his own personality.

"Was Miller around?"

Archie is vulnerable, he's very vulnerable. There's a big hook waiting in the wings.

"Marilyn Miller . . . not quite the same, really, is it?"

Up there all alone looking at a sea of empty faces. Praying for the first laugh. Nothing coming back at you but cold breath. What's known as the comic's graveyard? Is it the Glasgow Empire? Must find out. Think it's somewhere up there.

"Funny combination, isn't it, Miller and Monroe?"

The temptation to be good is always going to be there; must remember to avoid it. Archie, when I get to him, has had it.

"Mind you, I thought Vivien was wonderful on stage."

That really is the big problem: to be tatty, but entertaining at the same time.

"Vivien was divine."

What would Archie have made of Marilyn Monroe? That would have been a meeting, those two together.

"Wonderful timing, and she looked so good."

Wait a minute, perhaps they did meet. They could have been in the same show. Not Monroe—the character. The showgirl. Archie might well have fondled her breasts in his imagination. That's it—think along those lines.

What newspapers does he read? Does he read a newspaper? Of course he does. But does he read one daily? Yes. Why? To see if his name's in the obituary column.

"Have you ever thought of doing an Arthur Miller play?"

He's read a paper to keep up with events: political

patter—always good for the act. Let them think you're brighter than they are. How does he vote? Has he ever voted? Perhaps not. That would be being too much part of the Establishment. That way the tax man would find him. The tax man *will* get him. His bogeyman.

"You'd be wonderful as Willy Loman."

What does Archie drink? Draught Bass of course . . . of course. They don't have it in Canada, do they? He'll never survive in Canada, he'll never survive out of his own small pond. Archie Rice, he's . . .

"More coffee?"

It's happening; my God, it's happening. I'm beginning to fall in love with him. Tony Guthrie, it's happening all over again.

"Well, shall we sit down and read?"

We sat down, and Archie was alive. Archie Rice was on board and the train was pulling out of the station, destination unknown.

Of course, I had worked very hard at the text before the first reading, as I always do; but no matter how hard you work at it or how well you know the lines, you still have to take that first leap, and that doesn't happen until you meet your fellow actors. Then, and only then, can you get the true feel of your character, for it is then that he is seen through other people's eyes.

I often feel that you have to pick at the warts to find the real person, and in this Archie Rice was no exception. It is not a question of adding them; it is a question of dissecting them and seeing what is underneath. You can add them again afterwards if you want to. With Archie I really had to dig, and down in there I found gold. The gold that had been planted by John Osborne. It was like lighting a firework with a long fuse: a slow burner, but when it touched the gunpowder, the sky became a blaze of color.

I learned to dance, I learned to sing the way I thought Archie would, and I learned the loneliness of the stand-up comic.

The uninitiated would think that one of the most difficult things for me to attain was Archie's mediocrity. Sorry to disappoint you, but I can find plenty of that in myself. Everything inside the actor is geared to making things work successfully: the timing spot-on, the singing correct and the dance routines perfect. Here everything had to be slightly out of kilter, and yet the actor inside me still had to hold on to the audience. It was a very exciting period, and a difficult one. Very exciting.

John took me around the music halls that were left, and I slowly began to piece together the background. The jigsaw puzzle began to fall into shape.

To be able to do things badly, you first have to be able to do them very well, so my dancing went along the lines of Fred Astaire and my singing towards Mario Lanza. I slightly exaggerate, of course. I think, by the time I was ready, I could have made a decent attempt at standing up on my own and hurling someone else's patter at an unsuspecting audience in Hull. Or could I?

Step, ball, change; step, ball, change . . . it looks easy when you see them up there doing it, relaxed smile on the face, but believe me, it's not. Find the face in the

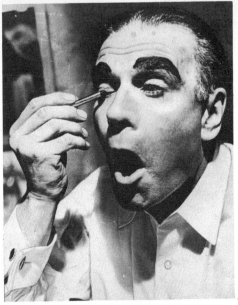

1960, *The Entertainer* on film; with Joan Plowright

audience, the woman who's going to giggle . . . where
is she? Ah, there she is. Come on, laugh, you bugger,
laugh. Here's a latecomer. Play off him, give yourself a
minute to breathe. Pause, beat, pause, tag line. Not a
titter—try again. "Have you heard the one about . . . ?"
"Yes."
Who said that? Ignore it; it will go away. "Well, I'll
tell you anyway."
"No, thank you."
Why doesn't he shut up? He's getting more laughs
than me. Christ, I need a gin. A large one, several large
ones. Should have had one before I came here. I did.
Perhaps that's the problem? Timing—nothing wrong
with my timing. I'd be all right if that idiot would shut
up. Give him his money back—send him home.
I'm dying up here. You're killing me, you bastard.
You're throttling me. Get your hands off my throat,
will you?
"Get off, you're rubbish."
Think of something witty to say. Come on, you can
do it. Say something.
"You're about as funny as my dog's arse."
Someone shut him up. If I had a gun, I'd shoot him.
If I had a machine gun, I'd shoot the lot.
"Bring the hook on and get him off."
Why does everybody think he's so funny? Somebody's
paying him, that's what it is. He's in one of my rivals'
pockets. Cutthroat world, this. Somebody's after my job.
"He's drunk; I can smell the gin from here."
If he doesn't shut up, I'll be off the circuit, and there

aren't any others after this. I've gone right through the lot from the Palladium to the Scunthorpe Music Hall.

"Bring on the girls, give us some tits."

That's not funny; that's not funny at all. What are they laughing at? Morons, all morons.

"Rubbish . . . rubbish . . ." He's chanting now.

That's all I need. In a minute they'll all join in. He's destroying my life. After this demonstration I'll be out of work, out of money and out of food. Doesn't he realize what he's doing?

"Come on, get on with it or get off. . . ."

God, someone else has joined in. I'm going to be lynched.

"Come on."

You think you're so clever, you come up here and do it. Trouble is, he probably could. No, he couldn't. It's easy from down there; even *I* could do it from down there. Think of something—come on, think of something . . . nod at the conductor and get into the song and dance. That's it . . . right . . . music . . . come on, Bill, music.

Well, perhaps I'll leave it to those who have been schooled in it, those unsung Archie Rices who tread the boards of the clubs and halls, the holiday camps and the summer seasons. Those valiant troupers, that breed of vaudevillian who never become more than a pimple in the Hall of Fame. I take my hat off to the hero of the gin palace, the little man who is courageous enough to attempt to get a laugh out of a chunk of stone, the smiling jester who is forever being pulled off by the managerial hook. I leave it to them.

Archie Rice was a landmark in my career, and one that
I'm very proud of. But whatever is said about my performance, we must always look to the man who made it
possible, the man who, with *Look Back in Anger*, *Luther*
and *Inadmissible Evidence*, painted great, huge, exciting
brushstrokes across the theatrical sky.

I thought of John Osborne sometimes as a young lion.
Another such was Trevor Griffiths. John Dexter (one of
my associate directors at the National Theatre, when it
was still performing at the Old Vic in Waterloo Road,
because the South Bank site had not yet been built)
dropped a script on my desk one morning and said,
"Read that. You won't like it, but read it all the same.
I think we should do it. *You* won't." Clever John, he
knew what he was at. First create a challenge, provoke,
poke, stir, then sit back and see what happens. Naturally
I read *The Party* immediately and found it fascinating.
It was a political piece, but it wasn't overloaded with the
author's political bias. He was too talented for that.
There was no doubt that Trevor Griffiths had a considerable talent, and to my mind, one that should be given
the facilities of the National Theatre to stretch its
muscles.

I suggested I should play the role of Tagg—not the
leading part, but a very good one, and one with two
enormous challenges for me: a twenty-minute speech and
a Glaswegian accent.

This was to be my last performance in the Old Vic
theater, about which Joan said, "If you do *King Lear* for
it, I'll kill you"—and there was no point in going out the

easy way. I have never been one for creeping out the back door.

What I was not aware of at the time, or perhaps had not given it any thought, was that it was to be my last performance on any stage—professionally, that is. Strange, looking back now: would I still have made the same choice? Yes, I surely would. Point to the future always. Be positive and look ahead. Anyway, as far as I was concerned at the time, it was just my last appearance at the Old Vic. I still had many more boards to tread. I was already thinking about a Lear, and more.

During the summer I worked at the speech day and night for four months. I knew from experience that it was essential to get the words first. Then, when I'd got the words absolutely so that they were tripping off my tongue, I'd get the accent. Trying to learn the words and the accent at the same time was dreadfully unwise, for then you had twin problems to contend with. Every morning between six and eight I'd worry away at it like a terrier, slowly putting more lines into my head, inch by inch, word by word, syllable by syllable. Driving it into those old, decaying brain cells. I was sixty-four then, and the memory was not backing me up as it had in the old days. I began to bully myself like an irate schoolmaster: "Come on, Olivier, it's not all that difficult. I mean you learnt James Tyrone two years ago, a much bigger part than this."

"That was two years ago."

On and on I went, any stray visitor getting the script thrust into his or her unwilling hands. "Just hear a bit

TWO PHOTOS: FRIEDMAN-ABELES

1960, *Becket,*
as Becket,
with Anthony Quinn
as King Henry;
and as King Henry,
with Arthur Kennedy
as Becket.
1960, *Rhinoceros,*
with Alan Webb

ZOE DOMINIC/CAMERA PRESS

1967,
A Flea in Her Ear;
and 1973,
*Saturday, Sunday,
Monday*

of that, will you?" I am sure the weekend guests used to hide behind the bushes: "Watch out—Larry's in the garden." Slowly and painfully I got myself in order. The first rehearsal approached. I was determined to have it ready by then.

We all met in the rehearsal room at Aquinas Street, where the National Theatre offices were—Nissen huts—in those days. As I described earlier with *The Entertainer*, the usual first-rehearsal jitters were in the air. Some actors get so introverted they decide not to let you hear a word at all, every line directed at their jumper. I hasten to add I am not one of these; I just let it all out, regardless.

We started the reading and in time got round to my speech. I could sense that the company was waiting. Right, I thought: here goes. Down went the book and on came the speech. Here it was; here was the first hurdle. I plunged. I knew all eyes were on me. Twenty minutes later I had done it. Word-bloody-perfect. I can't quite remember, but I think there was a signal of appreciation.

The rehearsals appeared to go well, but the nearer we got to the first night, the further away the lines seemed to go from me. I knew them, by God I knew them, but did they know me?

In no time at all we were there—the first preview of my last performances at the Old Vic. The stage on which I'd played princes and kings over the years since 1937 was to greet me in 1973 as a Glaswegian revolutionary in a baggy suit. Really very comical, I suppose.

By the time I made my first entrance, the rest of the

cast had been on for some time, and had settled. That cozy area under the warm spotlights had become their home for the evening. They were comfortable and at ease—or if they weren't, they appeared to be. Here was I, the newcomer, the intruder, the outsider in my crumpled suit, without any disguise but a Glaswegian accent. "Here he is," I could feel them thinking in the audience. "All right, show us!" They probably weren't thinking that at all, but that's what I thought they were thinking. Laurence Olivier had entered their room thinly disguised as John Tagg. Word had got round that I was going to attempt to speak for twenty minutes, and they had come to see me roasting on the spit of my memory.

I sat down on the sofa, center stage. I glanced out front. . . . My God! were they checking their watches? There is always a fear when you've been at it for some time and have had a certain amount of success that there is going to be someone in the audience who is seeing you for the first time and, after a bit, is going to turn to his companion and say, "My dear, what is all the fuss about? *That* is Laurence Olivier?" This fear was with me now. There were bound to be people sitting out there who had never seen me before and, to judge by the number of Japanese, had never even heard of me. Hands on my lap, looking perfectly relaxed (Ha! always make them think that you are confident) . . . I started.

Twenty minutes is a long time, a very long time. I could feel the eyes of my company willing me on. The two brains started to work—the one saying the lines, the other in charge of the lines. This is John Tagg speaking, not Larry Olivier. Trevor Griffiths for John Tagg, John Dexter for John Tagg. Thirty seconds into the speech John Tagg takes over. Suddenly we are all together. That's what it's all about; give it to the man himself, let him talk, let *The Party* talk.

When the actor begins, it is the moment when the director and the author feel at their most vulnerable, for there is no longer anything they can do about it. Once the actor is up there on his side of the footlights, he and he alone is in charge. Good, bad or indifferent, he is the boss. The director and the author must remain silent: as far as they are concerned they are impotent, they may as well go home. You, the actor, are the "guv'nor," and they must trust you. Weeks and weeks of rehearsing, rewriting, working are now being tried out up there where the actor belongs. He is in his territory, and no one may enter save another actor.

The door at the back of the theater opens, then shuts again. Someone has left. Who? John, Trevor? Doesn't matter now. I'm on the speedway . . . I'm motoring.

"Don't get too confident, Olivier. That's when he'll get you, the bogeyman who steals the lines before they reach your lips. Have respect."

"Must be halfway through. Not too many coughs. They're listening, by God; they're listening."

Suddenly it was all over. I was at the other end of the tunnel and had crossed the tape that stretched over the author's vocabulary track. I'd gone through. I'd made the journey. I may not have been line-perfect, but I'd got there. No night was easy with John Tagg: every perfor-

mance was an immense challenge; but then, that is how
it should be.

I trust that Trevor won't think I was more concerned
about my speech than about his play. His play is superb,
and I'm sure will be done again and again. And I'm
grateful that he gave me such an animal to fight with,
night after night, as I prepared to say farewell to the Old
Vic and the National.

I have talked in this chapter about two plays in particular, because they were both of special personal interest to me: *The Entertainer* marked my entry into "new
wave" theater and also introduced me to the black-eyed
actress who was to become my third wife. My choice of
The Party for my exit naturally received much encouragement from her and John Dexter, both of whom had
been protégés of Devine's Royal Court. In between, of
course, there had occurred a major change in my life
and career, beginning with the directorship of the new
Chichester Festival Theatre in 1962 and followed by the
formation of the National Theatre Company in 1963.
It was an exhilarating time; I had a new purpose, a new
toy in the shape of the open stage, and the exciting task
of planning the future. George Devine had opened the
way for me and I knew he would not mind if I purloined
some of his best talents for my new enterprises. Apart
from being a showcase for contemporary writers (Pinter,
Wesker, Ionesco, Beckett, as well as Osborne) the
Royal Court had produced a new breed of actors and
directors which it was my business to get to know. They
included Albert Finney, Alan Bates, Robert Stephens,

Franco Zeffirelli directing *Saturday, Sunday, Monday*; Frank Finlay leaning over Joan Plowright

Frank Finlay, Peter O'Toole, William Gaskill and Joan Plowright; and together with Maggie Smith, Anthony Hopkins and Derek Jacobi, they came to join my company at the National. Most of them were part of the influx of regional talent in the sixties (when the Beatles took the world by storm). They had a reality, inventiveness and spontaneity which brought richness and variety onto the stage; I sensed immediately that they made the sort of company I had had around me at the St James's look a wee bit old-fashioned. Once a thing has been done in a fresh style and manner the atmosphere be-

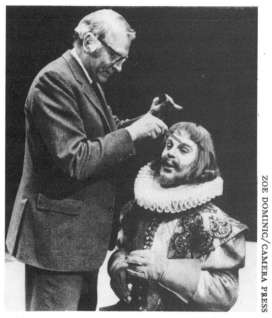

Touching up Derek Jacobi's makeup
The opening of the Olivier Theatre. The Queen is in the
Royal Box

comes charged with it, and you can't escape breathing it into your lungs. Of course acting styles change about every fifteen years, and in this country they are invariably linked with social and political change. Any young English actor with a public-school background and a much too upper-class accent was going to have a hard time of it for the next fifteen years or so. (Not a few of them would resort to disowning their families and claiming a Cockney barmaid for a mother!)

As Tynan wrote of Osborne's generation:

> For the first time I was recognising people on the stage that I'd lived with, that I'd shared bed-sitting rooms with, that I'd queued for buses with, that I'd been in the local amateur dramatic society with in my home town, Birmingham. For the first time my own generation was on stage, not by tolerance but by right, saying the kind of things we'd spent nights at the university arguing about; but now saying them in public to an audience that wasn't used to hearing them. . . . They were a fully educated generation. They'd been in their early teens I suppose during the first post-war Labour governments and they'd come to maturity with no doubts in their minds that they had a stake in the country's future. They had a stake in what society meant and was going to do, and they were no longer prepared to be admitted to the arts on sufferance; the arts were their business and their business was the arts.

This new breed of actors were, in part, a product of their material but I felt myself most happily in tune with many of their qualities. It remained to be seen whether they could perform with equal success in the classics. But my instincts told me that a judicious combination of the old with the new was the only way to achieve the kind of acting ensemble I was determined to form. All my life I had struggled to raid the audiences' consciousness and appreciation of acting as an *art*, not merely an interpretive craft. It was to be one of my main goals at the National Theatre.

CHAPTER THIRTEEN

Colossus
of the Drama

EUGENE O'NEILL is the father figure of modern
American drama: his shadow touches all the modern
American playwrights from Tennessee Williams and
Arthur Miller to Sam Shepard and David Mamet, as well
as a great many British playwrights. O'Neill was a colos-
sus of twentieth-century drama: he dared and succeeded.

His wife describes how he wouldn't talk to her for
weeks and weeks when he was writing, but would lock
himself away. If he did come down to a meal, he'd just

sit there, forking up odd bits, his eyes red with weeping. Though all playwrights must write from a certain amount of actual experience, I always felt that O'Neill had really done everything he described.

He put his true experiences on paper and so it looked like an early photograph, all sepia and misty, past memories—the biographical playwright.

He was a writer with a heart the size of a melon, which he sliced open from time to time and dipped his pen into. I suppose it is not surprising that he would not let *Long Day's Journey into Night* be performed until after his death. It was too close and too personal, too much blood and pain, though it must have been odd never to see your masterpiece performed. A musician with all the sounds in his head and unable to hear instruments play them; a bit like Beethoven, I suppose. All the same, something inside him must have regretted that. But then again, to spill your life out onto a stage and say, "This is how it was" can't be easy. And when the raw truth is spoken, as I believe it is in this play, nobody really wants criticism.

He must have thought a lot about the reaction it would cause, for he knew that people would want to see it as soon as they possibly could. Indeed, he must have wanted the world to look at him: otherwise he wouldn't have written it, or he would have burned each page as it left the typewriter.

It was almost as though he were saying, "There, that's what it was like, that's what it was really like, that's the pain that I've lived with all my life. You may call me a romantic but I know that I'm a realist. You think I choke on my imagination; I have no imagination, my brain is burning with only true, stark facts."

It is fascinating to look at his early work and see the playwright emerging. It was very raw and the brushwork naive. He splashed ideas and imagination on paper with, it would seem, no respect for proscenium or theatrical format at all. He wrote movies for the stage. "Scene One: a boat in the Caribbean"—that sort of thing. No more your French windows and your polite cups of tea. A boat in the Caribbean, a dockside bar in London. Fog and whores, pimps and press-gangs. He put the sea on the stage, the moon and the stars, engine-room oil and death. Warts, spots and boils—they were all there. He exploded a theatrical myth and went back to the basics. He put the earth back into the theater and made you smell the sweat.

From *Long Voyage Home* through to *Long Day's Journey* the development of the writer is incredible; and yet you can see the same hand in both, pen poised ready to jab like a sword.

In his middle plays you can see the young man and the mature man walking side by side, hand in hand; eventually, in the later plays, the mature man tells the young man to hold his peace and not pop up every now and again like a jack-in-the-box. The older man's pen slowly pushes aside the pencil of the boy O'Neill who passaged the world in a boat and gazed at the stars and dreamt of what would be.

He was every inch a writer, and I think we are very

fortunate that he did not put his work down in the form
of novels, which at the time would have seemed the obvious way to go. I mean, if you want sea, stars, moons
and fog, you go straight to the novel form—but not
O'Neill. He was, of course, familiar with the theatrical
format, his father being an actor.

I was about to say it couldn't have been easy to have
an actor for a father and then realized that having four
children of my own, I was pointing a finger at my mirror.
I think what I meant was, it couldn't have been easy to
have *that* actor for a father. No . . . maybe I shouldn't
have said that either. Never mind, I've said it now.

Of course, one is allowed to look at O'Neill's father
only through O'Neill's eyes. Perhaps the old man wasn't
so bad after all. He was rather successful, and they did
live in a certain amount of comfort. Maybe O'Neill felt
bitter because his father hadn't fulfilled his potential and
had opted out for what might have seemed easy money.
But then again, maybe the father did fulfill his potential,
and that was as far as he was going to go anyway.

Whatever, the man who created modern American
drama was given to us by that father and mother: the
actor and the drug addict. Interesting to think that the
background that bred him was that of a maker of illusions and a taker of illusions. Does that say something
about all of us? I wonder.

It was suggested, again by Kenneth Tynan, that I play
James Tyrone in *Long Day's Journey into Night* in the
early days of the National. But I didn't want to do it.
Having seen Fredric March play it in the original produc-

1971, *Long Day's Journey Into Night,* with Constance Cummings

tion, I was wary of the role. It wasn't that March put me off, though it was a giant performance to follow; it was that I didn't really want to play the part of an actor. I sensed that I would be very good in the role, but something kept telling me not to. I felt a strong resistance to playing an actor and yet, strangely enough, I'd happily produced a play about one some time before at the St. James's: *Winter Journey*, in which Michael Redgrave gave a superb performance as the alcoholic. Quite frightening and true.

Why is it that when he is given life under the author's pen, the poor old thespian is invariably portrayed as a drunk? We're not all like that, you know. I have known some sober ones in my time. In fact, I've actually met some teetotal ones . . . not many, but some.

However, in 1971 I decided to take on this marathon, partly aided by Tynan, but also forced by a decline in funds at the Old Vic. At the time, if we were to be frugal, it seemed the ideal play to put on. One set, and five in the cast. So the great god Money, and Ken, won.

To look at it romantically—and why not?—O'Neill stretched his hand across the Atlantic and put us back in motion again.

So, not for the first time, lack of funds set me off in a new direction. The rogue and vagabond with his box of tricks and his sticks of paint always worked harder when the upturned hat was empty.

I'll never regret James Tyrone, and would be very sad to have missed him. But then, if I'd not played him, I would never have known. Strange how parts can turn on

1971, as James Tyrone

you, consume you, regurgitate you, and make you ask yourself why you had any doubts in the first place.

It was a long part. The cast met once a week for five weeks to talk about *Long Day's Journey* and to read it through; this encouraged us to think about our parts all the time, mulling them over, dreaming about them. It's not the number of times you've rehearsed that is crucial, but the length of time it's been in your heart.

If you play an actor, you have to be a bit florid, a bit theatrical, and even with all that, the audience may not be quite sure if it's you, or the part you are playing. I gave the part twelve lines of Shakespeare—quite short, but enough to assert my role as an actor, enough to create that stillness you need in the theater.

Long Day's Journey into Night is without question O'Neill's masterpiece. Infinitely better than *The Iceman Cometh*, in which he went overboard and tried to outdo himself. The part of Tyrone is one of the richest ever written: very long, but nearly perfect. The repetition's a challenge, a delicious little problem to overcome; but then, I enjoy challenges.

As it turned out, it became a huge success and seemed to be the beginning of a new era for the National Theatre's coffers: we became the darlings of the subsidized theater. The swings and roundabouts of West End fashion had stopped at our particular door. We followed it quickly with Tom Stoppard's *Jumpers*, *The Front Page* and *The Misanthrope*. We were back on top again.

It's strange how the public and the critics (maybe the public because of the critics) sway from one major company to the other. Today the National Theatre is flavor of the month, tomorrow the Royal Shakespeare. Nothing wrong with it, of course. Rivalry in the theater is very healthy and can only lead to superior work. But what the fans sometimes forget is that it is the same pool of actors moving back and forth across the river, according to which company is offering the better parts. There are loyalties, of course, and these seem to remain with the actor's original theater—in my case the Old Vic, which eventually became the National.

The rivalries have always been there, and have been

encouraged by the public and critics alike. You can list them from Shakespeare's day, and historians could obviously go back further. The Globe and the Bear then; later, the Theatre Royal and Covent Garden; then on to the Lyceum and Her Majesty's, followed by the Old Vic and the Stratford Memorial, to the present day.

It is interesting to note that there have always been two major companies around, where at some time or other you will be able to watch the leading actors of the day. Even those who have been lured away by the money in the beckoning hand of the film world will always come back again, just to dip their roots in the hormone powder of their beginnings. Well, almost, anyway—those who really believe that they owe the empty boards a thanks or two. Those who have not returned probably didn't have it in the first place, and are welcome to their bear pits in Beverly Hills.

Part Four

THE
SILVER SCREEN

CHAPTER FOURTEEN

Early Hollywood

WHEN I went to Hollywood in 1930, aged twenty-three, I was very snooty about moving pictures. I went for the money—it was the Depression—and the chance of fame: to have a go at something different, rewarding or not. More likely not.

The Jazz Singer, the first "talkie," had been released in 1927, and the studios were desperate for actors with good voices. I considered myself a Shakespearean actor and was sure I could outtalk anyone. I still didn't have great confidence in my looks, but RKO had seen me as Beau Geste in a London stage production, directed by the fearsome Basil Dean, and thought that I was rather dashing and would be another Ronald Colman on its books. In fact I'd slavishly modeled my stage appearance on Colman's in his silent film. Basil Dean, a master of spectacular productions, had based his whole concept of the play on the film; one medium aping another, with the usual disastrous results. He had a bad reputation for his bastard bullying methods. He bullied me to his heart's content. I was lost among the hundred legionnaires, the smoke, the real sparks of fire, all that timber of the massive sets; and he screamed at me from the dress circle of Her Majesty's, "Show us some charm, boy. More charm, boy!" My performance badly needed some big close-ups.

I knew even then, I think, that no one, not even Douglas Fairbanks, could match Ronald Colman's screen close-ups. They were marvelous because he had a beautiful face, and because he had a deep but gentle masculinity: the ideal of the dark Englishman. In all my acting up to then, especially at the Birmingham Rep, I'd taken pride in submerging my personality so that the audience wouldn't recognize "me" in one part after another. I went to Hollywood with no great confidence in my personality. I might become a star; I was sure I could act, and I had what was thought to be essential in the earliest talkies, an English accent.

RKO gave me no great acting parts, and I gave RKO no marvelous close-ups. I could talk, all right, but my performances were precious, lacking in vitality, charm-

less. But I felt comparatively at ease in my last film for
RKO—*Westward Passage*, with Ann Harding—and Greta
Garbo liked my performance. She asked me to be her
leading man in *Queen Christina*, and naturally, I accepted. What a breakthrough! But after two weeks on
the set, she'd found me out. The director wanted to
shoot a love scene first, which was Hollywood logic, I
suppose—to see if the lovers jelled before too much
money was spent; but it unsettled me. I took Garbo in
my arms to "awaken her passion." There was no famous
flicker of an eyelid or of the corner of her mouth, however faint; only shyness and cold eyes. I was miserable
and overacted. She became bored with my twitchiness
and saw my lack of personality, a mouse to her lioness.
All the great sceen double acts had equal personality:
Tracy and Hepburn, Bogart and Bacall, Garbo and John
Gilbert.

"We want you to know, Larry," said Walter Wanger,
the producer, when he fired me from the picture, "we're
all crazy about you here at Metro." He tried to make me
feel better by offering me a screen test for Romeo to
Norma Shearer's Juliet. "I don't believe in Shakespeare
on the screen," I said, and left Hollywood. Ronald Colman stayed, thrilled audiences with his voice, doubled
his charm when he talked and won an Oscar for his brilliant performance in George Cukor's *A Double Life*—
the story of an actor playing Othello on the stage who
takes his work home with him with disastrous results.
(Alas, this was one of Vivien's abiding problems.) I
went back to the stage and to films in England, trying

hard for variety, and leaving my work in the dressing room or the studio. I saw *Queen Christina* and thanked my lucky stars I'd been turned down by the greatest star of them all. The part was a bad one, and I wouldn't have had a hope in it. It was simply a bad part; even Gilbert didn't manage to make anything of it. Fancy having a bad performance immortalized in a Garbo film!

Ronald Colman became a dear friend, and he revealed his sweet and honest nature. Vivien and I honeymooned on his yacht *The Dragoon*. Years later, George Cukor—another friend and hardworking professional—told me Garbo was upset at the way I'd been treated. I asked him to get a message to her in retirement: "I applaud you for getting rid of me. I have no bitterness. Only admiration."

English films in the 1930s were cast with London stage actors, and Alexander Korda, who wanted an English Hollywood, had more grand ideas than most on either side of the Atlantic. He gave me opportunities, which I took only disdainfully because I still despised the medium; I felt unhappy in it, and was using most of my energy trying to build strong performances on the stage in the evenings, after shooting all day in the studios. Korda's English crews and electricians too thought films were inconsiderable because they were to do with an ephemeral and untrustworthy thing called entertainment. They had not learned respect for the medium. Hollywood, along with every other place in America, had a healthy respect for money; and if movies made money, boy, they deserved respect. A much healthier attitude.

If you want to be a happy film actor or technician, get rid of your snobbery.

While I was giving a "real" and bravura performance of Mercutio on the stage to John Gielgud's Romeo (we were alternating the roles), I was trying to play Orlando in a film version of *As You Like It* to a Rosalind with a German accent, whose impersonation of a boy hardly attempted to deceive the audience; but they loved her whatever she did. I made my humble most of Orlando, but the circumstances were too much charged against me. The director's flocks of sheep ran away with the film, and if Walter Wanger had asked me what I was doing in such a mess I would've had to say, as Ralph Richardson did, "Getting £600 a week." (Tax five-sixths of that, of course.) Korda provided me with a very good costume part in *Fire over England* with Vivien (and Flora Robson as Queen Elizabeth), but I emoted too much, and in the American version they had to cut one of my scenes because the New York preview audience got the giggles.

Then along came a man who pulled me up by the jockstrap and dragged me down to earth! If any film actor is having trouble with his career, can't master the medium and, anyway, wonders whether it's worth it, let him pray to meet a man like William Wyler. In 1938, when war was rumbling and I was still worrying about how bad my face looked on the screen, I received a telegram: ARE YOU INTERESTED GOLDWYN IDEA FOR VIVIEN YOURSELF AND OBERON IN WUTHERING HEIGHTS? This wasn't enough to get me back on the first boat and train

1936, *Fire Over England,*
with Flora Robson
and Vivien Leigh
1936, *As You Like It*
1941, *49th Parallel*

1939, *Wuthering Heights*, with Merle Oberon

to dreadful Hollywood, because it smelled of Goldwyn corn—with a pinch of Merle Oberon tartness—and Vivien was to play Isabella, not Cathy, which certainly didn't fit into the way she should have been planning her career. Slowly we were learning that actors have to manipulate their careers with cool, determined heads.

Then the excellent script arrived: very versatile, very American, by Ben Hecht and Charles MacArthur, who had written *The Front Page.* But I still wasn't won over, for what is any Hollywood film against a grand Victorian novel?

William Wyler then came in person to see me, perfectly charming and obviously in love with his medium. Although at first he struck me as a little naive, he did seem to understand the character of Heathcliff. I too had done my homework this time. I'd learned that from Garbo, who had known everything there was to know about Queen Christina. But I still said no. I went to see his current success, *Jezebel,* and realized that he had a telling way with camera and with dialogue. Vivien saw that I liked Wyler, liked the part of Heathcliff, and persuaded me. Often your partner's head is cooler than yours. But she'd never had a wretched time in Hollywood.

What happened on the *Wuthering Heights* set is well known. I'm glad. Whereas Garbo was cold, Wyler was vicious: a Hollywood version of the nasty Basil Dean. At about this time, I'd had a God-given blinding flash—not from anything Willie Wyler said—about my goddamned face. Just take it, settle for it and use it; and stop thinking about it, because it's spoiling your acting. There was not a great deal of paint used in Hollywood in those days, and for *Wuthering Heights* they just daubed my face here and there; I decided to forget about my image, to give the role a true personality. Flora Robson, who played Ellen, and I more or less mastered the Yorkshire accent—who were the Americans to argue about that?— so I felt unfettered and gave my all to the emotional, passionate, disdainful and arrogant Heathcliff.

But Sam Goldwyn didn't think much of me at all. I remember one day he arrived and I had a very bad foot. I was limping, and as I approached he held out his arm, and I put my shoulder underneath his hand where it rested, and he said, "Willie, if dis actor goes on playing the way he is, I close up the picture. Will you look at that actor's ugly face." That actor was standing there. "Will you look at that . . ." As if I were an object of some extraordinary horror. "He's dirty, his performance is rotten, it's stagy, it's, it's just nothin', it's not real for a minute, I won't have it and if he doesn't improve, I'm gonna close up the picture." The vicious Wyler just kept on saying "Lousy" and told me to do it again and again, without explanation, while giving Merle Oberon all the attention she wanted.

Wily old Wyler was softening me up. With the occasional violent ego blow: "That was lousy overacting. What dimension have you climbed up to now? Get off your ass and come down from that cloud. Crawl back down here to earth and join us." It was probably then that I said his medium was too anemic to take great acting, which shows how pompous and opinionated I was,

although I remember with absolute horror hearing myself say those words. Wyler was a marvelous sneerer, de-
bunker; and he brought me down. I knew nothing of film
acting or that I had to learn its technique; it took a long
time and several unhandsome degrees of the torture of
his sarcasm before I realized it. "Do you think you could
try seeing if our little medium could capture one of your
frowns instead of a frown and a glare?" He knew I
couldn't be told anything. He knew I'd come to my
senses in time, to some true feeling. Very flattering. I
didn't know it at the time. I merely thought him a cruel
bastard!

Wyler was a professional. He liked me, and enjoyed
talking to me at his house in the evenings. (Or was he
trying to prevent my catharsis from taking place on the
set? His cunning was quite up to that.) "I want you to
be patient about this," he'd say. "But you're quite wrong
to take up this despising attitude. I believe with my heart
and soul this is the greatest medium ever invented in the
field of expression. There's nothing in literature, Greek
drama, in anything you like, be it the most primitive,
which is beyond it. If you put your mind to it. Don't
sneer at that *As You Like It* Shakespeare film. Shakespeare can be done as anybody else can be done if you
just think out how. Just think and keep thinking. Do it
right, and *anything* can be done on film. Don't worry
about your personality, just get on with getting on with
your medium, and acting. Regard the camera as another
actor, if you like, who shows the audience your subtlest

reactions. And don't bring your personal problems to the set."

He was right—again. I think I was being high-handed because my emotions were in a bit of a whirl. I was most deeply in love with Vivien, and I could think of little else. Merle and I had been spitting at each other all day, in real hate, and he suddenly made us do a love scene, which went beautifully in one take. The camera does lie sometimes, but it doesn't like lies, insincerity or superficiality in others. It loves true feeling and isn't too concerned about what goes on on the surface, provided it's subtle. Okay, tricks of the trade. Okay, it's an art. What Willie Wyler was really trying to teach me was humility. I'll say it now—instead of at the end—as a homage to him: my stage successes have provided me with the greatest moments outside myself; my film successes the best moments, professionally, within myself.

Wuthering Heights was a success. I experienced my catharsis; Merle and Willie and I became friends, and the only Goldwyn corn was the heather on the Yorkshire moors, which was as high as an elephant's eye. When I had asked Ralph, when I was first offered the part, whether I should take it or not, he had said, "Yes, dear boy. Bit of fame. Good." In Hollywood, fame meant power. Then came Darcy in *Pride and Prejudice* for MGM, which I accepted because Vivien was to be my costar and George Cukor the director. But no. Greer Garson became Elizabeth Bennet and Robert Z. Leonard the director, and I was very unhappy with the picture. It was difficult to make Darcy into anything more than an unattractive-looking prig, and darling Greer seemed to me all wrong as Elizabeth. To me, Jane Austen had made Elizabeth different from her affected, idiotic sisters; she was the only down-to-earth one; but Greer played her as the most affected and silly of the lot. I also thought that the best points in the book were missed, although apparently no one else did. I'm still signing autographs over Darcy's large left lapel. MGM always got its costumes right.

The story goes that David Selznick was reading Daphne Du Maurier's *Rebecca* in bed (he'd read at least one other book, *Gone with the Wind*). When the description of Max de Winter's face came along—"arresting, sensitive and mediaeval in some strange, inexplicable way . . ." (I hate playing inexplicable characters)—he wrote my name in the margin. If true, this shows my face had become my fortune and I was no longer the poor man's Ronald Colman. Selznick was also shrewd enough to choose an Englishman to direct, Alfred Hitchcock, who was wise enough to choose an English cast and to advise me to gray up my temples because, at thirty-two, I looked too young. I admired and liked Hitchcock tremendously, and we had a jolly time; all English pros together. He didn't treat us like cattle—although he boasted that that was what he thought about all actors, and although my leading lady docilely obeyed him like a female of that species. I loved his little bits of business and the way he always avoided the obvious. Do you remember the confrontation scene in the sitting room in that sea-

1940, *Rebecca*, with Joan Fontaine

side hut? Instead of plonking me in the obvious big armchair, he put me around a corner in the shadows, where
the girl—Joan Fontaine—had to find me. But he didn't
give me much help with the part.

I could manage the smooth, impervious Englishman;
but the haunted quality, the mystery element, was thinly
written. I was used to tragedy; this was melodrama. I
couldn't find the reality of the part. Joan Fontaine played
the young wife beautifully, but I was never sure how
much she was to be deceived; nor, indeed, how much the
audience were to be deceived. For example, when she
wears a copy of Rebecca's dress—a childish mistake

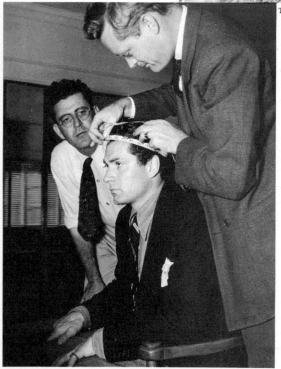

1941, making up as
Lord Nelson for
That Hamilton Woman

The older and
the younger
Nelson

which has been wickedly suggested to her by Mrs. Danvers—was I meant to be cross or furiously angry? But why? What about?

I had not been happy with Wyler, but he had taught me more than I knew. When Alexander Korda came to Hollywood with the script of *Lady Hamilton* and a juicy offer which would mean security for a few months, I decided to accept, although the war had now started. I acceded to the Hungarian's patriotic zeal and played the English hero, Lord Nelson, not as the neurotic I discovered in my researches, but as the gallant yet gentle sailor in the patriotic convention of the times. Nelson had the most extraordinary girlish mouth, so I wore rose lips because I was now becoming relatively at ease in the medium, didn't have a star's face that couldn't be changed from one film to the next, and wanted to practice my craft of acting.

Korda, with his cultural knowledge, was a particularly sophisticated director; he had ideas and the acumen to put them into practice. A highly practical man.

I then returned to England to join the Fleet Air Arm. They'd bring us actors down from time to time to make Ministry of Information films, and I was released for *49th Parallel*, a film with a patriotic theme directed by the imaginative Michael Powell, who allowed actors to act. I was happy with my simple and gentle French-Canadian trapper, which I established in only ten minutes' screen time. Had I learned something about the economy and directness of film acting from my days in Hollywood?

CHAPTER FIFTEEN

Shakespeare on Film

I HAVE been luckier than most because I was ultimately given the opportunity to take Shakespeare from the "wooden O" and place him on the silver screen. "Not possible," I was told. Initial attempts to do this had been absolutely appalling. The audiences had stayed away in their multitudes. But I had the good fortune to be something of a movie star; I already had a following, so whatever I did was looked upon with curiosity.

As far as I was concerned, *Henry V* might as well have

been the first Shakespeare film. To me, it *was* the first Shakespeare film. Somehow it worked, and I think it had much to do with the way I adapted the sound of the lines to the modern ear. In the speaking of Shakespeare, you do not give way entirely to the music of Shakespeare because that is too much in one direction. In the other direction, it is wronger than ever to pretend you're speaking prose. That is very wrong. What you have to find is the truth, through the verse.

The filmgoing public, many of whom had never been in a theater in their lives, understood, enjoyed and were entertained. I appealed to a new public, to those who had thought that Shakespeare was not for the likes of them. When actor and audience communicate well, the sense of freedom is unbelievable. It is like flying together. Once the public had been wooed and won by *Henry V*, the critics and the studios came round to the idea that it was possible to put Shakespeare on the screen. *Henry* was a box-office success. Shakespeare had been given to the people. He was no longer for a small band of the select. Film, of course, can never give the actor the real sense of urgency that happens between curtain rising and curtain falling, but it can project a man's thoughts to millions of people who would never have had the opportunity to hear them had they simply remained upon a stage.

From the beginning of England's war with Germany, I realize now, I was being tuned up for the undreamt-of film of *Henry V*. As I flew over the country in my Walrus, I kept seeing it as Shakespeare's sceptred isle. I was

thirty-seven and in fine fettle. I asked Wyler to direct,
but he said, "No, if it's Shakespeare, it must be you." So
I went away and thought and thought about what was
practicable. I could think of the play sideways, upwards
and outwards, because I knew it backwards. I saw its
nuances of rhythm and movement in my mind's eye, and
then heard its dialogue.

In *Henry V* more than in any other play, Shakespeare
bemoans the confines of his Globe Theatre—"Or may we
cram / Within this wooden O the very casques / That
did affright the air at Agincourt?"—and all those short
battle scenes, in a lot of his plays, are frustrated cinema.
I was amazed how easily I thought in the language of
film: panorama shots, tracking shots, dolly shots, medium
short, close-ups, and the movement and prying of the
camera. Flash upon flash came the problems. Flash
upon—no, perhaps a little longer—came the solutions.
How I loved the problems! How I loved the medium's
ingenuity! How I loved the medium! Wyler's medium,
mine, William Shakespeare's. The main problem, of
course, was to find a style which Shakespearean actors
could act and yet which would be acceptable to the audience of the time, used to little other than the most obvious propaganda.

I have sometimes been lucky in my thoughts. "You've
been lucky in your friends too, dear boy," Ralph would
say. During the preparations for the shooting of *Henry V*
I was acting in a film called *Demi-Paradise*, directed by
Anthony Asquith, who'd directed Wendy Hiller's *Pyg-
malion* and many other things English. Under his sensi-

tive direction I played another gentle and bewildered person—this time a Russian visiting England—but it was an undemanding part. Asquith was not a demanding man, and he was happy to help me gather my *Henry V* crew of film technicians, a happy band of brothers because they were fired by my enthusiasm and I seemed to know what I was talking about. Filippo Del Giudice— bless him—was the moving force behind the project; an Italian interned by the English for the first four months of the war, he kept all financial worries from me and left me with complete artistic control, including every bit of casting.

What sort of man was Shakespeare's Chorus to be, narrating and commenting his way through the play, showing his frustration that the Globe audience weren't in France? Get rid of him altogether? Have him as a voice-over, appearing at the end to wrap up the show? Ah! No voice-over, but if the Chorus at the end, why not at the beginning as well, where Shakespeare put him? And in the Globe, as Shakespeare had him. And then I wouldn't have to cut his question: "Can this cockpit hold / The vastly fields of France?" The goddamn play was telling me the style of the film.

Dress the Chorus as an Elizabethan actor (which he was), get him—with broad gestures—to challenge the imaginations of the unruly audience in the pit. Maybe that way the film audience would be challenged. Play the first few scenes on the Globe stage in a highly, absolutely deliberate theatrical style; get the film audience used to the language, and let them laugh its excesses out of their

systems before the story really begins. I was determined
to bring in the comics—Falstaff as well as his friends
Nym, Bardolph and Pistol—for without them, it would
have been two and a half hours of Henry, Henry, Henry:
the film cried out for light relief.

Henry, historically and in Shakespeare's eyes, had an
unheroic beginning, so I would start with me, the Elizabethan actor playing Henry, waiting in the wings, while
the audience got to know the other characters, especially
Pistol and his wife, the former Mistress Quickly. Bring
on Falstaff, give him some lines from *Henry IV Part II*
and to hell with the purists, because he was a leader of
the comics, an old friend of Henry's, and later, Mistress
Quickly tells us of his death. I wanted the audience—the
universal audience—to have a concrete image of the dear
old man. Surprise, surprise, the purists approved.

"If you really want to shock or delight an audience,
get them a little bored first," said William Wyler. You
need some confidence and courage to take such advice—
maybe not, just be true to your instincts—but I wanted
the film audience to get a restless feeling of being cribb'd
and confin'd in the Globe's wooden O, irritated by the
silly actors speaking in their exaggerated way, so that
when at last we leave the place, with a flourish of William Walton's music, and I speak my lines beginning
with "Now sits the wind fair, and we will aboard" real-
istically and with a modern tone, there's a tremendous
feeling of relief and anticipation. The language may be
archaic, but it's not strange. It's charming. It's sincere.

But how to make the language seem real all the way

1945, *Henry* V on film

through? To the end of the story? One of the original ideas was to use Kenilworth Castle for the French settings. Lovely. But all that stone, dust and patchy grass would seem too familiar, *too* real to a modern audience, who'd be thinking: "Yes, nice, very real, absolutely real castle. You can see it's absolutely real. And those trees, they're absolutely real and quite normal. But why are they talking so funny?" And that was what I had to avoid. I didn't want the eye to quarrel with the ear; what the eye saw had to bolster the seeming reality of the language. No eyesore like crumbling Kenilworth stone; but something artificial, very pretty and unreal, and yet real to the mind's eye's vision of a romantic tale of an heroic medieval king. Oh, how I prayed to God—or to the Willies, Shakespeare and Wyler—that I would have the courage to be absolutely true to that vision: not fudge it. The difficulty was the language, and my only hope was for the background to be more unreal than it was, so that the language would seem real.

Then, out of the sometimes divine collaboration between expert art designers (Paul Sheriff, Carmen Dillon and Roger Furse—my thanks to them) and a director with a vision, I decided to base the costumes and scenery very meticulously on medieval illustrations in storybooks, especially those of the Limbourg brothers, with their bright and pastel colors, prettiness, odd perspectives and, sometimes, no perspectives at all. I wanted the characters to spring out from the beautiful, stylized, almost cutout scenery, alive and kicking and speaking in a vigorous and varied language; the actors to dominate, to feel confident

and sometimes to dwarf the scenery. Thus, when I'm
telling the audience the wind's set fair for France, I'm
standing at the mast of a miniature and colorful ship
soon to approach the French town of Harfleur, which
is miniature, pretty and an odd shape—undaunting to
the characters, uninhibiting to the actors and intriguing
to the audience.

"Action!" The power and responsibility of a film director directing two actors from his canvas-backed throne,
or two thousand from behind a tracking camera, can be
awesome: sometimes his ego drives him into arrogance
or a dreadful feeling of vulnerability. Not with *Henry V*,
though. There we were, a band of artists and technicians,
humble in our souls because Hitler was killing our countrymen, imbued with a sense of history, gallantry over-
coming wartime shortages and problems. We had no
quick-cranking Technicolor camera to slow down the
smoke from the chimneys or the tidal waves in the
Thames on the model of Elizabethan London at the beginning of the film. Horses were as rare as kingdoms, but
how we loved our problems and reveled in our resourcefulness! We were inspired by the warmth, humanity,
wisdom and Britishness just beneath the surface of
Shakespeare's brilliant jingoism. (The play has its Welsh-
man and Irishman, too, as well as the former Mistress
Quickly.) And there I was, an Englishman with a mission to bring Shakespeare to the screen, to bring caviare
to the general audience; not in a snobbish sense, but
because I love caviar. Both its own and Shakespeare's
esoteric natures are overrated, and it's certainly not

Shakespeare's fault they are not for more universal con-
sumption. (If he were around now he'd be writing new
Carry On television comedies, or soap-opera cameo parts
for aging actors.) I had a mission; I was physically and
emotionally very fit; I'd learned about coordination and
balance while flying my Walrus; my country was at war;
I felt Shakespeare within me, I felt the cinema within
him. I knew what I wanted to do, what he would have
done, and every sinew was stiffened because the budget
was so tight. Between "Action!" and "Cut" things went
very smoothly, with only the usual number of cock-ups.
No temper. The war cleared the head, but it was love of
the medium—my band of brothers', mine, Shakespeare's,
Wyler's, the modern audience's—which summoned most
of the blood.

However, I did not direct like Wyler. I would not have
had enough film in my stockroom to have someone come
down the stairs, pause at the newel-post and walk off just
right of the camera sixty-three times—something he had
made me do. I mapped out every movement first and
knew exactly what every shot was going to be. I couldn't
afford to reshoot, so I designed every angle in advance,
knew every move, every cut; all was pretimed and pre-
planned.

We'd found a setting for Shakespeare's dialogue. Now
we had to find out how to create a Shakespearean battle
sequence, free from the fetters of the wooden O and
made up of short scenes, yet full of his drama, reality
and humanity. I was particularly anxious to maintain
purity of intention in the way the scenes were handled.

Directing *Henry* V

I felt myself to be an agent of his imagination. I looked at the old masters like Eisenstein and D. W. Griffith for inspiration, but saw that only Shakespeare's spirit and the spirit of his drama and characters (from the comics to the heroic King himself) could conjure up the stirring images and the unique pattern, rhythm and movement of the screen's first Shakespearean battle: a battle which encompasses typical Shakespearean twists of high seriousness and low comedy. The telegraph poles, the pylons,

the gray and stunted foliage meant there were no medieval battlefields in England, and no horses. So we went
to Ireland, where I lived in a trailer like a modern field
commander, ordered the day's shooting like military ma-
neuvers, coordinated and played my roles of director,
producer, leading actor, script and film editor with gusto
and sincerity and, with 150 willing Irish horsemen and
500 willing Irish foot men, worked for six hard weeks to
produce ten minutes of film action.

Every second, half-second of that action was clearly in
my head before the six weeks' action began. I invented
the charge of the French cavalry for reasons of pace,
rhythm and conflict, and because Shakespeare would
probably have done so—better: my small, but confident,
talent's homage to his expansive genius. I shot the charge
with an exciting tracking shot, full of technical problems
almost on the pinnacle of the imaginative concept itself.
I added Walton's music and realistic sound effects; and
when the dramatic action needed a pause, I sent the
sound of a thousand arrows through the air.

There was, at least, one insuperable problem. I made
the soldiers on both sides fight vigorously and realisti-
cally—no backs-to-the-audience stuff—but I showed no
bloody gashes. The bright medieval costumes tended,
too, to emphasize the formal elements and patterns of
the battle. But to be true to the film's overall style the
battle should have been fought on green velvet—and
that, clearly, was impracticable. Once again the play itself saved us. Between the pretty parts in the French
palaces and the Battle of Agincourt, Shakespeare has a

long and contemplative night sequence, which gave the screen neutral colors and tones to cushion the contrast between the artificiality of medieval picture-book castles and the earthiness of Irish fields, pretty and green though they were.

I always looked to the text of the play to give me the movements of the camera, and towards the end of that night sequence I had the camera look through Henry's eyes as he reviews his thoughts and the serried ranks of his soldiers, then cut away to see him climb into a cart and then come into a big close-up as he says: ". . . Now, soldiers, march away; / And how thou pleasest, God, dispose the day!" Not a few moments before, Henry has been talking about Saint Crispin's Day, so the audience's mind is truly attuned to a day of death or glory; and its eye—as it turned out—would not be offended by the day's stylistic change of setting. I feel Shakespeare and God disposed the day well. They got us over a stylistic anachronism which grieved only the pedantic and mean-spirited. We had faith in what was practicable. If it comes off, it's good. If it's practicable, it can be exciting— given the spirit and the faith.

In the early days of preparation I puzzled over previous failures of Shakespeare on the screen, worried about his verse and worried about the Shakespearean actors who were to speak it. Even earlier, when I had been flying my Walrus, I'd said to myself, "This flying is going to help my acting if I ever get back to it." I was perfectly all right in my physical coordination—some actors aren't, you know—but I as sat at the controls, very basic controls

which bound you very close to the aircraft's behavior, my
mental coordination was all askew, giving me and my
Walrus rough rides and crude movements: relaxing too
much on the control stick, or holding it too tautly; using
it as a "joystick" when its power was no more than equal
to that of the rudder or the throttle. Of course, being me,
I achieved my aerobatics, but only after hours of practice.
Learning to fly an aircraft effectively, you need poise, a
sense of balance and utmost mental coordination. I was
getting quite mischievous and daring—but always with a
necessary coolness in the head—and I was the only one
in my squadron ever to roll a Lysander . . . before they
plucked me out of the sky for the heaven-sent *Henry* V.

I looked at all the old Shakespeare films. *The Taming
of the Shrew*—with additional dialogue by Wayne Z.
Snooks—contained little verse. Katharina was played by
the world's sweetheart, Mary Pickford, but it showed
Shakespeare's knockabout rumbustiousness. My performance in *As You Like It* looked eccentric, the film was
excessively "rural-pictorial" and Rosalind still crucified
the verse with her German accent. But it was *Romeo
and Juliet*, directed by George Cukor, a man I loved and
a director I admired, which puzzled me most. "What's
wrong?" I said to myself. "Norma Shearer and Leslie
Howard are fine; Barrymore is Mercutio, overplaying his
mannerisms but not the part; Basil Rathbone is marvelous as Tybalt and on the screen his pale blue eyes
make him look deadly dangerous. The scenery and production values are perfectly respectable and first-class:
and yet, it is not succeeding. . . ." I felt there was a

quarrel between the eye and the ear, between the behavior of the camera and Shakespeare's verse. In the potion
scene, for instance, that "dismal scene I needs must act
alone," the camera lens was just two inches from her
nose. Shakespeare deliberately gives Juliet a large vocal
climax (with even a ghost to shout at):

> Oh, look! methinks I see my cousin's ghost
> Seeking out Romeo, that did spit his body
> Upon a rapier's point. Stay, Tybalt, stay!
> Romeo, I come! this do I drink to thee.

But alas, George Cukor had shot the scene in the way
he'd learned to create film climaxes—brilliantly, of course,
but he'd crept the camera forward, ever so skillfully, to
end with a mighty big close-up. Norma Shearer was so
close to the camera she had to do "Romeo, I come!" in
a whisper to avoid distortion or even laughter of the rib-
ald kind; whereas Shakespeare moves his actress upstage
(to a bed with curtains) so that she and the audience
can take the strain of a big climax. Time and time again
I saw actors who had to come down on the big Shakespeare moments because of the proximity of the camera.
More flexibility, poise and balance were needed between
Shakespeare's words (and stage directions) and the actions of the camera. Coordination.

Big discoveries creep up on you and later, seem naive.
They swirl out of the mists of half-forgotten words of
advice—Hamlet's "Suit the action to the word, the word
to the action." If Shakespeare has a flourish and a big
speech, bring the camera back; if he has moments of
humor and poignancy, bring it forward. I first tested this

out in *Henry V* with an early scene in which Henry, on receiving a gift from the French Dauphin of tennis balls, remarks,

> We are glad the Dauphin is so pleasant with
> us. . . .
> When we have match'd our rackets to these
> balls,
> We will in France (by God's grace) play a set
> Shall strike his father's crown into the hazard.

I wanted a big climax on that, so from "We are glad" (I got a laugh on that) I crept the camera back and back until I stood up suddenly and said "crown into the hazard" in a full theatrical climax which, to my utmost delight, I saw the camera could take. This was the way to do it. When all the big climaxes come along—"Once more unto the breach, dear friends"—I was at ease, I didn't have to throttle back. And what's more, all the other Shakespearean actors, Robert Newton as Pistol included, didn't have to either.

Henry V taught me to love directing on film: taught me to love the medium, taught me how versatile it could be. I'd pull the celluloid through my fingers saying, "What shall I do with this bit?"; holding it up to the light and thinking, "How can I get round that mistake?" Film taught me to be ingenious, and I learned how to do what the Americans call a Fox-cut. Wonderful expression: comes from the time when American companies made quota pictures, and the firm that had the worst reputation for doing this was Fox. They used to make these terrible cheap films then. They'd find that they had shot the footage so badly that they couldn't cut it. They couldn't just cut back to the love scene or whatever it was, so they would shove in a few tiny lines of inane dialogue to cover up and cut to something irrelevant in between. When a love scene had got too broad, they would cut down to the street outside to a kitten rubbing itself against a lamppost.

The most beautiful Fox-cut I ever managed was in *Henry V*. I had shot the whole film and long since taken down the Globe Playhouse when I found myself in trouble. When I put the film together, there was no link to explain, at the end, how we had got back into the Playhouse. So I ran the whole film through until I came to "In your fair minds," turned it round, reversed the action, cut to the long-shot take and then used "O for a Muse of fire" and inserted it. Instead of leaving, the actors were now returning. You might think they were walking backwards, but they weren't. Marvelous. I am forever sold on a medium that can do that. Absolute glory.

I enjoyed being the director; I enjoyed being the leading actor. The responsibility is a major challenge, and one's grown up to like challenges. But I didn't enjoy the act of acting a great part on film. I don't think any actor does. I'm always haunted by anxiety, an underlying, constant dread. So when I say my "discovery" made me feel at ease acting Shakespeare to the camera (provided it coordinates its movements and angles and lights and shades to my words and actions, sometimes drawing back to a responsive distance to avoid my spitting in its eye), that ease was relative, as it was to all the other Shakespearean actors too. I was so happy and relieved I'd found a way of lessening an actor's anxiety. On the stage, a tentative actor can hide behind his technique, or the other actors, from which he regains his confidence. On film, a tentative actor looks haunted.

Henry V was a success with the critics and the public. Some said—probably Americans who enjoy celebrating success, enjoy contributing generous praise—it was the best first film since *Citizen Kane*. Servicemen on leave, and ordinary housewives from the Home Front, queued outside the Empire, Leicester Square, for eleven months. It ran for forty-six weeks in New York. Its opening night was just a few weeks after D-Day. I was so delighted about its success that I would have died a happy man if they'd sent me back flying and my Walrus had blown up.

Arthur Rank, who'd gained control of Filippo Del Giudice's production company in return for money to finish the film, told me I should have cut the "unimportant" scenes like Henry's wooing of Katharine—played with delicious humour by Renée Asherson, and part of the delicate balance of the play—and I said, "All right. But the film would have seemed twice as long. I'll show you!" I did, and it did.

The film won an Academy Award—which did wonders for my prestige, and for my chances of having another go.

Hamlet, of course.

I soon felt that the film of *Henry V*, which had in reality been a marvelous, innovative achievement, was kindergarten, end-of-the-pier stuff: "Look at this man Shakespeare! He's accessible!" Not quite film, not quite play: a new form of entertainment, an exuberant concoction made (with love) to show that Shakespeare could speak to us from the screen. It lacked a director's personal, interpretive vision which, if faithful, always shows the breadth and depth of Shakespeare's vision and the immediacy of his speech and the universal power of his thoughts; always gives each member of the audience his own personal vision.

I'd played Hamlet twice in 1937 in London and at Elsinore, and once you've played Hamlet, the play's thoughts and actions are part of you forever, and so are your thoughts about the play. As I've said before, Hamlet is spectatorproof. He fascinates every member of the audience, who recognizes—always—something of himself or herself in the dramatic ebb and flow of Hamlet's moods, his inhibiting self-realizations and doubts, his pitiful failure to control events. But I wasn't inhibited in my realization that everyone has his own idea of Hamlet; no, far from it, I was exhilarated.

As Shakespeare's interpreter, I would of course have to be true to his idea of tragedy and make up my mind about the vicious mole in Hamlet's nature. I remembered seeing a Warner Brothers seafaring picture in which Gary Cooper asks an intellectual and sensitive belowdecks crewman (Alan Ladd, I think) what book he's reading. "*Hamlet,*" the sailor answers. "A story about a guy who couldn't make up his mind"—which showed that not every Hollywood scriptwriter was ignorant of Shakespeare or lacking in respect for him.

My earliest and deepest resolutions were to find a cinematic interpretation of the play. Emboldened (and slightly chastened) by the popular success of *Henry V,* I didn't initially want to play the part of Hamlet myself. Not because I didn't think I was suited (my stage Hamlet and my stage Romeo—Hamlet's younger brother—had been passionate and successful), but because I didn't want the audience to think, "Oh, that's just a repeat of Laurence Olivier's Henry V, only this time he's dressed up to look like Hamlet." That's one of the reasons I gave myself blond hair when I did decide to take the part, for I wished to get well away from the glamorous dark-haired medieval king, from my usual image; it was also to make me conspicuous in middle and long shots—not because of any actor-manager conceit, but because Hamlet is always central to the story. The story is seen through his eyes and, when he's not present, through his imagination—his paranoia. This subjective element, paradoxically, I think, has encouraged many subjective interpretations over the centuries in many different media: theater, opera, mime, ballet and Emlyn Williams's very much abridged version for touring before the troops. Much of the verse has been cut out, and even though traditions are handed down, John Gielgud's 1930s Hamlet was quite different from Richard Burbage's original. I thought it quite legitimate to make my own subjective contribution, to make a filmic interpretation to add to the universal consciousness of Hamlet.

If my blond hair was archetypal of the Dane, so much the better; Claudius and Gertrude were dressed as the king and queen of universal playing cards, Hamlet in the timeless doublet and hose of a romantic young prince. The core of Hamlet is his loneliness and desolation after the death of his father, and his feeling of alienation from the new court. In my mind's eye I saw the camera seeing most things through Hamlet's eyes, wandering, or running, through the empty corridors, piercing the vast shadows of Elsinore's great rooms of state for some joy or the sight of some familiar object; but in vain: as lonely as a cloud, with no color, no silver lining. I was having a flaming row with the Technicolor people at the time—another reason, perhaps, for thinking in black-and-white—but I would have overcome my sulks if I'd really wanted Technicolor. I liked its subdued shades—grays, sepias and black. But I was terrified by its tangerine and apricot faces, which were not the faces I wished to haunt my melancholy Hamlet.

Black-and-white had another big, big advantage. I could use deep-focus photography. Deep focus is simply this: the character in the foreground (usually Hamlet) is in focus, so are the characters in the middle ground, and so are the characters in the far ground. I say "simply this": technically it was very difficult—but Desmond Dickinson, my lighting cameraman, was a genius.

People said I was far too interested in moving the

1948, *Hamlet* on film

Directing *Hamlet*. Opposite, the duel scene, with Terence Morgan as Laertes; the fifteen-foot leap

camera, and in *Hamlet* I was accused of being overly self-conscious about film directing. But I wanted to exercise myself with the camera. Maybe I overdid it. But it pays off sometimes. For instance, at the end of the very first soliloquy when the camera simply goes all the way across an interesting courtyard, goes up, shows a very interesting bedroom, which you know wasn't shown you for nothing. That works nicely.

With deep focus I could beset Hamlet with faces around him which were, to him, too, too solid; I could create distances between characters, creating an effect of

TWO PHOTOS: KOBAL COLLECTION

alienation, or of yearning for past pleasure as when Hamlet sees Ophelia, in her innocent Victorian dress, an eternity away down the long corridor (150 feet away, actually), sitting on a solid wooden chair—in focus—with love clearly in her eyes. While the camera was showing much of Hamlet's melancholy and the decadence and desolation of Claudius's court, I was able to use the empty spaces for exciting physical action, showing Hamlet's athleticism which is in the play's text—and in my repertoire as an actor, or at least, it was.

That climax really was tremendous. That fifteen-foot dive, with an open sword, onto Claudius! I first saw the finished version of the film in Australia, and I heard the ladies in the audience go 'Wow!' And then, of course, the film ends with the dead Hamlet's sad, drumbeat journey up the dark flights of steps and battlements of Elsinore towards his father, the blackness lit by firelight (and if I may say so, by William Walton's music, which is where my first images of the film began).

Nothing pretty or artificial about the stone of Elsinore; gray, black, sometimes crumbling, sometimes oppressive, sometimes cavernous. At the ends and beginnings of sequences I dissolved the solid flesh of the deep-focus characters away from and into scenes, so that they looked like ghosts. At the beginning of a long walk towards Hamlet, Ophelia looked like a specter; and it seemed the most natural thing in the world to have Hamlet's soliloquies as words in his head, with his "To be or not to be" uttered to the sound of a roaring sea, like the sounds which fill the ears of troubled spirits. I once said the film was "An Essay in *Hamlet*," but that's not quite right. A bit demeaning to the creative impulse which Shakespeare inspired in me and my team; a bit insulting to the resourcefulness of the medium. Why not "An Interpretation of *Hamlet*"? Or just "A Film of *Hamlet*."

Of course, I had to be ruthless in the cutting. Half of *Henry V* had had to go; so did half of *Hamlet*. *Hamlet* is the best-known play in the world. Everyone's got his favorite quotation. I approached the job with terror, and the utmost respect—not terror of the purists, but fear that my concept, and its execution, would be unfaithful to Shakespeare or to the medium; it must be utterly respectful to the spirit of Shakespeare and to the audience's consciousness of Hamlet. I kept bringing the concept sharp into my head so that I knew every second of the length of the film, without a loose moment.

Eileen Herlie, who played Gertrude as a sensual young-middle-aged woman, and I reveled in the closet scene, which, confident of the camera, we played as big as in Drury Lane. All the actors were confident; each gave a top-class Shakespearean performance: Jean Simmons as Ophelia, young and sensitive, and Peter Cushing as Osric, one of the best screen actors. Little makeup was worn, and the deep focus showed their confidence—and their sincerity. I used only actors who could speak the verse, either from experience or from their natural talent—like Stanley Holloway, who was the gravedigger. It would be foolish to do a Shakespeare film with actors who'd never been in any of his plays before: he presents his own volumes of technique to learn. I rehearsed them before each shot, with a stand-in for me, telling them what I had in mind, telling them the length of each cut, but otherwise giving them their freedom. Restraining them occasionally, perhaps, but never inhibiting them, and never letting the camera inhibit them. It's not a director's job to teach actors how to act. It's his job to make the most of the talent they already have: to make actors feel relaxed and happy in their work. Of course we missed—those of us who'd known them on the stage— some of the favorite characters, like Rosencrantz and Guildenstern, who enriched the four-and-a-half hour pattern of the play which I was changing to the tighter pattern of a two-and-a-half hour film.

If the shooting has been successful, editing a film is the pinnacle of a director's joy; if not, he must make it so, with no regrets about what exists or does not exist on film, because it's only his joy which will transform the lengths of film and sound track into the realization of his imagination. No human mind is big enough to forestall all problems, strong enough to quell the insistence of a last-minute inspiration, but problems in the editing room are usually part of the joy because that's where the medium of film really comes into its own, solving all the difficulties within itself. I was lucky in my editor, Reginald Beck, a consummate technician and a brilliant friend, who saw the point of the camera's changing directions in ways hitherto unknown and against the rules, of a character's being shot from the left instead of from the right. He realized the drama through Hamlet's eyes and noticed his odd moments of nervous agitation. I was lucky in my composer, my friend William Walton, who absorbed Hamlet's every mood—and mine. We coordinated his music and my sound effects: the sound of cannon shots on Hamlet's last journey on the battlements, Hamlet's heartbeat as he sees the ghost of his father for the first time (an effect I borrowed from Jean-Louis Barrault, for which Arthur Rank paid him £500—which was nothing compared with the royalties he didn't pay to Shakespeare).

The editing room is where the author, medium and audience have their most vital meeting; where the medium—for the others' sakes—must assert its own rhythm, pace and movement and, I suppose, its visual dominance, although it is a big mistake to regard the film as only a visual medium. Shakespeare sometimes poses problems, even to stage directors, with his sudden bursts of "purple poetry" coming from the most unlikely characters—for instance, the Queen Mab speech from the usually macho Mercutio. So when Gertrude—sensual and articulate, yes, but hardly poetic, and presumably grief-stricken—describes the drowning of Ophelia by saying "There is a willow grows aslant a brook" followed by some pretty complicated imagery difficult for the modern audience to understand, I thought: "God, they're going to say to themselves, 'Why is she suddenly talking the gobbledegook they talked in the Globe at the beginning of *Henry V*?' "—which would have done Shakespeare no service, either. So I thought: "Why not let Gertrude speak the lines, but take them away from her visual image, put them in a more universal context? The death of Ophelia, after all, is a vital event in the story. Let it be seen on the screen. Give it full dramatic weight. Reinforce Gertrude's imagery, simplify it, let the audience really see what she is talking about. Clothe the nakedness of her 'poetry.'" This had to be most delicately edited, and I suffered and enjoyed the dread of doing something new, of being charged with the offense of trying to improve upon Shakespeare's verse. My main aim was clarity. And the result was not tawdry. Another important part of the story is mentioned in a letter from Hamlet, read by Horatio: so I showed Hamlet's sea battle with the pirates—just a glimpse, not too long, but long enough to show his physical courage, and to establish a vital event in the audience's mind.

"How all occasions do inform against me / And spur my dull revenge!" I should quote the soliloquy in full, it is so marvelous, ending with "O, from this time forth, / My thoughts be bloody, or be nothing worth!" which, as I said, I think the most important lines in a play full of important lines. I had the soliloquy in my original concept of the film, firmly imprinted on my mind, down to the last second. I shot the Fortinbras bit, which was all right, and the scene with the Fortinbras captain, which was excellent; but during the speech I was wearing a ridiculous tam-o'-shanter hat—designed for me by the beloved Roger Furse—whose edge fell down over parts of my face, and I felt uneasy, and feared that the audience would wonder why Hamlet was suddenly dressed as another person, away from the shadows of Elsinore, look-

ing at a back-projection seascape, white and glistening—
another country. Whether from my unease or from a
sudden failure of vitality, the speech seemed lifeless—especially flat and stale after the high drama of the way I
had filmed "To be or not to be"—and the more I looked
at it on the moviola, the flatter it seemed. Murderous to
my pride as an actor, murderous to my thoughts about
Hamlet, murderous to the text of the play; it had to be
cut.

But murder most foul? No! I spared the audience!
The tension between text, medium and audience, at
this stage, demanded that the story go forward swiftly towards the death of Ophelia from sorrows which did not
come singly: first, her father slain; next, Hamlet gone
away; next, Laertes returning, speaking revenge, and seeing her final madness. If I'd interrupted this with Hamlet
ruminating, debating, discussing, lacerating himself into
action, interrupting the action by examining inaction,
the audience would have got bored and as irritated by
the funny hat as I was.

Hamlet was a success with the public, and with un-
pedantic critics. I receive a Best Actor Oscar, which was
good for my career, and wise of the Academy; the Hollywood Establishment had recognized an innovative screen
performance which had sprung from one of them—
Wyler.

I was not too happy at the way I'd had to cut the final
film, for I was a dreamer at heart even if I was also one
of Wyler's practical men. Perhaps I'd been too keen on
being on budget, on schedule, on being a professional

film director. For instance, the dueling—if it's bang bang bang and you know it's all rehearsed for the Letchworth Amateurs or something. It has to be very real, and you have to practice it a lot. And you have to be gifted towards it; you must like it. If you are afraid of hurting your opponent, you don't like the game. You must really go for him and he must really go for you. That's why that looked good, and that's why it was long—because it was good; and the audience enjoyed it as they did in the Elizabethan days. I had succeeded, but at a cost. I had ruthlessly cut the volume of Shakespeare's verse. But then, in trying to put on film Shakespeare's creative genius, I had no other option.

In the end, I judge the film of *Hamlet* as a rattling good story, inside and outside Hamlet's mind, told cinematically; and that makes it my favorite Shakespeare film. My acting performance was thrilling enough, but not, perhaps, as satisfying as Richard III.

I'd made Richard III very much my part in the theater, and I wanted to make another film. I longed to put Shakespeare, the film director and the film actor together, to bring a classic stage performance to the screen to create a classic film performance. I hoped that I was sufficiently attuned to the part and to the medium to be able to use the intimacy of the camera to create an even more thrilling and insinuating performance on screen than on the stage. I would woo and charm the audience with my devilish villainy, using close-up and long shot to devastating effect.

Alexander Korda welcomed me with relatively open

arms when I took him the idea of *Richard III*, and I was able to gather my trusted team of Roger Furse, Carmen Dillon and William Walton with Anthony Bushell as associate director. But alas, not Filippo Del Giudice, whose soothing presence had seen me through *Henry V* and *Hamlet*. Instead, my new cameraman was Otto Heller.

I'd played Richard III so often on stage, I'd let ham fat grow on my performance. This I had to rid myself of before the cameras got me. So for two weeks I hid myself away and studied the text and my inflections anew, hacked off the extra flesh and the broad gestures I needed on stage to reach the back row of the upper circle some fifty yards away, made myself lean and austere in my expressions, and changed the phrasing, because Richard would be flirting with the camera—sometimes only inches from his eyes—and would lay his head on the camera's bosom if he could. He is the classical actor's favorite bravura part, but he must be kept credible, and the bravura must be carefully marshaled. On the stage his hideous wooing of Lady Anne works brilliantly, but if it's too sudden on the screen the unaccustomed audience would cry, "Hold it. We don't believe this!" So I cut the scene in two, let time pass and gave Richard two glorious climaxes: "I'll have her, but I will not keep her long" and "Was ever woman in this humour woo'd? / Was ever woman in this humour won?"

I took Richard's misshapen body and his sardonic smile, but I wanted to convince the audience of the mind behind the mask. A demonic mind, a witty mind.

But there's something of the flirting, calculating witch about him, so I kept the long black curls to insinuate this femininity. I made his nose and hump smaller than for the stage, but the nose was big enough to have the effect of concentrating the focus on the eyes: the only way to the mind when the speech is sardonic or false—unless the mind is dead, like Archie Rice's, which Richard's is not.

Shakespeare's genius fills the play with images of eyes: "Out of my sight! thou dost infect mine eyes," "Thine eyes, sweet lady, have infected mine"; of looking glasses, shadows, the sun. What a gift to the cinema! And what a part to immortalize your acting on the screen! How to pay homage to an acting tradition and to actors over the centuries, including Shakespeare! When an actor gets his eyes right on film, he's reached a peak in his professional life. Imagine my joy when Richard is trying to make Buckingham agree to the killing of the Princes in the Tower and I got just the right sort of hatred in his eyes on "Cousin, thou wast not wont to be so dull. / Shall I be plain? I wish the bastards dead," and on "Tut, tut, thou art all ice; thy kindness freezes," while cheering up my face. After the shot, for the first time, I didn't have to ask Anthony Bushell, "How was my expression?" because, for the first time, I was absolutely confident it was what I wanted. The scene ends with Richard turning on Buckingham: "I am not in the giving vein to-day." One of cinema's chilliest moments. The coldness in the eyes was just right. Richard's veins, his mind, were all ice.

I understood the venom in his mind. I felt its mood. Should I say there's a streak of venom in my own nature?

1955,
Richard III
on film

With John Gielgud as Clarence; the bier scene with Claire Bloom; and Ralph Richardson as Buckingham. Below, "I am not in the giving vein."

No more than in the next man's. No more than in Shakespeare's, who, by all accounts, led an exemplary life apart from a few default summonses, a writ of libel and some minor disputes over land, which should make us feel even warmer towards him. On the set I was able to treat Claire Bloom, Richard's Lady Anne, with the warm affection I felt for her—constantly—and if, off the set, I sometimes talked to her in Richard's tones, they were insubstantial echoes which made us laugh.

I made a mistake casting Ralph as Buckingham, but he wanted to play him. He wasn't oily enough. There was always a twinkle in his eye. I should have got Orson Welles. Not that he was oily—he had perhaps the oily aura of medium-dry sherry—but he was such a marvelous film man, as was seen in his bravura performance in *Citizen Kane* and its demonic, rule-breaking editing. Welles was a great Shakespearean; his Falstaff in *Chimes at Midnight* is hugely enjoyable, if not a little more demonic in the eyes than Ralph's would have been. Shouldn't there be something of the demon in Buckingham? It was Orson Welles who alarmed the American public by making a spook broadcast about space invaders, which was too real. He would have been admirable.

At the beginning of *Richard III* I let roll the following words—on an illuminated medieval scroll, as we makers of "historical" films are wont to do—which I quote in full (for the record):

> The Story of England, like that of many another land, is an interwoven pattern of History and Legend. The History of the World, like letters without

poetry, like flowers without perfume and thought without imagination, would be a dry matter indeed without its legends, and many of those, though scorned by proof a hundred times, seem worth preserving for their own sake.

I doubt very much if Richard was as evil as Shakespeare makes out, but the legend Shakespeare creates is so lively it's worth preserving.

"Now is the winter of our discontent . . ." is the most dramatic opening speech of any Shakespeare play; a direct, frontal attack on the audience's sensibilities, more brutal than Richard's upon Lady Anne's. It's a well-documented tradition of the part that Edmund Kean leaned his stunted body against the proscenium arch and mesmerized the audience with his eyes, taking them into his confidence or alienating them from the action at his will. What a gift to the cinema Edmund Kean would have been!—properly directed. On film, I had to get the audience in the mood, give them some background, before the opening soliloquy. So I gave them the coronation scene, the last scene from *Henry VI Part III*, as I had done on stage at the Old Vic, which has plenty of medieval color and courtly costumes and a pompous Shakespearean speech from a weak king soon to be overcome by the cunning and strength of Richard's irony. And there he was, dressed sparingly in brown and black: a slightly restless Richard, holding himself apart from the crowd, ridding himself of his sparse finery to an agitated attendant, glancing anxiously at the camera to make sure we—the audience—are still watching. I used a

magnificent VistaVision camera which gave us distinct
and solid figures in wide shots, precise and true features
and vivid eyes in its big close-ups. The King and the
others begin to leave, but Richard holds us back with the
air of a man anxious to get us alone behind locked doors
for a private parley.

Even thinking about the way I shot the soliloquy fills
me with pleasure: ideas springing naturally from the text
(which, admittedly, I manipulated) and from the main
idea of having Richard speak direct to the camera. Ideas
which worked because I had the confidence to enact
them boldly. The camera goes through the thick wooden
door, which closes with a firm click behind us—and there
is Richard waiting for us, standing beside a small throne
at the end of the room. The music of the court continues
softly, martial at first, then ending with the lascivious
sound of a lute. He briefly pretends to be in a meditative
mood, looks at us standing by the door, blinks a modest
hesitation, and sways towards us at a commanding pace
curtailed a little by the courtesy of a new acquaintance-
ship and the dragging of his left foot. His disproportion'd
gait, his big nose, his stiff black curls add meanness and
power to his eyes, whose lids flutter and blink like a gos-
siping noblewoman's as he stands a foot or so from the
camera and speaks to us in clear, crisp tones. For the first
seventeen lines of the speech he speaks as though to each
one of us personally—you can do that on film—as he explains how he's missed out on the glorious summer of the
sun of York because he's not shaped for sportive and
amorous tricks. But upon:

> I, that am curtail'd of this fair proportion,
> Cheated of feature by dissembling Nature,

he turns away from the camera to list his deformities (I used ten lines from Act III, Scene II of *Henry VI Part III* for this), to save us embarrassment perhaps, to gain our sympathy certainly, to shout a bit, to show his righteous anger. Upon:

> Why, I, in this weak piping time of peace,
> Have no delight to pass away the time,
> Unless to spy my shadow in the sun
> And descant on mine own deformity

he's standing at the entrance to the large throne room, expecting the camera to come closer to him. So upon "Then, since this earth affords no joy to me" (the beginning of another five lines from *Henry VI*) he moves toward us,

> But to command, to check, to o'erbear such
> As are of better person than myself,

and—flatterer—he goes to put his arm around the camera, and we almost feel the gentle touch on our arm, like an importuning uncle's, as we follow him closely towards the big throne room, telling us how he'll make his heaven to dream upon the crown. But we lag behind; so he turns—a little agitated—and puts his arms around our shoulders:

> And yet I know not how to get the crown,
> For many lives stand between me and home.

Then we follow him as he gets entrapped in that glorious simile of "one lost in a thorny wood," and leave him for his big theatrical climax, standing at the throne:

Torment myself to catch the English crown;
And from that torment I will free myself
Or hew my way out with a bloody axe.

But he's back at us again, telling us to our face that he
can smile, and murder while he smiles, and pushing us
back towards the small throne as he lists the way he'll
frame his face to all occasions:

Can I do this, and cannot get a crown?
Tut, were it farther off, I'll pluck it down.

He takes a garment from the throne, walks jauntily
past us, up some stairs, and leans against a wall near a
window. The last thirty lines of his speech were from
Henry VI. He says to us, after a modest smile: "Mean-
time, I'll marry with the Lady Anne. Here she comes"—
we see her through the window—"Lamenting her lost
love." (Not Shakespeare.) And taking us down a dark
passage towards two huge doors which open into the
courtyard, he explains who her lost love is:

Edward, the Prince of Wales [my words], whom I,
      some three months since,
Stabb'd in my angry mood at Tewksbury.
A sweeter and a lovelier gentleman . . .
The spacious world cannot again afford; . . .
And made her widow to a woeful bed.
                              (RICHARD III, *Act I, Scene II*)
That from his loins no hopeful branch may spring
To cross me from the golden time I look for!
                        (HENRY VI, *Part III, Act III, Scene II*)
. . . and he pushes open the doors. We see Lady Anne

walking behind her husband's coffin, and the circle at the top right-hand corner of the screen which tells the projectionist the reel of film is about to finish.

It's very bad practice to have a reel break in a dramatic scene: a sleepy projectionist can ruin everything. Most film processes have ten-minute reels, but VistaVision, because of its technique for producing such clear images, had only five, so throughout the soliloquy I was aware of a shortage of time, and that gave the performance an extra edge. Ah! Sweet problems of film that add to the dread and the adrenaline of acting! No doubt to the horror of schoolteachers, and the confoundment of their pupils, I left out the lines

> And therefore, since I cannot prove a lover
> To entertain these fair well-spoken days,
> I am determined to prove a villain

because I simply don't believe them. Even Shakespeare makes him a "credible" lover. Improving on Shakespeare? Sacrilege? The part was the thing. Within his own extraordinary world I had to keep Richard credible, and film audiences are the most difficult to convince. Besides, I had difficulty saying the lines. They didn't seem real to me, and might have affected the brilliance of the rest.

Richard talks and nods and winks to us while things are going well for him; and if he doesn't lean against the proscenium exactly, he leans against the half-open shutter of a window, giving a commentary on the politics of the court below, a report on the success of his plotting. He's very self-conscious about his clothes, and after the successful wooing of Lady Anne, he's so pleased with himself he barely notices us, and talks to himself and the sun:

> Shine out, fair sun, till I have bought a [looking]
>   glass,
> That I may see my shadow as I pass.

He changes brown and black with blue accessories (blue is for boy, but his had feminine tones) to an elaborate deep red costume, with white lace and the white figure of a hog stamped on each glove. But back to the plain garb when he says his prayers with the bishops, and swings down the bell rope to call back the citizens of London to proclaim him king. But when he's king, he behaves badly and has to go to battle, his long hair looking incongruous and ugly in his black medieval armor; and he's no longer talking to us because troubles and ghosts have come betwixt us and him. He'll have to offer more than his kingdom to get horse and sympathy from us.

"Here pitch our tent, even here in Bosworth field"— curses to Richard for that. We shot the battle scene in Spain, and those stunted Spanish trees and the silver grass were not Bosworth. When Richard insisted on a view of his battlefield, I was forced to use a painted picture of Leicestershire with the trees a little less stunted. Who has the faintest idea what Bosworth field looks like—except people who live near Bosworth, and they're not medieval?

I was injured at Bosworth, as I was in the other Shake-

Bosworth Field

speare films. I was in the battle on a horse, padded with cork. I got a technician to fire an arrow into the padding over the horse's body (I'd pull the horse up, someone would unsettle its hind legs, and thus the horse would fall in battle), but his arrow missed the padding and went into my leg.

"Impossible!" the stubborn English technician said, several times, in the Spanish sun.

"Pull the arrow out and see my blood on the end of it," I said.

He did. "I still don't believe it," he said, absolutely

aghast that his skill had been imperfect. Not worried so much about my wound.

The film got several awards for its craft and technique. *Richard* was nominated for an Oscar, but the vote went in favor of another king—Yul Brynner. It lost money the first time round, was revived successfully in 1966, is now enjoying a fresh release in the cinema with a new print, and who knows, in a hundred years' time it may be a cult cassette. But the film's initial flop made it impossible for me to get the money to make *Macbeth*—in my mind a director's film (I've found him to be a difficult acting part), a blood-colored, murky picture. And the British craftspersons now working brilliantly on Star Wars pictures would have helped me create an absolutely real and believable supernatural world: the lizard's legs and the poison'd entrails Hecate's witches throw into the hell-broth would be horrifyingly real. I could have taken stalwart Scottish actors, like John Laurie and Andrew Cruickshank, to Scotland to sup full of the horrors of the blasted heath or, if the budget was small, to Yorkshire, where *Wuthering Heights* should have been filmed. But no money, no budget. One may be daring, bold and resolute, even a bloody dreamer, but one cannot laugh to scorn the power of moneymen. So posterity is dispossessed of another version of the Scottish play to compare with Orson Welles's or Roman Polanski's.

CHAPTER SIXTEEN

In Front of the Camera

I HAVE always been an actor who molds characteristics to hide his personality. I take parts of the character *into* myself—not onto, or they would fall off. I do not search the character for parts that are already in me, but go out and find the real personality I feel the author created. I work all this out before I begin to rehearse the part and build up the role from within, knowing that the camera will expose me if I am not true, if my imagination is askew or only at half-power; if I am doing anything unreal. I make use of my natural talents and make sure that I do not waste other people's time on the set.

After the grimness of Richard III and my disappointment over *Macbeth*, I thought it would be fun to work with the legendary beauty and comedy actress Marilyn Monroe as both her leading man and her director; but I had not bargained with the problems of "method" acting.

I went to one of Lee Strasberg's New York classes once and saw him bullying a boy who I saw had a good feel for character. "He's got so many faults," Lee said, and went off into a lot of hot air, sprinkled with clichés. "The only fault he's got is the confidence you are draining from him," I said, or words, I hope, to that effect. Probably more pompous because I was angry. No doubt Strasberg thought English actors knew nothing of Stanislavsky, but we had all read him avidly when his books came out. Some of us—misunderstanding him—even used to come in an hour earlier and smell the furniture on the set. He was no highfalutin phony, he was an intensely practical man in the Wyler mold. By all means have Stanislavsky with you in your study or in your limousine or wherever you are three hours before the scene; but don't bring him onto the film set, where the schedule is tight and the time is ripe for fizzing action to carry along the story.

My feathers were considerably ruffled by Marilyn's erratic behavior on and around the set; her spikiness and spite were frightening, split from her sweetness and vulnerability. Half the time her head was so full of the rigmarole of "method," her natural talent was suppressed.

She'd take ages over a shot, keep people waiting for hours. "Marilyn, I've got the whole film in my head and this shot's fifty seconds long. You've got to make it thirty-eight seconds shorter. . . ." However, she could be a dream, listening and understanding my idea of a scene, taking off-camera direction beautifully, and proving her physical beauty and comic timing to be historical facts.

At one point, when Marilyn had to talk in a silly, drunken way, I told her to get on with the scene and not take the slightest bit of notice of what I did or said. Then I began to embroider around her, talking at the same time: an idea the Lunts invented in the 1920s. The audience can hear the bits they need to know, but the effect is killingly funny and can be magical. Difficult to do, though.

I had been amused by Terence Rattigan's original script for *The Sleeping Prince* on the stage, but found it hard to love the character in the film version, which the moneymen had christened *The Prince and the Showgirl*, making it sound like an Edwardian musical. As the Prince, I needed something real to grasp on to (the man *was* odious), so I based the accent on Alexander Korda's (though he wasn't), and some of the mannerisms, including a lot of fun with an eyeglass (I was so confident with my eyes!), on King Paul of Greece, whom I had watched behave badly and unprofessionally at a reception—something minor royalty is prone to do, I believe. In the editing room I had a happier time than I expected. I loved cutting away to Marilyn's reaction shots;

1981,
Clash of the Titans,
as Zeus
1957, *The Prince and
the Showgirl,*
with Marilyn Monroe
1972,
Lady Caroline Lamb,
as the
Duke of Wellington

SNOWDON/CAMERA PRESS

KEYSTONE

BOB PENN/CAMERA PRESS

1952, *Sister Carrie,*
with Jennifer Jones

1968, *The Shoes*
of the Fisherman

1960, *Spartacus*

no one had such a look of hurt innocence or of uncon-
scious wisdom, and her personality was strong on the
screen. She gave a star performance.

I was fifty. What a happy memory it would have been
if Marilyn had made me feel twenty years younger—but
I was upset by her insolence, which showed my age, I
suppose. Still, my theater work and my film work with
people like Wyler had taught me discipline and a respect
for experience. I was usually directing fellow actors who
felt the same, telling them what I wanted, letting them
do what they wanted as far as I could, solving technical
problems by discussion and by drawing upon experience.
One of the glories of working in the theater or in films
is the teamwork, the trust; the cool trust needed to overcome the otherwise superhuman task of realizing the
imagination. Maybe I was tetchy with Marilyn and with
myself, because I felt my career was in a rut.

It did not remain so for long. The 1950s saw a major
change for me. As I have explained earlier, John Osborne
introduced me to the world of the young modern writer
through Archie Rice with his seedy bowler hat, his tatty
bow tie and dingy check jacket.

In some ways it was not as difficult for me to make this
change as it was for more mannered, effusive actors, for
those who built their characters round themselves. My
acting had always had contemporary characteristics: it
had always been inventive and as spontaneous as possible. I had always tried to be a real person. (But not at
the expense of verse, of course; if it was Shakespeare, I
would find reality *through* the verse.) At my first audi-

tion, the coach, Miss Elsie Fogarty, said, "Perhaps it would be all right if you could confine yourself in a speech like this to just one gesture." And I thought, "Well, that's very splendid, but how can I show her all I can do with one gesture?" And she said, "Sans eyes, sans teeth (sans whatever the next thing is), sans everything." And she did it so beautifully that I thought, "Yeah, I see. Thanks." And it was very good; lasted with me a long time—forever, in fact.

To me spontaneity meant talking as people do in everyday conversation. I hardly ever say a full sentence without at least four "ummms" and an "aaah," and I often pause for a time to find the right word. That's very much part of a natural performance for me: I would call that actual spontaneity. After I have produced my final performance by a process of selection made during my full-out rehearsals, I add spontaneity: the olive in the cocktail. It is hard to achieve, so I always put it in last. In a long run you have to reproduce technical spontaneity over and over again and make it real every night. On film you have to keep it diamond-sharp and never go over the top.

Film acting taught me to have sincere eyes on stage. There's no point in exaggerating your eyes in the theater because they reach only the first five rows of the stalls anyway, and there's a danger they'll become detached and flash to and fro across the footlights like coiled china eyes worn by clowns at children's parties.

Archie Rice had to have flashing music-hall eyes, which were dead underneath, and we achieved that much better on film. (Full circle from the passion I finally achieved in Heathcliff's eyes by ridding myself of the habits of the stage.) As with Richard III, the camera relished the intimate parts of Archie—and John Osborne wrote some more scenes to give the film of *The Entertainer* what it wanted, craved: more emotion.

I think the film allowed John to show more of Archie Rice. I tuned up my stage performance, often changed it. I looked to the subtlety, the expressiveness, the reality of his mannerisms and accent (based on music-hall chums I'd lived with in theatrical digs, and artistes I'd seen in my youth), rehearsed the cheap music-hall flickers and flutters for the surfaces of the eyes, and made him dance expressively (at almost full theatrical throttle) and badly—which I achieved by dancing as well as I could! And the camera caught the deadness behind the eyes. Archie Rice was a hollow man. We are the hollow men. I felt Archie's hollow mood because that was what the camera wanted. Or was I feeling middle-age disillusion at the time? I am not a hollow man, but I know what it feels like to be one!

We all acted well in that picture, and Tony Richardson, the director, made the most of us and the medium. Joan Plowright revealed the clear and honest eyes of a true film actress. (Am I not to be allowed a tribute to my wife?) Alan Bates, Albert Finney, Daniel Massey, Shirley Anne Field, Charles Gray, Miriam Karlin and Joan joined us older actors, Brenda de Banzie and Roger Livesey, with Thora Hird flitting delightfully, as ever, between; and all of us, and the music-hall acts, presented a pretty lively picture of mid-century blues. For the first and last time I was able to cry tears on the screen, in the scene when Archie hears that his son's all right as his mistress is washing after fornication. I don't know how it happened. Relief at the news of the son. Maybe the challenge that a cheap music-hall artist would have the versatility to cry to order.

John Osborne's *The Entertainer* lifted my spirits to new heights. I was no longer in a rut; I immensely enjoyed the challenge of the new, the chance to adapt my knowledge and abilities into fresh channels. Details of all the films I have made since Archie Rice are in my autobiography. I cannot discuss them all again here. I will just comment on a few aspects of some of them which I remember particularly well and which may be of interest.

I enjoyed my supporting roles in modern films. As usual, I put all I could into the parts—undemanding though they were in many ways, for an actor who had played kings and princes—determined always to appear convincing. I was particularly amused by the dry irony of Shaw's Burgoyne in *The Devil's Disciple*; there's no harm in an audience's seeing an actor enjoying himself. Here again I was able to use my eyes to great effect and play the ironic, civilized soldier to the top of my bent. For Crassus in *Spartacus*, I was passing through a patrician phase, but I gave him a touch of that flirting femininity of Richard III, the cool eyes, suddenly aflame—second cousin to Coriolanus, several times removed.

Several theater productions of mine were made into

1970, *The Three Sisters*, as Chebutikin, with Joan Plowright as Masha

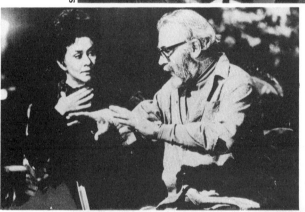

films, including *Uncle Vanya,* a play with which I had great success at the Chichester Festival Theatre; and *The Three Sisters,* based on a beautiful production from the National with a marvelous cast. It was a celebration of the acting rather than a thoroughly conceived filmic version of the play. That would have been a mammoth task for which we had neither time nor money.

I had a couple of "visual" sequences, such as Irina's dream of a better future in Moscow, and the camera seemed to like Chekhov's dialogue and his shifts of mood. I had little to do with the screenplay, which made it not-a-director's film in my book. All encouragement to the film man who will tackle Chekhov wholeheartedly. He could reap much reward. Too wordy, maybe, but I've a feeling that as we go further into high tech, cassettes and private entertainment, people will have a yearning for more words. Especially if conversation dies.

But films based on obvious stage origins sometimes misfire. Stuart Burge directed the film of the National's *Othello,* and he did it marvelously, within its limited concept. Alas, my performance was tired. I mistimed effects. Somehow I was lacking in confidence and full vitality; perhaps, subconsciously, I was being gnawed by the question "Why aren't we making a full-blown Shakespeare film of this?" Certainly I regret that now.

Immediately after *Othello,* I played the Mahdi in *Khartoum,* with Charlton Heston playing Gordon. His seven feet down to my five feet. A consummate actor who (it is said, and I happily concede) acted me off the screen—not from want of trying on my part. Making up

1966, on the set of *Khartoum*

as the Mahdi, I put white greasepaint along the lower edge of each eye to increase its size, as I had done for both the play and the film of *Othello*.

"Oh, no, oh, no, don't do that, black is what you want," they all said.

"Won't it make my eyes look tiny?"

But they were right. I kicked myself for not having discovered this before. Black on the lid and quite a lot of black round the eye is far more effective; it made me look much more African.

When making *Khartoum*, I was relaxing after *Othello*, recharging my spirits and my bank account, prepared to experiment a bit with the effects I'd learned from *Othello* but on a less demanding level. This is not putting down the part of the Mahdi. Tony Guthrie told me not to. But in epic pictures there's not much time for deep characterization—sometimes the dialogue can be anybody's—and you have to rely very strongly on the pictorial effect. Every epic film has its flamboyant part—usually played by Peter Ustinov. The secret is to play the part up to the audience's expectation of it—a healthy tradition from Shakespeare to Westerns and Mae West—and the real amusement is the little extra. A great deal more extra, if it's real. We all loved Charles Laughton for his big performances. I've had a lot of fun being part of that cinema tradition.

And I'm not diffident about playing the ordinary man again, as I did with Simone Signoret and Sarah Miles in *Term of Trial*. Not boring myself. Getting closer to myself, perhaps. Not boring the audience. And learning all the time. Franklin Schaffner, who directed *Nicholas and Alexandra*, was having a bit of a go at Michael Jayston, who played Nicholas: "Make him weaker!" So Michael, one of our finest young actors, tried to make him weaker, but it just looked like weak acting. Then we noticed that

when he acted anger, his eyes watered—just something
he could do, lucky man, a marvelous natural gift. You
can hardly do better than that as a symbol of weakness.
Show the camera his eyes. I played a rather little man in
Bunny Lake Is Missing, probably bullied onto me by
Otto Preminger—a real bully, who never let up. Noël
Coward and I didn't like the man much. Almost put me
off his *Carmen Jones*, which I thought an inspired piece
of work. I have a taste for mixing forms, for experiment,
and *Carmen Jones* was an innovative film. It's a miracle
it came from such a heavy-handed egotist. Have a pleas-
ant atmosphere on the set and a director is in less need
of a miracle.

I found *The Dance of Death* by Strindberg a pretty
claustrophobic piece in which you can't open out too
much, unlike *Miss Julie*. Strindberg is *veritas*, perfectly
straightforward, no undercurrent, no subtext, no sneaky,
subconscious underneath thought that he is either un-
aware of or hiding from himself. Quite unlike his fellow
Scandinavian Ibsen, who has a subtext of pure filth and
a very strong undercurrent which can have an extremely
bad effect on the actor. The subtext is so dirty, really;
well, if not dirty, then salacious. The part of Strindberg's
Edgar is a big one—intense and emotional—and that's
how I played it on the screen, daring and risky; and if
occasionally I appeared to go over the top, that didn't
ruin the performance or discount the screen's potential
to contain a big performance. You have to follow the
rhythms, the death-dance rhythms of the play. My feelings for the part were right. My intentions for the film

1967, *The Dance of Death*

were right. I swam along with the other actors, especially Geraldine McEwan, my antagonist. Any flaws, put down to professional misjudgment in a profession whose watchword should not be caution.

The physical disorders which, at times, drained me of vitality started in the mid-1960s. Cancer when I was sixty. Actors, like other devout professionals, don't like talking about their diseases. (If a man has attained a memorable professional achievement, it's very likely he'll forget—if he knows—the spur his illness gave him, or whatever the upheaval was.) If you haven't the vitality, don't act. If you can't do it, don't do it. An actor must be constantly vigilant about his energy, even when he's young and he thinks his body can take every abuse. The body is a vital part of the equipment. I used to keep very fit—best for the movement, the gestures—and only a few years before the cancer I'd reached a peak in a Stratford *Coriolanus*, appearing heroically half-clothed without any feeling of unease. The vitality doesn't disappear altogether, of course; that would be the end of life. You have to nurse it.

I would have to do cameo roles for the sake of my health, the balance of my professional life, the balance of my social life—and my bank account. Working with friends. Working for friends. I did a sort of double act with Frank Finlay in that film in which my friend Anthony Quinn wears *The Shoes of the Fisherman*. (Brave man, Frank Finlay. He had a very shaky start with Iago on the stage, but he persevered and ended by giving the best performance in the film.) Richard Attenborough

1959, *Coriolanus* at Stratford-on-Avon

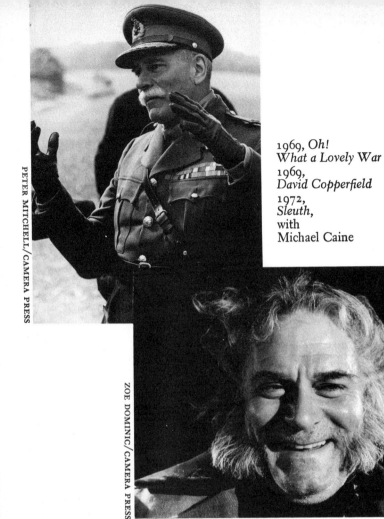

1969, *Oh!
What a Lovely War*
1969,
David Copperfield
1972,
Sleuth,
with
Michael Caine

asked me to do Field Marshal French in his brilliant directing debut *Oh! What a Lovely War*. That meant a bright couple of days in Brighton—which may have been the trouble with the film, in which the songs didn't have the same eerie effect they had had in the theater. Richard and I did another double act, Mr. Creakle and Mr. Tungay, in an American television version of *David Copperfield*, which wasn't made with as much love and humor as George Cukor's 1934 film. A magnificent British cast, though. No cameo parts in Dickens: they're all gems. Cameos are sparkling gems set it strong relief against a subdued background. Film producers put them into their epics to ensure some sharpness, bitterness, humor—flash some money on a bit of class. They assure an actor of an income, and meeting with old friends. I always chose interesting parts and usually had the chance to be relatively relaxed, to be the larger-than-life character audiences want, and have wanted, since pantomime, music hall and early film Westerns. Vital to me, these cameos—spiritually and financially. I've always managed to give them all the animation they need.

Time, strength and the opportunity to do a full-length film part arrived with *Sleuth*—an amusing script by Anthony Shaffer, from his stage play. Very clever, if a little repetitive, as with his brother Peter, who has made a habit of repeating his stage successes on film: I understand *Amadeus* is a veritable feast of color and music, impossible to achieve on the stage. I suppose I've reached an age at which I can see the massive further potential of the cinema—well, film in its broadest sense—and when

I can wholeheartedly admire other people's contributions to its development, feel pleased about my own, but feel regret at what I didn't achieve or do, even for my own pleasure.

The making of *Sleuth* was tinged, for me, with nostalgia and hope for the future. The part was big and good enough to test my powers to amuse on a sustained level. Joseph Mankiewicz, its director, has always been concerned with words on the screen—a wordsmith, a screensmith. He made *All About Eve*, with its witty dialogue and voice-overs; a very fine screen version of Shakespeare's *Julius Caesar* with brilliant performances by Marlon Brando as Antony and John Gielgud as Cassius (not so different in style as they may seem); and *Guys and Dolls*, with most of the lyrics kept intact—a film which broadened the public's consciousness of the American stage musical, and no doubt contributed to my wish to do a stage production at the National, in which I would play Nathan Detroit as well as Frank Sinatra did (but differently), and dance as well as Archie Rice, and sing like Macheath in *The Beggar's Opera*. Michael Caine was an absolute delight in *Sleuth* (except that he didn't like rehearsing—I went through my lines with the continuity girl). The camera loves him just as much as we who work with him do. I can see him in the Gary Cooper role in *High Noon*—but with his Cockney charm, the townsfolk would all have been his deputies by 11:30 A.M. No! His professional discipline is too powerful for that. He has the true personality of a star, and in *Sleuth*— in particular the scene on the staircase—he showed deep and difficult emotion. He's restless to widen his range. Mark my words: the mark of Caine on the cinema will be deeper yet.

Michael Caine is young enough to be my son. For the last ten years I've worked in films with technicians and actors who are a generation or so behind me—or in advance of me, if you look at the ways of professional leadership (I've provided the example)—and finding fresh ideas for and from the medium. It warms my heart to see young people—any people—expressing their talents. I've had a family, and I've wanted to help them do what they want to do in life. I've wanted to be a contented family man. I've never been a star who gets paid a million dollars a picture; and when I was a dashing young stage actor or a Hollywood star, or a stage and film director, a theater administrator, when I was acting classical roles, I didn't set up educational trusts for my children, and when you are ill you become very anxious for your wife and family.

Actually, I was pleased with the parts I played—not wholly for the money—in films like John Schlesinger's *Marathon Man* (particularly good), *The Boys from Brazil* (interesting and heartening seeing Gregory Peck play an unsympathetic part) and, yes, even *The Betsy*. They were usually shot in exotic places, or the sun shone and life was relatively easy. They were all rattling-good "entertainment" pictures, expertly made, with touches of the innovative. The parts I played were lively and expertly done, which is amusing in itself, both for me and for the audience. I can't go along with the critics who say I lowered myself playing these parts. On no account should a critic consider an actor's domestic and physical problems, but I wish he (or she) would be more aware of the so-called classical actor's need for his enjoyments— like Graham Greene's "entertainments," or Shakespeare's, Chaucer's, T. S. Eliot's (who would have given him a cat's chance of being a hit on Broadway? Didn't he get a Tony Award for the best lyrics?).

An actor's entertainments refresh him, reach other parts, get him tuned up for the arduous classical roles. It's an English tradition for the highbrow to feed on the vulgar, to be subsidized by light relief—English eclecticism. Get a New York "method" actor to say that! Get a snooty New York film critic to think that! Not that I'm snooty in turn about film critics as I used to be snooty about films. I regard the best of them as partners. We love the medium. We enjoy making new discoveries together. Critics like Dilys Powell, and most of the modern-day ones. Every actor—workaday, classical—needs his critics. We are in early days yet for the film. Early days for the film actor. Early days for the film critic. I hope we keep up with each other and keep away from the highfalutin cant which has sometimes affected the stage.

Fundamentally, I think, television is a more "hearing" and "listening to" medium than the cinema, where the picture is bigger and the eyes can wander only to darkness. So you can use more words, more details in characterization, you can give a more intimate performance. Startling effects are permissible if you've got the audience in the mood for them. You can sustain emotional effects

1959, *The Moon and Sixpence*, with Jean Marsh
1976, *Cat on a Hot Tin Roof*, as Big Daddy
1984, *The Ebony Tower*

SOME TELEVISION ROLES

THAMES TV

1982, *A Voyage Round My Father,*
with Elizabeth Sellars
1978, *Daphne Laureola,*
with Joan Plowright

for long periods, with relatively bare settings, as the Royal Shakespeare Company did with their studio *Macbeth* with Ian McKellen and Judi Dench.

I had the marvelous opportunity of doing a number of well-known plays for Granada Television: Pinter's *The Collection* (those Pinter pauses on the TV screen are fascinating), *Cat on a Hot Tin Roof, Come Back Little Sheba*: I found that the medium can take any play, any performance, provided—yes, back to it!—the feeling is right. I can do anything if I am prepared. I can look the littlest man in the world if I am *ready*. I could play so little, you wouldn't recognize me. But it takes time. Get your integrity together and you'll integrate with the medium.

I always go to endless trouble to learn American accents, even for small television parts. If it's north Michigan, it's bloody well got to be north Michigan. If its Kansas, it's goddamn well got to be Kansas. I go to endless trouble to find someone to teach me. The fact that you learn to say the lines with an inflection that a local person would use automatically from birth doesn't mean you are not playing the part. The teacher is not teaching me how to act. Of course there were times when I said to the teacher: "I know that isn't quite right, but I feel I need a variety of tonal touches in that scene, so I hope you won't mind if I say it a little wrongly. Sometimes tonal values are more important to a scene that a perfect accent. The audience'll have a helluva lot of perfect accents, but I hope I will have won their trust by that scene. If I haven't won them over by then, I never will."

When I wanted a Mississippi accent for *Cat on a Hot Tin Roof*, I couldn't find a single soul at the American Embassy in London who could cough me up one. The nearest was a nineteen-year-old girl from Tennessee. It worried me that she wasn't very Mississippi. She'd already begun, of course, to ape the English accent, and there are very few nineteen-year-olds who have what it takes to tell me what to do and how to do it, so I was very worried. Maureen Stapleton and the director kept saying I was fine, but I wondered whether it was Mississippi enough.

My fellow National Theatre actors and I successfully brought our stage performances of *The Merchant of Venice* and *Long Day's Journey into Night* to the television screen—successful, but not conceived as television performances. Of course, there have to be adjustments— my false teeth for Shylock were slightly smaller—but the barriers are down. English eclecticism, Wyler's "Do all that can be done" are thriving. Film—in its widest sense—is indeed a great medium. I'm just sorry I stood aloof from television film for so long.

Maybe I haven't said enough about the technique of film acting. The technique of film direction, yes, perhaps. I've talked about making an actor feel at ease. Take a cricketer. The groundsman gives him a perfect wicket. The bowler gives him the perfect ball, and he executes a beautiful cover drive which gets him four runs and has the spectators on their feet. Ask him how he does it, and he'll explain that his back-lift was short (miraculously so) and his bat straight.

"But how do you make it so sweet and beautiful?"

"I don't know. All I can tell you is it feels good."

And John McEnroe. He's got a beautiful backhand. But at the Wimbledon Celebration Ball, what's his dancing like? I bet, with a few lessons, he'd be closer to *Come Dancing* than ever Archie Rice would be. You can't teach a man rhythm if he hasn't got it. McEnroe's serve, I understand, wasn't as strong as usual after he fell in love with a beautiful actress. Perhaps he should have taken a million dollars, taken a year off and given vent to his versatility, and so saved his game. "There's nothing wrong with my game!" Yes, of course: how can I possibly say? He may have shown signs of feeling a little out of sorts with his game. He could hardly blame his "technique," as though it were an independent willful creature. When I see an actor like Michael Caine, who's never out of sorts with the camera or the world, give a performance of natural feeling and power without any apparent technique, I wonder if technique should be given any independent identity. Mind you, I'm almost as "natural" as Michael is. I'm naturally more of a show-off than he is. I'm more versatile—as yet! I have more technique!

I do wish we'd see more actors of Marlon Brando's caliber on television. More classically trained stage actors should appear regularly on the box, explore its possibilities as I explored film's, and create classical television roles. John Mortimer's father in *Voyage Round My Father* is a classical television role in the sense that future actors will want to play it, and will, specifically on tele-

vision. Try to forget its so-called stage origins. John wrote
it from his mind and soul, with love and knowledge of
his father, and with love and knowledge of the television
medium. Some critic or other said I played the old man
as though rehearsing my own old age—something absurd
like that. Was I rehearsing my own death as Lord
Marchmain in *Brideshead Revisited* (if so, it's going to
be a most giggly, lighthearted affair)? My own madness
and death in *King Lear*? Lear, of course, is a classical
stage role; it needs the resonance of the theater. I might
try it if I had a bit more confidence about being able to
do it. If I thought I could develop the voice again and
if I thought I could develop that particular pocket of
energy which a stage actor has to have, which a film actor
or a television actor is better off without. But you can
capture the intimate very well on television; the fond,
foolish old man. Doing *Lear* on television was an exercise of will for me, with a great deal of help from my
friends, especially Michael Elliott, the director—alas, now
dead. The will to get the right vitality and reality. Physically it was arduous. My frailty suited the old man. I suppose I felt his mood. Loved him. I felt the moods of all
my old men.

My wife, Joan, threatened to feed me nothing but
bread and drippings and to have Otto Preminger as a
houseguest if I ended my acting career at the National
by doing *Lear*. Happily, I did *The Party* instead. (Incidentally, Trevor Griffiths also writes very well for television.) As it turns out, Lear is to have been my last
major role, on stage or screen. But if you'll excuse a bit

1981, *Brideshead Revisited*

With Jeremy Irons and Anthony Andrews

of sentimental fancy, *The Tempest* was Shakespeare's acknowledged last play, and reputedly, Prospero was Richard Burbage's last role. As Prospero's charms are all o'erthrown and what strength he has is his own, and as he prepares to leave his magical island, Shakespeare has him say:

> Our revels now are ended. These our actors,
> As I foretold you, were all spirits and
> Are melted into air, into thin air:

1975, *Love Among the Ruins*, with Katharine Hepburn and George Cukor

Just a moment or two of nostalgia. I'm happy, witty, wise and unpretentious, especially when I'm with friends like George Cukor and Katharine Hepburn, as I was for the American television production of *Love Among the Ruins*. (Actually, George was very good at pretending to be pretentious.) That was my happiest professional film experience. Master and mistress of the medium, and it must have shown in our performances. With Hepburn— as with all the great stars—you have a deep sense of her personality, of her strong and still center of gravity which radiates her wit, her vulnerability, her courage and her outspokenness, the way Shakespeare's verse radiates from his Rosalind in *As You Like It*. I could never aspire to Hepburn's star quality, I didn't have Cukor's knowledge of technique or his great knack with screen actors, but we felt equal and comfortable in our shared love for the medium. All actors are egotistical and competitive—that's where we get our energy. It's our love of the art of acting (and its camaraderie) which makes us artists. You can feel the vitality in the performances of Hepburn and Richardson, for example, in *Long Day's Journey into Night*—superb examples of ensemble playing and film acting.

Ralph Richardson, John Gielgud and I competed with each other in those scenes when we were all together in Tony Palmer's marathon *Wagner*—there was very little else to do. So often the case when you're blockbustering. We certainly competed in the classical stage roles. Do you know the most affecting thing about my "affair" with *Richard III?* John Gielgud passed on to me the sword Edmund Kean had used in his performance. A great and unselfish and typical act of friendship, but a greater act of love for the art of acting. Actors' camaraderie stretches back to Shakespeare, at least, and it must continue. The stage will be all right, in varying degrees of flourishing. But you might have to form a television repertory company.

As the center of gravity of my body moves closer to its grave and my soul thinks of Heaven, I'm expected to show a touch of *gravitas*, to give advice. I would be appalled if I met a modern film actor who didn't love his medium—snooty now as I was snooty then. The wonder

BEING DIRECTED

Brideshead Revisited

The Ebony Tower

The Collection

Daphne Laureola

Cat on a Hot Tin Roof

of Willie Wyler's medium and the reality of his predictions are everywhere to be seen; television is showing the medium's growth and history. Film will go anywhere you want to take it. If I'd been born ten years earlier, say, in Hollywood, I wonder if I would have found my way to words, Shakespeare, the stage and the classical roles. Certainly I'm prejudiced to say "Get a classical training," but you must act as the spirit moves you. (Work on a building site rather than go to a "method" studio.)

If you love your art and your medium, what can be added to Tony Guthrie's "Love the character you play"? If you're having trouble with your relationship with the camera, look to your makeup, gestures and expressions; look to your eyes; look within yourself. And get your feeling and mood right. If all else fails, talk to the director!

Unlike the fading Prospero in Shakespeare's final Epilogue, you lack neither spirits to enforce nor art to enchant.

Part Five

REFLECTIONS

CHAPTER SEVENTEEN

On Acting

Acting is like that first sip of beer ever, the one you probably steal as a child, the taste that you never forget, it makes such an impression on your palate. No other sip ever tastes the same. Always just a little different. When I was sixteen and had been seeing my brother off to India, and my father and I were both very sad, I said to my father, "When can I follow Dickie to India, please? How long shall I have to wait?" And my father said, "Don't be such a fool. You're not going to India, you're going on the stage." Acting is often put down by outsiders, who are not interested anyway, as a game played by adults who ought to know better. It is not; it is a great art, and when it is done well it stands out on its own, supreme and satisfying.

Mind you, the same philistines who call us children in long trousers would more than likely find a Turner painting not much to look at—"Those shadows are purple, aren't they?"—and a Van Gogh a botch of colors that didn't compare with their children's kindergarten finger paintings. These zombies who share the planet with us would think Beethoven a painful cacophony, Bach a Welsh choirmaster, Chopin something you do when you split wood for kindling.

I have been acting all my adult life. And before. It has stood by me and I have stood by it. It has given me much joy and some sorrow. It has taken me to places that otherwise I would not have seen. It has given me the world and great happiness. It has brought me friends and good companionship, camaraderie and brotherliness. It has taught me self-discipline and given me the retentive eye of the observer. It has enabled me to love my fellowmen. It has clothed me, watered me, fed me and spared me from a bowler hat and a nine-till-five desk. It has given me cars and houses and holidays, bright days and cloudy ones. It has introduced me to kings and queens, presidents and princes. It has no barriers. It has no class. Whatever your background, if acting decides to embrace you and take you to its heart, it will hurl you

up there among the gods. It will change your wooden
clogs overnight and replace them with glass slippers.

I have been lucky, I admit—nay, boast—for I have
been successful for most of my working life. But the
wonderful thing about it, this business, is that it can
thrust accolades on you at any moment, at any time. It is
never too late. At eighty when you are about to suck in
your final breath, it can turn you into a star. It is always
just round the corner.

Once you have been to the tree and tasted the fruits,
some sour, some sweet, you will never be able to leave it
again. It will get under your nails and into your pores, it
will mix with your blood, and nothing will ever take
it away from you. It has its ups and downs, twists and
turns, great fortune and bad luck. It has its own super-
stitions and its own language. It has its "in" crowds and
its "out" crowds, its jealousies and its loves. It can destroy you in all sorts of canny ways, with drink, with
drugs, with success, with failure. It can change charming
personalities into monsters, and big egos into even bigger
ones. It can make you believe your own publicity. It can
make you sit on your behind and feed yourself with past
glories. It can leave you in a pile of yesterday's press cut-
tings and laugh at you as you wonder what happened to
your real self. It is selective and very surprising. It can
make you give up everything else. It will blinker you from
personal relationships, destroy marriages and families. It
can turn even twins against each other. It can rape you,
bugger you, bless you and succor you. Its moods change

with the wind. Once it takes you, you must go with it
and let each new day shower you with surprises. Once
you have made your decision, if you believe enough,
there is positively no turning back. Above all, you must
remain open and fresh and alive to any new idea. . . .

It's all very well to have your head full of the past; we
can all sit in bed and dream our dreams of yesterday. I'm
sure I could fill a waking day without moving from the
bedroom. But that's not important; that's merely cozy
and comforting, like a child's blanket. What is important is tomorrow. You must never let that get beyond the
periphery of the eyeball. Hold on to it strong and fast.
Keep it firmly fixed inside you so that you are looking
ahead at all times. Reminisce, by all means . . . talk of
the past as I have; but always keep your eyes fixed firmly
on the future; otherwise, you may as well stop now, at
this very moment. Stop and bury your toes in yesterday's
concrete. Plant your sticks of No. 5 and No. 9 in an in-
fertile plot, and watch them slowly atrophy.

I have always been fascinated by the theater in all its
aspects. I like to know how every nut and bolt fits together. I've attempted to learn every little detail. I've always believed that you can't ask a man to do something
unless you've been there yourself. So I made a point very
early on to understand how a theater breathes. Believe
me, when you are second assistant stage manager at eighteen for Sybil Thorndike's company, you learn very
quickly. . . .

I learned too, very early on, from Noël Coward. In
Private Lives, Adrienne Allen and I were obviously mere

feeds to the glorious Gertie Lawrence and the great Noël. Not that there is anything wrong in this in the beginning, but it really is most frustrating when you are desperate for a part of the apple to bite. Noël, of course, was the author and admitted in frank honesty that his own part and Gertie's could be equally well played without any other characters to support them. Charming. But I knew that beneath all that bravado, they both needed us as the tinderbox is needed to fire off the rocket. I mention this only because it is a state of growing in our business. I knew that to be fed well, your feed had to be perfect. And that the better you feed, the more likely one day you will be fed. Early days . . . but never to be forgotten. Lessons, blackboard, chalk. In those days of support, I learned, remembered and retained.

I suppose I am fortunate to have sat at the feet of such masters. But even the worst actor can teach you something, even if it's something not to do. How not to time, how not to inflect, how not to move. There is always something to learn.

I suppose it was because of my complete involvement in the theater that I eventually became an actor-manager. I've always been determined to try everything. I had dabbled before the St. James's, but suddenly here was my own theater. Unlike the Old Vic, where Ralph, John Burrell and I were a triumvirate, this was my very own. For twelve years I was to be my own man.

I was not a successful manager by any means, but I think it could be said I was a pretty courageous one. I was adventurous rather than cautious, and eventually

ended up at the thin end of the box-office takings. I was
probably always too ambitious, and my theater, even
when full, could not cope with this. For example, when
I put on the Cleopatras we were packed every night of
the run, but the only profit I could make was £40 a week.
You can imagine how long I'd have to run a show to
gain any real capital out of that. So you see my success
record was not high; it may have been artistically, but
not financially. Consequently, the ordinary moneyman
("angel") was not prepared to back me without reserve,
so I had to plunge more and more of my own into it. By
the time my twelve years were up, and fate was about to
do permanent desecration to my beautiful St. James's, I
had spent all my savings in trying to keep it alive: £60,000
in all. The money I'd made and saved in Hollywood. At
least the only pockets that were emptied were my own,
so I had to pick myself up and get on with life and go
out and earn my daily bread. And that's what I did. It
hurt to lose my theater, it hurt very much, but there was
nothing I could do about it. The roof had been shifted
by the bombings in 1940; it was an old theater, built in
1820, and a fire hazard. It could not be licensed by the
London County Council any longer unless £250,000 was
spent to make it safe. No investors were available.

I successfully stayed away from management until
1963, when I was appointed the first director of the National Theatre—though in a way this was a million miles
away from the sort of actor-management I had been involved in before. I was about the best person for the
job—I had had so many failures as a manager, which the

1951, *Caesar and Cleopatra*

governors had the sense to see meant I had learned a lot. I had been an actor, I'd been an actor-manager, I'd been a director time and time again. And I had been a manager above all; and therefore very few actors had had quite the same breadth of experience as I in every area of theater. I was the artistic director, but I had a board to answer to, I couldn't just go out on a limb and do as I wished. But I cover most of this in *Confessions of an Actor*. In spite of the disagreements over policies in those years, I would like to think that all of us had one thing in common: the continuation of the theater as a fine art.

I was proud of my position as director of the National, and always will be. And I'm certain that the work we did there was a great credit to the British theater as a whole. I am convinced that pound for pound, for a moment we were the best troupe of players in the world. They were a sensational company, and they were a company in the true sense of the word. Anyone of my team, at any time, could have taken the helm and steered a play into safe harbor. A wonderful company from the second assistant stage manager to the top. I felt I knew them all individually, and I think I did. I may have been the father figure, but not in the Victorian pattern: my company *did* speak and *were* heard. The proof of my boasting is to look at some of the unknown names of my company then, and how many are known now. I think you'll find that quite a percentage are now in lights above the West End bills, in their own right. I hope we all learned something from each other; I'm sure we did. I was able to pass on to them what had been passed on to me. For although I maintain we must forever look forward, we must still hold fast to our theatrical roots, and listen.

Out of seventy-nine productions at the National, I acted in only seven and directed only seven, so as to create opportunity for other, younger directors. I never seized the reins and drove the horse single-handed. We had wonderfully versatile actors; enough people to cast an entirely Scottish play or an Irish one, and what other company could do that? We discovered new plays: the complete spectrum of modern writers from the right to the political left. The whole operation, especially casting, fascinated me: moving actors from one part to another, constantly polishing them up, constantly letting them emerge in new forms that would stretch them and make them absolutely first-class. When I was directing I always encouraged them to invent like mad, and then it was up to me to see that they didn't foul up the rest of the production. Those were great years.

I will never forget that it was Guthrie's remarks to me which changed my approach as an actor. The transformation didn't issue out of my own heart: it was sold to me by the one man from whom I'd never expected sage advice. Stage directions and practicalities, yes, but never soul matters. I was staggered, and my opinion of him improved enormously, as did my acting.

Our calling is the art and craft of presenting a personality to an audience. There are said to be two kinds of actors: straight and character. But everybody who is respected in the profession thinks of himself as a versatile performer. The use of hands, the use of feet, the use of face; but above all, the acknowledgment of life.

I have always been fascinated by surgeons. Theirs too is a dramatic art. The theatricality of the surgeon, in the heat of the operating theater, fighting for the life of a patient, under the winged shadow of death, is drama at its height.

I have been through a series of illnesses during the past few years and have had to venture under the surgeon's knife myself. The more I discover about my body, in sickness or in health, the more fascinated I become.

I had a friend who was a very fine surgeon and for some time I begged him to let me attend one of his operations. He took much persuading because he thought that for all my intrigue and bravado, the moment I saw the knife slice into the flesh and blood gush out, I would slide to the floor and need to be revived myself.

I was eventually able to convince him that my legs were more stable than a seasick sailor's, and he allowed me into *his* theater. Very strongly came the statement "You're in *my* theater now; if you decide to meet the floor before your good-night mattress, we'll just have to leave you there. We've no time to look after the disarranged stomach of a *well* man." Fighting, aggressive and understandable words. I was in *his* world now.

"I'm fine," I said.

"Well, if you pass out, pass *out* and not *in*. If you feel queasy, get out of the way."

There was a pause. I nodded. He began. There was no

likelihood of my passing out; I was totally absorbed. From the moment the knife went in I was riveted.

I feel that actors should know more about their bodies than perhaps they do. Maybe they should have a copy of Gray's *Anatomy* on their bookshelves along with Shakespeare. I'm not suggesting they should all go and storm the galleries of their local operating theaters, but then again, perhaps it wouldn't be a bad idea if they did. Actually to see and be aware of the way the motor works. The blood and the pound of flesh.

After the operation the surgeon realized how intrigued and sincere I was. He knew now that my stomach and head were mine, they did not belong to the nursery floor. I think he was impressed. I certainly was with him. I asked him if I could come again. Later, if anything came up that he thought might interest me, he'd always let me know.

You might think this morbid or macabre, but for me it wasn't at all. I simply wanted to know more and more about myself. I wanted to get under the makeup, really beneath the skin. I wanted to know every part of me. Every inch, duct and vessel.

I'm sure it helped me during my illnesses. I knew exactly what was up, and where it was. I was never frightened, I was just determined to fight. I refused to give in.

When recently I had a kidney removed, I asked quite sincerely if it was possible to be operated on under a local anesthetic, and watch the whole procedure in a mirror. The doctors declined. A pity.

I had always been very athletic, running and lifting

weights, using the gym as often as I could. When illness curbed this form of exercise, I took to swimming and to this day swim half a mile most mornings. Sixty-six lengths. Monotonous, but worth it. Never give up.

To be fit should be one of an actor's first priorities. To exercise daily is of utmost importance. The body is an instrument which must be finely tuned and played as often as possible. The actor should be able to control it from the tip of his head to his little toe. He must be able to send messages to any part of it with the speed and skill of a computer. We are living in a machine, a machine of great complexity, and in order to use it properly we must try to understand as much of it as possible. Perhaps an actor's course should include a few months of medical studies. Perhaps he should follow the rounds of a physician in one of the major teaching hospitals, listen in on the lectures and observe. If I were starting today, I know that's what I would do.

Daily exercise is essential when you're working in front of an audience in the evening. Getting tuned up before the performance. The actor should be as fit as a boxer, as poised as a matador, as agile as a ballet dancer. During the course of an evening he may have to work on high voltage for long spells. As Hamlet he must be at top energy level for four hours or more, and then complete the evening with a sword fight. Shakespeare made the actor work for his bread and butter.

My exercising was for aesthetic as well as athletic purposes. I was always terribly thin. I am still. It was years before I dared expose my nobly proportioned limbs be-

fore the public. I first had the courage when I played
Oedipus, after I'd done so much exercising to remedy the
situation. Whenever I played a part in tights, there was
that perfectly beautiful padding we used to get from
Bernetts in Covent Garden. You were always all right in
tights, and playing Romeo or Mercutio or anyone like
that, you didn't often take your top off, so you didn't
give away the wires hanging from your shoulders. And
after a while I did work up enough physique to *dare* to
show myself. I think I always kept my left arm sort of
covered in a cloak, but I was able to show the right, and
occasionally do a gesture flexing the muscle. . . . I
wouldn't now, for the audience's sake, expose myself very
proudly, because at age seventy-eight, I'm not Tarzan
anyway, and hardly godlike.

As well as the body, the voice must be toned up, and
when you're working it should be exercised before each
performance. Difficult if you are sharing a dressing room,
but there are always ways round that. Too many actors
use the performance itself to warm up, and it shows. It
is at least half an hour before everything is running
smoothly.

When the actor is not working it is even more important for him to keep in good shape, though when the
horizon is looking rather dark such self-discipline is hard.
It is easier to get under the blankets and hide.

Not only must the body be kept supple and agile, so
must the mind. As a writer must write something every
day, so should an actor study. And if there is not an immediate part to learn, then he must work on something

of his own choice. Anything—a speech, a complete role, a poem. Sybil Thorndike learned a sonnet or some lines of poetry every morning of her life.

This all must sound like blinkered dedication. But I truly believe that in this profession, if you want to reach the heights, that is what you must have. You must be prepared to sacrifice in order to succeed. You must set your goals high and go for them with the pugnacity of a terrier. But remember, to fall into dissipation is easy, for it is a glamorous profession, full of glorious temptations. Place a foot on the first rung and the serpents will appear beckoning with their silky tongues, flattering you and begging you to bite the apple.

So many talents, good, raw and rich ones, have been battered against the walls of dissipation and left to drown. The sycophantic serpents are everywhere. Because the profession generates glamour, the adulators queue up to stare at, touch, or if possible entertain something that they can never be. Their admiration is genuine . . . but beware, actor, beware. Beware the Greeks.

Above all, do not despair when the hand of criticism plunges into your body and claws at your soul: you must endure it, accept it and smile. It is your life and your choice. And beware, look to the opposite. Do not float toward the heavens when the same patronizing person places a hand on the crown of your head and breathes compliments into your vulnerable ear. Everything can change tomorrow. I suppose critics are a grim necessity. There are good ones and bad ones, and ones who simply masquerade as critics but are merely purveyors of columns of gossip. Tittle-tattle signifying nothing. Poor creatures who are pushed by their pens and not by their intellects. The good ones are essayists and of immense value to our work. They help, sometimes hinder, but most understand the problems and pitfalls of our profession. Without them some of the great performances of the past would have gone by unrecorded.

Sometimes I think that more critics should be encouraged to sit in on rehearsals so that they could see the amount of work, concentration, belief and love that goes into the construction of a piece, before they take their inky swords to it.

But a note of approval for the good critics, the ones who share the same joy that we the actors, writers and directors take in our profession. They're the people whose intellect and pen go hand in hand. They add to our world and very much belong to it. And I imagine it is as painful to them when something doesn't come off as it is to us. I suppose a critic on a daily paper will see more plays in a lifetime than most of us, and many more than once. So it is only natural for him or her to feel he knows more about it than we do. It must be so easy to think of the witty line to ginger up a column, and very tempting to use it. But so unfair on the poor recipient who has had the courage to stand up there and be counted.

I know that if we are foolish enough to parade ourselves between spotlight and reality we must be prepared

1964, Othello

1950, *Venus Observed,*
as the Duke of Altair

1935, *Romeo and Juliet,*
as Mercutio

1951, *The Entertainer,*
as Archie Rice

1967, *A Flea in Her Ear,*
as Plucheux

1945, Henry V

1945, Oedipus

1945, *The Critic*, as Mr. Puff

1966, *Khartoum*,
as the Mahdi

1955, *Twelfth Night*,
as Malvolio

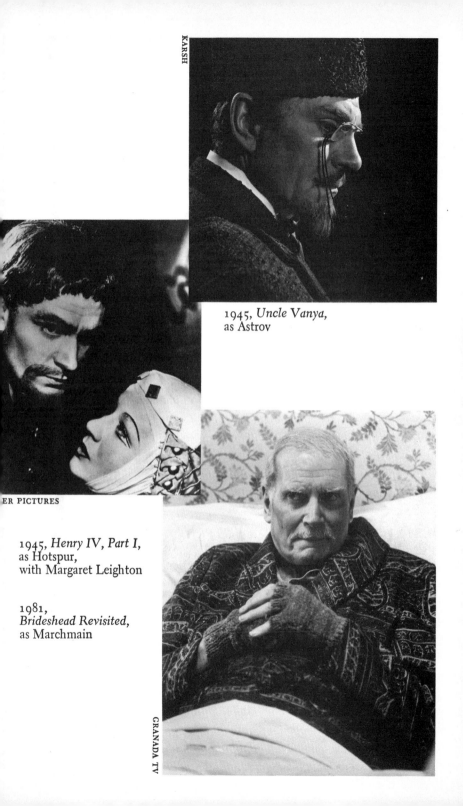

1945, *Uncle Vanya,*
as Astrov

1945, *Henry IV, Part I,*
as Hotspur,
with Margaret Leighton

1981,
Brideshead Revisited,
as Marchmain

to receive the attention of the pen. But let me plead for thought and care and sincerity, not for mere showmanship.

I have been battered and bruised, praised and lauded. I have laughed and cried, fumed and snorted; I have been beyond the moon and into the depths of despair. But in the end it has been myself I've had to turn to, believe in and listen to. When the time comes, it is you, and only you, who knows your truth.

I have concentrated most on my Shakespearean roles in this book because I have found them the most fascinating, and their construction still remains clear in my head. I can still see and feel them as though they were happening now. Unlike those of other parts, the lines have remained with me. They are part of me and I am part of them. The older I grow, the more I seem to understand them. What a shame I can't play them again.

Perhaps I should have spent more time with Shaw, Wilde, Ibsen, Strindberg, Coward, but I'll leave them to the next generation to make their mark upon. Once I saw myself as merely

> . . . a poor player,
> That struts and frets his hour upon the stage
> And then is heard no more. . . .

But now I know we can remain. We now have film, television, tape. We can stay hereafter to be referred to, looked up and criticized, laughed at or admired, a hundred years from now. But much as I love these media—indeed, I must owe at least a third of my acting life to them—they cannot truly show what it is like to have been there. Once printed they will never change; that moment is there forever. There will never be the smell of the adrenaline on celluloid. The real moment will have gone.

Film is the director's medium, television the writer's, but the theater is the actor's. When the actor is on stage, it is he and he alone who drives the moment. The audience have no choice but to remain in his faith or leave. That's the true excitement, the real magic of the profession. The actor on stage is all-powerful, for once the curtain rises, he is in control. There is nothing the director or author can do once the house lights dim and the curtain goes up. The actor can choose to do or say anything he likes; he is the governor, he cracks the whip.

It is the author and the director who bite their nails at the back of the house between overindulgent intakes of alcohol, not the actor. Once he begins to motor and the initial nerves are overcome, his inward smile is Cheshire-like as he flexes and enjoys the muscles of his art.

Breathing in the thick, warm air, feeling the expectancy of the house as it waits for your next moment. Timing a pause for perfection. Feeling the lungs bellow in and bellow out as the voice hits the heights of its power. Never giving too much; always making them want more. Making a gesture and holding it, knowing that all eyes have moved with you. Hearing laughter as it moves through the theater like a giant wave, aware that it has been caused by you. Knowing that tears are there for the asking. Controlling every eye in the house, making your thoughts theirs. Taking them on the journey with you, lending their ears to your mind. Frightening them, exciting them, loving them, holding them in the palm of your hand, Lilliputians and Gulliver. Cuddling them, cajoling them, caressing them. Without them you do not exist. Without them you are a man alone in a room with memories and a mirror. Without them you are nothing. An actor without an audience is a painter without a brush. Of course you can always perform in your head, but where's the satisfaction?

As I have already said, it starts at the very beginning by the family fireside, where the child demands attention: "Look at me . . . look at me. . . ." Once attention has been achieved, it's the keeping of it that's important. It is then that the talent to amuse, entertain, provoke shines through: you can soon see who are going to be actors and who stage managers. It is then that you can see the future.

Never underestimate the audience, never patronize them. Because if you do, they will know. They are far more intelligent than you may think. They pay your bills and fill your stomach. Without them you are in an empty room again with a bare cupboard. You must always treat them with respect, be they one or a thousand. If the house is small, never give a small performance. Never cheapen yourself or your profession. It is one of the oldest and best. Remember the court jester: he didn't dare perform badly; he was always on the high wire.

I can no longer work in the theater, but the thrill will never leave me. The lights and the combat. The intimacy between the audience and me during the soliloquys in *Hamlet* and *Richard III*; we were like lovers.

At my age you do things when you think of them. Because you don't know when the great axe is going to fall.

I am seventy-eight going on eighteen. Tomorrow I begin filming a new television series for Granada. I have made a hologram, which means I will appear nightly in a new West End musical next year. When the television series is over I will make a pop record . . . and so it goes on.

That's an actor's life. Complete freedom and versatility. Everything changes, as I have said. But then again, nothing changes. All we need is an old cigar box and someone to take notice.

1964, *The Master Builder*

Letter to a Young Actress

On 24 January 1947, I made a speech at the opening of the Old Vic School. This is part of what I said to the incoming students:

> An actor, above all, must be a great understander, either by intuition, observation or both, and that puts him on the level with a doctor, a priest, or a philosopher. If I can get more from him than just belief, then I feel fortunate and overjoyed. . . . There are many dimensions in the art of acting, but

none of them . . . are good or interesting . . . unless they are invested with the appearance, or complete illusion, of truth. The difference between the
actual truth and the illusion of the truth is what
you are about to learn. You will not finish learning
it until you are dead.

Present as I made that speech was a student in her
twenties who was to be a great influence in my life. She
was to go on to become acknowledged as a great actress,
and for twenty-five years has been my pride and joy: my
beloved wife Joan Plowright.

I had fallen in love with her Margery Pinchwife in
The Country Wife, marveled at her virtuosity as the Old
Lady in Ionesco's *The Chairs* and been quite knocked
out by her Beatie Bryant in Arnold Wesker's *Roots*.
Then she came to play Jean Rice with me in *The Enter-
tainer*. Later she went back to George Devine at the
Court to play the title role in Shaw's *Major Barbara*. It
was then that I wrote to a young actress:

Dear Joan,

I do hope you won't mind, pet, a few words of encouragement, and a few of criticism, as you said you wouldn't
last night when I was in a mad rush after your (very late
I must say) show, from your old Dad.

First of all I was really very impressed by how far you
had managed to go to collar this not at all rewarding part
along most difficult new lines for you.

By the way, please tell Georgie, who came to talk
about *All's Well That Ends Well*, that I am *absolutely*

happy, having seen you in this, that it will hold no terrors for you. You could knock off Helena on your dainty block head, darling. You have an absolute natural poetic quality and without any sign of strain, which is the whole bloody thing.

Now then. I think when you essay to alter your personality as radically as you are required to do for Barbara you must be prepared to throw out some of those qualities which have stood you in good stead in your earlier triumphs at this theater.

You have an absolutely marvellous uncalculated, impish sense of humor which is strongly laced with an aptitude for self-mockery. This last can be invaluable but also a dangerous quality which should be used judiciously . . . the first is priceless, but must not always be relied upon because it will not *always* get you out of a hole.

In any untoward circumstance which might make one unusually selfconscious, or when overtired, the basic elements of our personality will predominate naturally, as they are the first things within us we unconsciously grab hold of to make us think we can do it at all, as any mannerism is developed subconsciously to cover up some weakness . . . disjointed pauses by one who is frightened of drying up . . . exaggerated gait in one who thinks he is ungainly, e.g. J.G., etc.

But in this hole, or any in which the background is different from our own, we must be strong and prepared to face the fact that these elements may not be suitable and bloody well create something else that is.

Here we were last night, finding ourselves prepared for

the canopied presence of a South Kensington family, *one* member of which is a bit different. How? *Not* by a basic difference of natural type (although I suppose you could claim she took after Father) but by a basic difference of spiritual identification. In this case, the impish humour and self-mockery tends in these circumstances to say to the audience, "Just look at me, the rebel of the Royal Court, hobnobbing with all these stiff and starchy folk."

And that puts you at a disadvantage and takes away from your success in showing the *real* difference between Barbara and the society to which she belongs.

There is one word which describes what you should bring on to the stage with you in this part. *Radiance.* And don't be frightened of it, pet, and don't let self-mockery guy you out of it. Self-mockery can have its bellyful on other opportunities.

I think I told you how hard it was for me not to be selfconscious in the "Crispin" speech . . . it was 1937 and we were all a highly debunking generation.

You are a wonderfully gifted and beautifully disciplined actress . . . do not be shy of Dedication. Grasp hold of it. We can still keep our old sense of humour, but in its *place*; the indiscriminating allowance of it . . . has taken the top off many a brilliant actor. Acting is basically a humourless craft, and that's what makes people like us suffer so.

I think you are a little frightened of the part and it's hard to love anything you're frightened of. But you *must* love Barbara. Love her as she's never been loved before. Love is (among other things) the exaltation of understanding. Now *understanding* is the absolute *must* in our work, and the means whereby we can *inform*. Love is the means whereby we can bring that information home.

We must love Iago or Caliban, we must even love Jean Rice. Ours not to reason why, ours to apprehend and impart. We must never shirk the preparation in the wings, the practising of the old self-hypnotic act to transform ourselves completely before we step on to the stage.

Please don't think I am saying it is a bad thing to be frightened of a part at the beginning.

A humble approach to our work is essential and there is a dreadfully stern law which ordains that "No True Artist May Expect Satisfaction from His Work." But how do we equate the essential humility towards the work with the full possession of the confidence required to carry it off?

Not that last night's audience were given any other impression than that you were sailing along confident in your prowess and presenting a perfectly *plausible* Barbara for their enjoyment and approval. But you and I know that you have brought her towards yourself . . . and *into you* . . . instead of going out to her. And that is what leaves you with that niggling sense of dissatisfaction.

One or two things. Your back is straight and beautiful (Christ, those corsets in this weather) but don't be too far back on your heels. Keep your knees flexible and swing a *tiny* little more on the walk. Your hands are exquisite and you can afford yourself a little more consciousness of this. If you scratch your nose see that it is a charming gesture (I mean in this sort of thing).

Your voice gets better all the time and can be rich and lovely when you want it to . . . keep it clear and don't let emotion make it plummy. It is one of the hardest things to do in our work . . . to plumb emotion to its very depths and still allow the audience to hear every single f——g word. You don't know how lucky you are to be able to cry at will on stage . . . Johnny G. never stops . . . and as I've told you I've never been able to do it in my life. But I've been able to make people believe that I can . . . and that is what it's all about, isn't it?

I hope this has been of some use to you, my darling. I'd love to help any time I can . . . but only if you feel the need of it. You go your own sweet way and sweet may it be at all times. I know it will always be sweet to your devoted

Larry

PERFORMANCES

1907   Born on 22 May

THEATRE

1917   JULIUS CAESAR (Shakespeare). *role* Brutus, *dir*. Geoffrey Heald, All Saints School
        TWELFTH NIGHT (Shakespeare). *role* Maria, *dir*. Geoffrey Heald, All Saints School
1920   THE TAMING OF THE SHREW (Shakespeare). *role*
1922   Katharina, *dir*. Geoffrey Heald, All Saints School and Memorial Theatre, Stratford-upon-Avon

1923   A Midsummer Night's Dream (Shakespeare). *role*
        Puck, *dir*. W. H. A. Cowell, St Edward's School,
        Oxford

1924   Macbeth (Shakespeare). *role* Lennox, *dir*. Beatrice
        Wilson, Central School of Speech Training and
        Dramatic Art (CSSTDA), St Christopher, Letch-
        worth
        Byron (Law). *role* Suliot Officer, *dir*. Henry Oscar,
        CSSTDA, Century, London

1925   Henry IV, Part II (Shakespeare). *roles* Thomas of
        Clarence and Snare, *dir*. L. E. Berman, CSSTDA,
        Regent Theatre, London
        Unfailing Instinct (Frank). *role* Armand St Cyr,
        dir. Julian Frank, CSSTDA, Hippodrome, Brighton,
        and UK tour
        The Ghost Train (Ridley). *role* Policeman, *dir*. Julian
        Frank, CSSTDA, Hippodrome, Brighton, and UK
        tour

1925–26 Member of Lena Ashwell Players
        The Tempest (Shakespeare). *role* Antonio, *dir*. Lena
        Ashwell, Century Theatre, London
        Julius Caesar (Shakespeare). *role* Flavius, *dir*. Lena
        Ashwell, Century Theatre, London
        Henry VIII (Shakespeare). *role* First Serving Man,
        dir. Lewis Casson, Empire Theatre, London
        The Cenci (Shelley). *role* Servant to Orsino, *dir*. Lewis
        Casson, Empire Theatre, London

1926   The Marvellous History of St Bernard (Ghéon).
        role Minstrel, *dir*. A. E. Filmer, Kingsway Theatre,
        London
        The Barber and the Cow (Davies). small part, *dir*.
        H. K. Ayliff, UK tour
        The Farmer's Wife (Phillpott). *role* Richard
        Croaker, *dir*. H. K. Ayliff, UK tour

1926–27 Member of Birmingham Repertory Theatre Company

1927   Something to Talk About (Phillpott). *role* Guy
        Sydney, *dir*. W. G. Fay, Birmingham Repertory
        Theatre
        The Well of the Saints (Synge). *role* Mat Simon,
        dir. W. G. Fay, Birmingham Repertory Theatre
        The Third Finger (Whittaker). *role* Tom Hardcastle,
        dir. W. G. Fay, Birmingham Repertory Theatre
        The Mannoch Family (McClymond). *role* Peter
        Mannoch, *dir*. W. G. Fay, Birmingham Repertory
        Theatre

THE COMEDIAN (Chéon). walk on, *dir.* W. G. Fay, Birmingham Repertory Theatre

UNCLE VANYA (Chekhov). *role* Vanya, *dir.* W. G. Fay, Birmingham Repertory Theatre

ALL'S WELL THAT ENDS WELL (Shakespeare). *role* Parolles, *dir.* W. G. Fay, Birmingham Repertory Theatre

THE PLEASURE GARDEN (Mayor). *role* Young Man, *dir.* W. G. Fay, Birmingham Repertory Theatre

SHE STOOPS TO CONQUER (Goldsmith). *role* Tony Lumpkin, *dir.* W. G. Fay, Birmingham Repertory Theatre

QUALITY STREET (Barrie). *role* Ensign Blades, *dir.* W. G. Fay, Birmingham Repertory Theatre

BIRD IN HAND (Drinkwater). *role* Gerald Arnwood, *dir.* John Drinkwater, Birmingham Repertory Theatre

ADVERTISING APRIL (Farjeon and Horsnell). *role* Mervyn Jones, *dir.* W. G. Fay, Birmingham Repertory Theatre

THE SILVER BOX (Galsworthy). *role* Jack Barthwick, *dir.* W. G. Fay, Birmingham Repertory Theatre

THE ADDING MACHINE (Rice). *role* Young Man, *dir.* W. G. Fay, Birmingham Repertory Theatre

AREN'T WOMEN WONDERFUL? (Dean). *role* Ben Hawley, *dir.* W. G. Fay, Birmingham Repertory Theatre

THE ROAD TO RUIN (Holcroft). *role* Mr Milford, *dir.* W. G. Fay, Birmingham Repertory Theatre

1928 THE ADDING MACHINE (Rice). *role* Young Man, *dir.* W. G. Fay, Court Theatre, London

MACBETH (Shakespeare). *role* Malcolm, *dir.* H. K. Ayliff, Court Theatre, London

BACK TO METHUSELAH (Shaw). *role* Martellus, *dir.* H. K. Ayliff, Court Theatre, London

HAROLD (Tennyson). *role* Harold, *dir.* H. K. Ayliff, Court Theatre, London

THE TAMING OF THE SHREW (Shakespeare). *role* A Lord, *dir.* H. K. Ayliff, Court Theatre, London

BIRD IN HAND (Drinkwater). *role* Gerald Arnwood, *dir.* John Drinkwater, Royalty Theatre, London

THE DARK PATH (John). *role* Graham Birley, *dir.* Evan John, Royalty Theatre, London

JOURNEY'S END (Sherriff). *role* Captain Stanhope, *dir.* James Whale, Apollo Theatre, London

1929   BEAU GESTE (Dean and Mann). *role* Beau, *dir.* Basil
        Dean, His Majesty's Theatre, London
        THE CIRCLE OF CHALK (Klabund and Laver). *role*
        Prince Po, New Theatre, London
        PARIS BOUND (Barry). *role* Richard Parish, *dir.* Arthur
        Hopkins, Lyric Theatre, London
        THE STRANGER WITHIN (Wilbur). *role* John Hardy,
        dir. Reginald Bach, Garrick Theatre, London
        MURDER ON THE SECOND FLOOR (Vosper). *role* Hugh
        Bromilow, *dir.* William Mollison, New York
        THE LAST ENEMY (Harvey). *role* Jerry Warrender, *dir.*
        Tom Walls, Fortune Theatre, London
1930   AFTER ALL (Van Druten). *role* Ralph, *dir.* Auriol Lee,
        Arts Theatre, London
1930–31 PRIVATE LIVES (Coward). *role* Victor Prynne, *dir.*
        Noël Coward, Phoenix Theatre, London, and New
        York
1933   THE RATS OF NORWAY (Winter). *role* Steven Beringer,
        dir. Raymond Massey, Playhouse Theatre, London
        THE GREEN BAY TREE (Shairp). *role* Julian Dulcimer,
        dir. Jed Harris, New York
1934   BIOGRAPHY (Behrman). *role* Richard Kurt, *dir.* Noël
        Coward, Globe Theatre, London
        QUEEN OF SCOTS (Daviot). *role* Bothwell, *dir.* John
        Gielgud, New Theatre, London
        THEATRE ROYAL (Ferber and Kaufman). *role* Anthony
        Cavendish, *dir.* Noël Coward, Lyric Theatre, Lon-
        don
1935   RINGMASTER (Winter). *role* Peter Hammond, *dir.* Ray-
        mond Massey, Shaftesbury Theatre, London
        GOLDEN ARROW (Thompson and Cunard). *role* Rich-
        ard Harben, *dir.* Laurence Olivier, Whitehall Thea-
        tre, London
        ROMEO AND JULIET (Shakespeare). *roles* Romeo, then
        Mercutio, *dir.* John Gielgud, New Theatre, London
1936   BEES ON THE BOATDECK (Priestley). *role* Robert Patch,
        dir. Laurence Olivier and Ralph Richardson, Lyric
        Theatre, London
1937–49 Member of Old Vic Company
1937   HAMLET (Shakespeare). *role* Hamlet, *dir.* Tyrone
        Guthrie, Old Vic Theatre, London, and Elsinore,
        Denmark
        TWELFTH NIGHT (Shakespeare). *role* Sir Toby Belch,
        dir. Tyrone Guthrie, Old Vic Theatre, London

HENRY V (Shakespeare). *role* Henry, *dir.* Tyrone Guthrie, Old Vic Theatre

MACBETH (Shakespeare). *role* Macbeth, *dir.* Michel St Denis, Old Vic Theatre, New Theatre, London

1938 OTHELLO (Shakespeare). *role* Iago, *dir.* Tyrone Guthrie, Old Vic Theatre, London

THE KING OF NOWHERE (Bridie). *role* Vivaldi, *dir.* Tyrone Guthrie, Old Vic Theatre, London

CORIOLANUS (Shakespeare). *role* Coriolanus, *dir.* Lewis Casson, Old Vic Theatre, London

1939 NO TIME FOR COMEDY (Behrman). *role* Gaylord Easterbrook, *dir.* Guthrie McClintic, New York

1940 ROMEO AND JULIET (Shakespeare). *role* Romeo, *dir.* Laurence Olivier, New York

1944–45 PEER GYNT (Ibsen). *role* Button Moulder, *dir.* Tyrone Guthrie and Robert Helpmann, New Theatre, London, and Paris

ARMS AND THE MAN (Shaw). *role* Sergius Saranoff, *dir.* John Burrell, New Theatre, London, and Paris

RICHARD III (Shakespeare). *role* Gloucester, *dir.* John Burrell, New Theatre, London, and Paris

1945–46 UNCLE VANYA (Chekhov). *role* Astrov, *dir.* John Burrell, New Theatre, London, and New York

HENRY IV, PART I (Shakespeare). *role* Hotspur, *dir.* John Burrell, New Theatre, London, and New York

HENRY IV, PART II (Shakespeare). *role* Justice Shallow, *dir.* John Burrell, New Theatre, London, and New York

OEDIPUS REX (Sophocles). *role* Oedipus, *dir.* Michel St Denis, New Theatre, London, and New York

THE CRITIC (Sheridan). *role* Mr Puff, *dir.* Miles Malleson, New Theatre, London, and New York

1946 KING LEAR (Shakespeare). *role* Lear, *dir.* Laurence Olivier, New Theatre, London

1948 THE SCHOOL FOR SCANDAL (Sheridan). *role* Sir Peter Teazle, *dir.* Laurence Olivier, tour of New Zealand and Australia

RICHARD III (Shakespeare). *role* Gloucester, *dir.* John Burrell, tour of New Zealand and Australia

THE SKIN OF OUR TEETH (Wilder). *role* Mr Antrobus, *dir.* Laurence Olivier, tour of New Zealand and Australia

1949 RICHARD III (Shakespeare). *role* Gloucester, *dir.* John Burrell, New Theatre, London

THE SCHOOL FOR SCANDAL (Sheridan). *role* Sir Peter Teazle, *dir.* Laurence Olivier, New Theatre, London

ANTIGONE (Anouilh). *role* Chorus, *dir.* Laurence Olivier, New Theatre, London

1950   VENUS OBSERVED (Fry). *role* Duke of Altair, *dir.* Laurence Olivier, St James's Theatre, London

1951   CAESAR AND CLEOPATRA (Shaw). *role* Caesar, *dir.* Michael Benthall, St James's Theatre, London, and New York

ANTONY AND CLEOPATRA (Shakespeare). *role* Antony, *dir.* Michael Benthall, St James's Theatre, London, and New York

1953   THE SLEEPING PRINCE (Rattigan). *role* Grand Duke, *dir.* Laurence Olivier, Phoenix Theatre, London

1955   TWELFTH NIGHT (Shakespeare). *role* Malvolio, *dir.* John Gielgud, Memorial Theatre, Stratford-upon-Avon

MACBETH (Shakespeare). *role* Macbeth, *dir.* Glen Byam Shaw, Memorial Theatre, Stratford-upon-Avon

TITUS ANDRONICUS (Shakespeare). *role* Titus, *dir.* Peter Brook, Memorial Theatre, Stratford-upon-Avon

1957   THE ENTERTAINER (Osborne). *role* Archie Rice, *dir.* Tony Richardson, Royal Court Theatre, London

TITUS ANDRONICUS (Shakespeare). *role* Titus, *dir.* Peter Brook, Memorial Theatre Co. European tour and Stoll Theatre, London

1957–58 THE ENTERTAINER (Osborne). *role* Archie Rice, *dir.* Tony Richardson, Palace Theatre, London, and New York

1959   CORIOLANUS (Shakespeare). *role* Coriolanus, *dir.* Peter Hall, Memorial Theatre, Stratford-upon-Avon

1960   RHINOCEROS (Ionesco). *role* Berenger, *dir.* Orson Welles, Royal Court and Strand Theatres, London

1960–61 BECKET (Anouilh). *roles* Becket, then Henry, *dir.* Peter Glenville, New York

1962   THE BROKEN HEART (Ford). *roles* Prologue and Bassanes, *dir.* Laurence Olivier, Chichester Festival Theater, Chichester

UNCLE VANYA (Chekhov). *role* Astrov, *dir.* Laurence Olivier, Chichester Festival Theatre, Chichester

1962–73 Director of the National Theatre Company

1962   SEMI-DETACHED (Turner). *role* Fred Midway, *dir.* Tony Richardson, Saville Theatre, London

1963   UNCLE VANYA (Chekhov). *role* Astrov, *dir.* Laurence

Olivier, Chichester Festival Theatre, Chichester, and Old Vic Theatre, London

THE RECRUITING OFFICER (Farquhar). *role* Captain Brazen, *dir.* William Gaskill, Old Vic Theatre, London

1964   OTHELLO (Shakespeare). *role* Othello, *dir.* John Dexter, Chichester Festival Theatre, Chichester, and Old Vic Theatre, London

THE MASTER BUILDER (Ibsen). *role* Halvard Solness, *dir.* Peter Wood, Old Vic Theatre, London

1965   OTHELLO (Shakespeare). *role* Othello, *dir.* John Dexter, Moscow and Berlin

LOVE FOR LOVE (Congreve). *role* Tattle, *dir.* Peter Wood, Old Vic Theatre, London, and Moscow and Berlin

1967   THE DANCE OF DEATH (Strindberg). *role* Edgar, *dir.* Glen Byam Shaw, Old Vic Theatre, London, and tour of Canada

LOVE FOR LOVE (Congreve). *role* Tattle, *dir.* Peter Wood, tour of Canada

A FLEA IN HER EAR (Feydeau). *role* Plucheux, *dir.* Jacques Charon, tour of Canada

1969   HOME AND BEAUTY (Maugham). *role* A. B. Raham, *dir.* Frank Dunlop, Old Vic Theatre, London

THREE SISTERS (Chekhov). *role* Chebutikin, *dir.* Laurence Olivier, Old Vic Theatre, London, and Los Angeles

1970   THE MERCHANT OF VENICE (Shakespeare). *role* Shylock, *dir.* Jonathan Miller, Old Vic Theatre, London

1971   LONG DAY'S JOURNEY INTO NIGHT (O'Neill). *role* James Tyrone, *dir.* Peter Wood, Old Vic Theatre and New Theatre, London

1973   SATURDAY, SUNDAY, MONDAY (de Filippo). *role* Antonio, *dir.* Franco Zeffirelli, Old Vic Theatre, London

THE PARTY (Griffiths). *role* John Tagg, *dir.* John Dexter, Old Vic Theatre, London

FILMS

*Including films made for television. The year is the release
date. American film titles are given in brackets.*

1930   THE TEMPORARY WIDOW. *dir.* Gustav Ucicky
       TOO MANY CROOKS. *dir.* George King
1931   POTIPHAR'S WIFE (HER STRANGE DESIRE). *dir.* Maurice Elvery
       FRIENDS AND LOVERS. *dir.* Victor Schertzinger
       THE YELLOW PASSPORT (THE YELLOW TICKET). *dir.* Raoul Walsh
1932   WESTWARD PASSAGE. *dir.* Robert Milton
1933   PERFECT UNDERSTANDING. *dir.* Cyril Gardner
       NO FUNNY BUSINESS (THE PROFESSIONAL CO-RESPONDENTS). *dir.* John Stafford and Victor Hanbury
1935   MOSCOW NIGHTS (I STAND CONDEMNED). *dir.* Anthony Asquith
1936   AS YOU LIKE IT. *dir.* Paul Czinner
       CONQUEST OF THE AIR. *dir.* A. Shaw, J. M. Saunders, A. Esway and Z. Korda
1937   FIRE OVER ENGLAND. *dir.* William K. Howard
       TWENTY-ONE DAYS. *dir.* Basil Dean
1938   THE DIVORCE OF LADY X. *dir.* Tim Whelan
1939   Q PLANES (CLOUDS OVER EUROPE). *dir.* Tim Whelan
       WUTHERING HEIGHTS. *dir.* William Wyler
1940   REBECCA. *dir.* Alfred Hitchcock
       PRIDE AND PREJUDICE. *dir.* Robert Z. Leonard
1941   WORDS FOR BATTLE. commentary only, *dir.* Humphrey Jennings
       LADY HAMILTON (THAT HAMILTON WOMAN). *dir.* Alexander Korda
       49TH PARALLEL. *dir.* Michael Powell
1943   THE DEMI-PARADISE. *dir.* Anthony Asquith
1945   HENRY V. *dir.* Laurence Olivier
1948   HAMLET. *dir.* Laurence Olivier
1951   THE MAGIC BOX. *dir.* Laurence Olivier
1952   CARRIE. *dir.* William Wyler
1953   A QUEEN IS CROWNED. voice only, *prod.* Castleton Knight
       THE BEGGAR'S OPERA. *dir.* Peter Brook
1955   RICHARD III. *dir.* Laurence Olivier
1957   THE PRINCE AND THE SHOWGIRL. *dir.* Laurence Olivier
1959   THE DEVIL'S DISCIPLE. *dir.* Guy Hamilton

1960	SPARTACUS. *dir*. Stanley Kubrick
	THE ENTERTAINER. *dir*. Tony Richardson
1961	THE POWER AND THE GLORY. *dir*. Marc Daniels
1962	TERM OF TRIAL. *dir*. Peter Glenville
1963	UNCLE VANYA. *dir*. Laurence Olivier
1965	BUNNY LAKE IS MISSING. *dir*. Otto Preminger
	OTHELLO. *dir*. Stuart Burge
1966	KHARTOUM. *dir*. Basil Dearden
1968	ROMEO AND JULIET. voice only, *dir*. Franco Zeffirelli
	THE SHOES OF THE FISHERMAN. *dir*. Michael Anderson
1969	OH! WHAT A LOVELY WAR. *dir*. Richard Attenborough
	THE BATTLE OF BRITAIN. *dir*. Guy Hamilton
	THE DANCE OF DEATH. *dir*. David Giles
	DAVID COPPERFIELD. *dir*. Delbert Mann
1970	THREE SISTERS. *dir*. Laurence Olivier
1971	NICHOLAS AND ALEXANDRA. *dir*. Franklin J. Schaffner
1972	LADY CAROLINE LAMB. *dir*. Robert Bolt
	SLEUTH. *dir*. Joseph L. Mankiewicz
1975	LOVE AMONG THE RUINS. *dir*. George Cukor
1976	THE SEVEN PER CENT SOLUTION. *dir*. Herbert Ross
	MARATHON MAN. *dir*. John Schlesinger
1977	JESUS OF NAZARETH. *dir*. Franco Zeffirelli
	A BRIDGE TOO FAR. *dir*. Richard Attenborough
1978	THE BETSY. *dir*. Daniel Petrie
	THE BOYS FROM BRAZIL. *dir*. Franklin J. Schaffner
1979	A LITTLE ROMANCE. *dir*. George Roy Hill
	DRACULA. *dir*. John Bādham
1980	THE JAZZ SINGER. *dir*. Richard Fleischer
	INCHON (unreleased), *dir*. Terence Young
1981	CLASH OF THE TITANS. *dir*. Desmond David
1984	THE BOUNTY. *dir*. Roger Donaldson
	THE LAST DAYS OF POMPEII. *dir*. Peter Hunt
1985	WAGNER. *dir*. Tony Palmer
	THE JIGSAW MAN. *dir*. Terence Young
	WILD GEESE II. *dir*. Peter Hunt

TELEVISION

1937	MACBETH (Shakespeare). excerpts, *role* Macbeth, BBC
1958	JOHN GABRIEL BORKMAN (Ibsen). *role* Borkman, ATV
1959	THE MOON AND SIXPENCE (Maugham). *role* Charles Strickland, NBC

1967   THEATRE ROYAL, charity perf. *role* Prologue (Day Lewis), Rediffusion
1969   MALE OF THE SPECIES (Owen). *role* host/narrator, NBC
1972   LONG DAY'S JOURNEY INTO NIGHT (O'Neill). *role* James Tyrone, ATV
1973   THE MERCHANT OF VENICE (Shakespeare). *role* Shylock, ATV
1974   WORLD AT WAR. *role* narrator, Thames
1976   THE COLLECTION (Pinter). *role* Harry Kane, Granada
       CAT ON A HOT TIN ROOF (Williams). *role* Big Daddy, Granada
1978   COME BACK, LITTLE SHEBA (Inge). *role* Doc Delaney, Granada
       DAPHNE LAUREOLA (Bridie). *role* Sir Joseph Pitts, Granada
       SATURDAY, SUNDAY, MONDAY (de Filippo). *role* Antonio, Granada
1981   BRIDESHEAD REVISITED (Waugh). *role* Lord Marchmain, Granada
1982   A VOYAGE ROUND MY FATHER (Mortimer). *role* Clifford Mortimer, Thames
1983   KING LEAR (Shakespeare). *role* Lear, Granada
       A TALENT FOR MURDER (Choderov and Panama). *role* Dr Wainwright, BBC
1984   MR HALPERN AND MR JOHNSON (Goldstein). *role* Mr Halpern, HTV
       THE EBONY TOWER (Fowles). *role* Henry Breasley, Granada
1986   LOST EMPIRES (Priestley). *role* Harry Burrard, Granada

INDEX

389

RICK HORTON